A Countryman's Tale

A Countryman's Tale is the story of Eydon, a village near Banbury in Northamptonshire that existed before the Domesday Book, and in many respects represents a microcosm of rural England. A family memoir as well as a village history, it is the fruit of a long lifetime of curiosity and diligent research on the part of the local tailor. It explains the drastic effects of the Enclosures in the eighteenth century on the lives of country people, and the other historic influences which have made an English village what it is today.

Syd Tyrrell (1889-1976) left school at fourteen, worked for his father and later for other employers as a tailor. He served in the Great War, married and raised a family, and immersed himself in local affairs as a Parish Councillor for forty years, and as a Wesleyan lay preacher.

A Countryman's Tale

Syd Tyrrell

with an introduction by Byron Rogers

CENTURY

LONDON   SYDNEY   AUCKLAND   JOHANNESBURG
in association with the National Trust

To all our boys,
big and little

First published by Constable, London, 1973.

Published in paperback in 1991 by Century
Random Century Ltd
20 Vauxhall Bridge Road, London SW1V 2SA

Century Hutchinson Australia (Pty) Ltd
20 Alfred Street, Milsons Point, Sydney, NSW 2061, Australia

Century Hutchinson New Zealand Ltd
PO Box 40-086, 32-34 View Road, Glenfield, Auckland 10, New
Zealand

Century Hutchinson South Africa (Pty) Ltd
PO Box 337, Bergvlei 2012, South Africa

Printed and bound in Great Britain by The Guernsey Press Ltd,
Guernsey, Channel Islands

British Library Cataloguing in Publication Data

Tyrrell, Syd 1889-1976
A countryman's tale. – (National Trust Classics).
1. Northamptonshire. Eydon. Social life, history
I. Title   II. Series
942.559

ISBN 0-7126-4625-6

Contents

Introduction

I could not find it at first. I looked where I had been told to look, in a corner of the paddock where the village has buried its dead since the churchyard was filled. I found his parents, and his brother, but the last stone looked too old and the man I sought had died in 1976. Then I saw the name and, from the lettering, made out that it was to his little son who died in 1927. At the bottom half, hidden by grass, was this: 'Also the ashes of his parents Annie and Sydney, 1976.' Nothing else, nothing to indicate what he was, that at the age of 83 this man had a book published which one day should be as much a classic of English rural life as *Lark Rise to Candleford*, itself written about a village within walking distance.

Syd Tyrrell was the tailor of Eydon, ten miles from Banbury. In 1973 Constable, after ten publishers had turned it down, brought out *A Countryman's Tale*. ''S all about the Tyrrells,' grumbled his neighbours. 'Particularly good on his neighbours and friends,' said the *Times*, the only national to review it. 'A quite delightful read.'

Syd had intended it for his own family ('To my own folk our way of life will soon seem as remote as the seventeenth century does to our generation.'), but it became the story of the village. The strange thing is that then it became the story of England. It is not history. He had no sense of history as a series of events which are over, so he could be as cross or as amused by them as by anything in his own life. The same is true of people: the book becomes a room which fills with faces, thins out and fills again. He must have recognised this power in himself, for at one point he mutters: 'You may think these folks are all dead but all I can say is, they won't be quite dead while I am alive.' Nor are they now and the effect is extraordinary: there are no yesterdays in *A Countryman's Tale*.

You peer over his shoulder at the grim Methodist humour of Victorian England. 'Late in life Mother and Father did have a cup of tea at dinnertime. Mother said, "I think the time has come when we can indulge ourselves."' With the young Syd you stare reverently at the first artificial leg. 'Mrs Garner called me in to see it, carefully wrapped in a long cardboard box. It was a beautiful leg and no mistake; the joints worked and it had a most lifelike foot. Bill wore it only two or three times, for he never broke it in, saying it was too fast for him.'

You stand glumly with him as the enclosures come or the priest reads the burial service over an unknown man who staggered into the village to die of his wounds after Edgehill. And you begin to understand that most mysterious aspect of history, why a village *looks* the way it does, why one building is of brick and why one house is empty.

Some have written memoirs, others histories of villages, but this is something else. Syd Tyrrell, in addition to being the tailor, also sold insurance, and was a methodist lay preacher while his wife kept the village shop: nothing moved in Eydon without his knowing. He wanted the village to stay just as it was ('He threw a lot of spokes into a lot of wheels.'). Voted off the parish council, he got himself voted on to another one six miles away. Why? So he could see what was going on there. A tall, very thin man looks intently out of his fading family photographs, Syd Tyrrell, chronicler of Eydon.

You are in watercolour country, the ghostly wash between the trees rising from the flat Eastern fields to where the Cotswolds start, at Eydon on its hill like some Iron Age fort. You come to it through great brick pillars which once carried a railway bridge, but, bridge and railway being long gone, now have the grandeur of a palace gateway.

The name is Saxon, *'dune'* a hill or down and *'eye'* an isolated place. Now as then, two streets running parallel and two alleys between them: once a place where you remembered strangers. '29th October, 1642. One Birmingham, a soldier of the King's Army and wounded at Edgehill, was buried with us.' Trying to get home, thought Syd; probably only able to say the name of his home town.

You remembered the man at the manor too, for everything turned around him. John Browne, the Clerk of Parliament from 1641 to 1691 (as such, probably one of the most remarkable survivors in history), was in Eydon, a man much troubled by one Smallbone, a quaker steadfastly refusing to pay his church rate. Syd, a natural foe to squire and parson, noted the latter's appeal to Parliament against Smallbone, 'plotting, continuing and praying against the peace of church and state'.

The larger world intruded, imposing its Hearth Tax (Browne, muttered Syd, had fifteen hearths while forty cottagers had just the one). He revelled in the circumstances of its repeal, when the wives of the great complained to their husbands about men tramping through their homes to count fireplaces. The Window Tax came; in a lane in Eydon a farmer began quietly bricking his windows in.

In 1762 the enclosures came, but as far as Syd was concerned they could have come last Tuesday, so angrily does he round on the parson and his cronies who took away the common land which had made up a third of the parish. One man shaved away a road so that even today it is too narrow for traffic. 'If the Council should decide to widen that, I'll kick up a such a hullabaloo if they propose paying the owner for the strip of land necessary. I'll write to our MP. I'll enlist the aid of the *Daily Express*. Oh, I'll make such a shindy if they propose paying ratepayers money for stolen property.'

Syd was lucky in his villains. The Knightleys of nearby Fawsley were squires out of pantomime who in the Middle Ages had closed down whole villages to make way for sheep. An eighteenth-century Knightley, when enclosures came to the village of Badby, asked if he might grow a last crop on land destined for villagers. He was given permission and planted oak, ash and elm.

It is startling to be reminded of the quiet, largely unrecorded poverty of the villages. In the early nineteenth century a quarter of Eydon was on the Poor Law; a labourer in work was paid a shilling a day when the price of a loaf was a shilling. In the nearby village of Sulgrave an eccentric vicar sought to help the unemployment by getting men to raise a great earth mound in his garden. He had intended them to move it later, but the mound was still there in Syd's time.

Still, the Knightleys were as busy as ever. In Preston Capes lived a Knightley tenant who was a Baptist. The nineteenth-century Knightley, also a Tory MP, could not abide Non-conformism and – for once in his family's history – failing to evict a tenant, got men to remove the roof by night.

But in Eydon a strange cycle of pomp and decay was beginning for one house. In the 1830s the vicar had a new front built onto the rectory, raising it to three storeys so that it towered over the village. Twenty years later the man's successor moved out saying he could no longer stand the noise of a nineteenth-century village street. My dear, the carts, and the people . . .

For fifty years it stood empty, 'gaunt, forlorn and forsaken . . . too well-built to become a ruin, it stood like a proud old gentleman with dignity and poise, yet clad in tattered garments'. Its windows were regularly broken and it was thought to be haunted, though one old man told Syd the strange noises were caused by the wind in the wires of the bell system.

Then someone bought it, grandly restored it but left. Someone else was there between the wars and then, after more decay, it was bought by a Birmingham engineer for his parents. Now they too are gone, the windows are broken again, and, in a time when village properties are at a premium, the house has entered yet another cycle of decay.

This is the fascinating thing about this book, the feeling that this is an inside story.

Syd remembered the railway coming (the canal which came a century earlier to within seven miles of the village had lowered the price of coal; the railway brought its price within reach of most people, who, through enclosure, had lost the right to gather brushwood). He remembered the wages of the navvies, an unheard of three shillings and fourpence a week, and their swearing. In 1966 Syd saw the last train. 'It's strange we find ourselves quite unconsciously listening . . . Today, busy grubbing up weeds in the gardens, I pricked up my ears and said to myself, "Why that's a train on the branch line, in the cutting." It was only a combine harvester.' They were a remarkable family, the Tyrrells. They were Methodists and part of the radical counterpart to the squire and parson which came in the nineteenth century. Syd's father, the tailor, was a magistrate (a little moment of history in itself) and the chairman of Daventry Liberals; his brother later became Jeremy Thorpe's agent. With the chapels closing now, many of them to be converted into houses or garages, it is easy to forget the short but intense part Methodism played in the long story of village life. The old village families are in the book: the makers of sheep medicine, the coachman from the hall more snobbish than any duke, the labourer who in his far off drunken youth had killed his father. Searching for Syd's grave I came on names already familiar.

The King came to Eydon for the Army Manoeuvres and the Great War was not long behind him. Rejected for active service on account of his eyesight, Syd was recruited to sit it out on the cliffs of Gibraltar. A long life began: there was marriage and tragedy (his son, aged three fell into a sewerage tank and died of meningitis). The book came at the end of it and took him fifteen years to write in longhand in the small hours so that finally he and his wife settled for separate rooms.

In Eydon few know the squire's name now, though he is no longer the squire, merely the man who lives at the hall. He breeds racehorses and, with these so valuable, the villagers assume this is why they see so little of him. But then they see little of the neighbours for at night the lights come on in only half the houses, except at weekends when the large cars come on Friday nights to the immaculate locked houses. The stocks (last used in the 1850s for a man who beat up his wife) still stand on the village green, and are much loved by estate agents. The houses fetch upwards of a quarter of a million, so the old families have either gone or been swept neatly into the council houses. There is so much neatness. I walked past the notice-board with its details of aerobic classes and peered into empty houses at the rural dreams of strangers.

Byron Rogers, 1990.

Prologue

Many years ago Kitty Harrison told me that when her mother and father retired after a busy life they each wrote about their respective families, and the events that brought them together, and gave each of their children a copy. I remember thinking what a nice idea it was and why should we not have a history of our family? If I wrote all I knew now, maybe in years to come one of my grandchildren would carry the story a stage further.

Being a champion putter-off I did not get started till they began calling me 'old Syd'. That woke me up, just enough to get started. Having got started, the next problem was where to stop. I found myself on a slippery plane: how could I record one century of the life of Eydon, our village, and ignore the preceding eight? Yet to write an authentic history of those centuries was quite beyond my capabilities. Age, lack of mobility and our distance from the local Record Office were obstacles difficult to overcome. No doubt if one had unlimited time to search the records, scraps of village history are to be found in the archives of Lincoln Cathedral, and in the national records in London.

So it is possible that I have misinterpreted some items of ancient history, as well as over-simplified the problems that confronted the nation at the Reformation and in the eighteenth century. This is not written to suit historians; it's for my own kith and kin and for the man in the street. To my own folk, our way of life will soon seem as remote as the seventeenth century does to my generation.

In the first chapter I have put together as much information as I can find about the history of the village under successive lords of the manor from Domesday Book until 1762. Then in the following chapter comes the time when the common lands were enclosed and the village changed shape to become very much the place we know now. In the fourth chapter I talk about the Annesleys and all that they did in these parts.

Part Two concerns the nineteenth century, a period of great change and excitement, and also a time when Eydon seemed to be full of grand characters. Many of these were known to me when I was a boy; others I've heard tell of from family and friends. Part Three concerns the Tyrrell family, who first came to Eydon way back in 1841.

Strangers come to the village, stand and look at the old houses on each side of the street and say, 'My word, this is an old village, what's its history?' Well, this is the best I can do. I know full well much of it is scrappy, and that I make statements I cannot verify, for all my life I've been gathering scraps of information but, at the time, I omitted to label them in a business-like way with date and source of information. I plead that this book is written in good faith; where I let my imagination guide my pen it is simply in an attempt to put some flesh on the dry bones of recorded history. Fortunately many old friends have long memories; they listened when their mothers and fathers talked over old times by the fireside on wintry nights. Some remembered one particular item, some gave another glimpse into the past. Wherever possible I've checked one version with that told by a contemporary.

My thanks to all the good folk I have pestered with questions that made them delve deep into memories of past days, but there – they've loved it and so have I. I'm grateful, too, to the

Northampton Borough Council for maintaining the Abingdon Street Library and letting us country folk have free use of the Dryden Room with its splendid files of local newspapers. Thanks to Mr P. King of the Record Society for help in reading documents, and for his patience in helping me understand them. Thanks to Mrs Ella Austin for many peeps into the church registers on my behalf, and for access to the parish records. Lastly, thanks to a newcomer, Mrs Joan Plommer, for help in typing, kindly criticism and advice and, above all, encouragement when I was tiring of what seemed a never-ending task.

Now I lay down my pen, with the fervent prayer that one of the bright sparks now at school will, in a few years, carry on the story of this village in the heart of old England.

Part One

Eydon before the nineteenth century

Chapter 1

Lords of the manor

Close to the centre of England, where it is just as far to the coast at Skegness as to either the Somerset or Hampshire seaside resorts, stands the village of Eydon. It is situated in south Northamptonshire on the southern slope of a 580-foot hill on one of the last uplands of the Cotswolds just before they merge into the valley of the Nene and the Fen country.

The village consists of a street running parallel to a Roman road, joined by sundry lanes. The street is 'The Street', and the road 'The Back', so take no notice of the board that says 'Lime Avenue'. That is the posh name they have given 'The Back' lately. It's daft, for I don't see how you can call a row of lime trees an avenue; it takes two rows of trees to make an avenue according to my dictionary. The road was the back of the village. Very early on, the houses on the street stood on a strip of land about fifty feet wide from the street to the back. Their garden gates opened on to the back; their cows and horses went out that way to graze in the common pastures.

Just how long there has been a village here we shall never know, for our recorded history begins with the Domesday Survey of 1086. But it may well have been an old village when William's men came here to record and survey for the first time ever. The local historian Baker thinks that it was of Saxon origin for 'in Domesday, Egedonne, and in early records, Aydon or Eyndon, is of uncertain etymology, but may possibly be derived from the Saxon "eye", an isolated spot, and "dune", a down or hill; which is not altogether inappropriate to its elevated situation, approached from nearly every side by a steep ascent'.

Whatever its Saxon origins, the village grew on the side of the ancient Roman road from the villa at Chipping Warden to a settlement near Daventry – Benneventa to Brinavis, to give them their Roman names.

At the time of the Domesday Survey in 1086, 'one Hugh held of Hugh de Grentemaisnil, two hides of Eyedone'. The arable land was five carucates, two of which were in demesne with two servants, and the remaining three in the occupation of twelve villeins. There was a mill worth 2s. yearly and two acres of meadow. The whole had been valued at 40s. but was then raised to 50s. yearly. The mill mentioned is Burnt Mill, a water mill near Farndon, still inhabited with the meadow land around it. A holding of land unchanged since 1086 is surely a rarity. Nine hundred years is a very long time.

Hugh de Grentemaisnil came over with William the Conqueror and for his services was given over one hundred manors in different parts of the country. He died in 1096 six days after he had assumed a religious habit. The next owner of the manor of Eydon was John Beaufort, Earl of Somerset, followed by the Countess of Richmond and Derby. On her attainder for some misdemeanour, the manor reverted to the Crown and was then granted to John de la Pole, Earl of Lincoln. But John fought against Henry VII at the battle of Newark on Trent in 1487, was defeated and slain, so the manor again reverted to the Crown.

These great lords of the manor were all-powerful landowners who lived on their huge estates elsewhere. They may never even have visited Eydon – it probably seemed to them to be a small property of minor value. But there were families living locally whose names we know and who did have considerable impact on village life. They did much to help shape the village as we know it today.

During the fourteenth century there were two families in the village who owned considerable acreage, the FitzWales's and the Wakelyns. The Wakelyn family are first mentioned in 1329 and again in 1392 when William Wakelyn of Eydon bought more land roundabout. In 1506 Nicholas Wakelyn of Eydon, gentleman, sold one of his other manors and then in 1600 Allan Wakelyn sold his house in Eydon to Richard Wilbraham, so they appear to have lived locally for nearly three hundred years.

There is in the church vestry a recumbent effigy, believed to be one of the FitzWales family of about 1350, but it is so weathered and worn that no inscription can be deciphered. But it is known from the church records that Richard FitzWales gave the advowson of Eydon to the Abbey of St Mary de Pratis at Leicester some time between 1154 and 1167. Such generosity to the Church did not suit later members of the family, for in 1202 and again in 1255 there were attempts to recover the advowson; but the Abbey won both times. Thomas FitzWales had yet another try to get it back in 1291 and the Abbey finally held it until the dissolution of the monasteries in the reign of Henry VIII. It must indeed have been very trying for the FitzWales's to have a priest sent from Leicester Abbey to Eydon who could say what he liked against the FitzWales's with impunity whenever he felt like denouncing their wicked ways. The FitzWales's must have suffered badly to take legal action so many times against the entrenched authority and wealth of Leicester Abbey, for litigation has always been an expensive procedure.

If Richard FitzWales gave the advowson of the church away in 1154, there must have been a church here since that time. We still have the original Norman font and they do say that some bits of the nave are Norman too. But the church is a composite building and many others have had a hand in building it; the tower appears to be fourteenth century. Men toiled for years to build their parish church. They carved gargoyles to scare away evil spirits. That must have kept one man busy for weeks. To get the big stones up the tower needed a team of strong men with the primitive tackle at their disposal. An important local landowner was probably architect and clerk of the works, for he had the

labour of many men in the village at his disposal for so many weeks each year. He could set them to dig out stone and build walls instead of ploughing in spring and reaping in autumn. They did the donkey work under the supervision of one or two skilled masons and carpenters.

Having given a local landowner credit for building the church, my quandary is, which? I think most of the honour should go to the FitzWales and Wakelyn families. Perhaps they enlarged the original Norman building or maybe they pulled most of it down and rebuilt it. But I am sure they erected much of the church as we know it. It would have been smaller of course in their time and the roof of the nave and chancel may well have been thatched with straw. There would have been no pews or seats, just a ledge on the outside walls on which the old folk could sit; hence the saying 'the weakest go to the wall'. Church attendance on Sunday would have been compulsory but the local folk would never see the Bible in English. No Bible, or prayer book, no singing of the psalms; the spoken word would be in Latin, a language the folk could not understand. What a do! On Sundays everyone would have met outside the church after mass. Then they would have dispersed to their homes. What were these like in the fourteenth century and what was everyday life like in Eydon in those far-off days? We know that the old manor house was near the church and parsonage, and the houses on the west side of the street evidently once had a strip of land stretching from the street to the back road, about fifty feet wide. Some are still intact, others have been broken. In several cases the original strip can be traced and one can see where a plot was sold on which a house was built at a later date.

There were probably only about four or five houses built of stone in Eydon five hundred years ago. One or two might have had glass windows but these were rare; a few might have used oiled linen cloth to admit a semblance of light and to keep out the rain. But the poorer houses were just hovels made by thatching long poles with straw or turf, with no walls at all. No windows either, just a hole in the roof to let the smoke out. The fire was in the middle of this lean-to house and the family would huddle round it to sleep at night. Each labourer would have the right to take turf and wood from the waste land round the village to keep his fire going. It provided not only warmth and heat for cooking but light as well, for why should a working-man burn a rushlight when there was nothing to look at, and reading was an accomplishment that few labouring men had mastered?

Some of the men would own their cottage, others would have to pay rent, but all would have rights, great or small, in the common lands: rights to pasture, to meadow-land and to a strip or two of arable which the village would cultivate together. What they grew and when was fixed by the local court where all the men with rights would attend to take part in discussions and to vote. They would grow vegetables (but not the potato, for that had not been heard of yet), rye for bread and barley for beer. In the common pasture they would graze their cow or a few sheep and they would fatten their pigs on the stubble or let them roam the woods for acorns. Cattle fodder would be short in the long winter months so some would be killed and salted down for beef in the autumn. Salting was expensive, though, for salt was produced by evaporation of sea water and a couple of bushels often cost as much as a sheep. They used it sparingly and it must have been common to find the bacon rancid and the ham alive with maggots. The only source of sweetening was honey and people not only left their hives to their children by will, but might actually bequeath a summer swarm of bees to their friends.

The poor man's loaf was as dark as mud and as tough as shoe leather, for wheat bread was a delicacy for the rich. Food was seldom plentiful all the year, even after a good harvest; the people must have been near starvation at the end of some hard winters. The absence of vegetables for most of the year, the personal dirt of the people, sleeping at night in the rough clothes worn in the day, as well as other causes, made skin diseases common.

Men and women worked hard, rose early, toiled all day and went to bed as soon as it was dark. Certainly in Eydon some people must have prospered for, although we have no record of medieval life in Eydon, by the sixteenth century Eydon folk were being uncommonly generous with their gifts to the church. Maybe they had a good parson who not only reached into the hearts of the people but also touched their pockets. In 1512 I. Strawynton gave 6s. 8d. to 'bye a masse boke', and R. Heyward 'two brass basons for the Rode loft and money for a light above our Blessed Lady'. Richard Tew gave 12s. to buy a banner, and to our Lady of Eydon, two sheep. These gifts were made on the eve of the Reformation that swept out of the church the 'masse boke' and 'our Blessed Lady' and other frills and fancy work. The Pope was deposed and Henry VIII became supreme head of the Church. The Prior of Leicester and his monks had to take other jobs or retire on small pensions. During the next century a

Bible in English was placed in the church, to be read by anyone who could read, and the Book of Common Prayer was used morning and evening on Sundays.

Not all these radical changes would be appreciated here, I am very sure. I can hear some of the old men saying, 'I don't loike these 'ere new-fangled ways.' But there was no great local lord to whom to complain at the time, for since John de la Pole's death in battle the Crown had held the land, and continued to hold it for nearly a hundred years, until Henry VIII finally decided to give the manor to Sir John Cope of Canons Ashby. From that time on it has always been known as Cope's manor.

During Sir John Cope's time, in 1552, it is recorded that there were 'two bells in ye skepe and a raumcte bell'. Did Sir John give these perhaps, or did he give only one of them? Maybe some of them had been there for some time, for even now each of our church bells was made by a different bell-founder at a different period. What an assortment they are! These five bells still make a joyous noise at Christmas and on special occasions. They are inscribed:

1. M. Bagley made me 1770
   Wm. Hudson and Thos. Ivens, church wardens

2. J. Briant of Hertford, 1822
   W. Lines and J. Ivens

3. Thos. Mears of London
   Joseph Blackwell and Thos. Ivens

4. Be it known to all that doth me see
   that Newcombe of Leicester made mee, 1603

5. J. Taylor & Co., Loughborough, 1872

Sir John Cope must have been a powerful personality for his name to remain attached to his house all these centuries. He was followed in Eydon by another determined character, Richard Wilbraham, who seems to have bought the Wakelyn house and some land in about 1600, and then done that which he ought not to have done. For he converted by means of an enclosure two acres of the common tillage to pasturage and this land is still recognisable today. If you go up the Byfield road you find a field that is almost square, with roads on three sides of it. This is so out of the ordinary that for years past I always wondered how it came about. In spite of G. K. Chesterton and his rolling English drunkard, the surveyors who laid out our roads knew their job. A big tree here, a boggy plot there, an old gravel pit in another place had to be avoided, but to go three sides round a field was most unusual. But what surveyors had to respect were ancient rights. No doubt by the time the surveyors were finalising the roads in the eighteenth century this field had come to be classed as ancient enclosure land, so they very carefully put the road round three sides of it.

Indeed if we look up some of the ancient records we find traces of this field. For in the late sixteenth century there were riots in Northamptonshire caused by the enclosure of land that was converted from tillage to pasturage and complaints were so widespread that there was a government enquiry. In 1607 the returns of the depopulation commissioners state: 'Eydon: Richard Wilbraham converted from tillage to pasturage, 14 acres that belonged to Wakelyn's farm in Eydon. There is a highway leading from Eydon to Southam turned out of its usual course by means of the inclosure of two acres by Richard Wilbraham.' So we know for sure which field it was exactly.

When Richard Wilbraham died he left the estate to his son Thomas, a lad of sixteen years of age. Five years later Richard Wilcox either owned or was a tenant of the Wakelyn manor.

During this time there was an unusual entry in the church register: 'John Hinton the sonne of Henry Hinton of the Graynge and Jane Warde whome he gott with chylde being his mayde, was baptised the 30th Jan 1623. . . .' In some villages, if John had been a single man it would have been the constable's duty to take

him and Jane to church for the parson to marry them, the fee and
expenses for this being paid by the rates.

Another incident that must have aroused much interest also
occurred at this period. On 29th October 1642 the rector made
this entry in the register at the church: 'One Birminham a
soulder of ye King's army and wounded at ye battel of Edgehill
was buryed with us.' Evidently a severely wounded man trying
to get home, who was so far gone when he was found, or when he
reached the village, that he could only say something that
sounded like Birminham. If he was trying to reach Birmingham,
the poor man was coming the wrong way.

In those days there was no standing army; the militia was called
up when necessary. Each lord and each parish according to its
size had to find a man and equip him with clothing and weapons.
We were one of nine villages in the Warden hundred and the
men from all these villages were mustered every so often, and
drilled so that they'd know how to go on in actual warfare. In
1559 the muster roll reads, 'Eidonne, Mr Waklyn is chargid to
furnyshe a byll man and the rest of that towne a byll man.' By
the time of the great Civil War battle of Edgehill, the 'byll' or
pike had no doubt been replaced by a musket. Although we do
not know their names, we can be sure there were Eydon men
fighting at Edgehill that sad Sunday in 1642.

Very soon after that year a very illustrious man came to live
at Eydon. This was John Browne, Clerk of Parliament from 1641
to 1691. John Browne had legal training and was a member of
the Middle Temple. He was born into a rich City family, and
belonged to the inner group of civil servants both socially and
professionally. It was his job to keep a Journal of the House, a
list of peers present daily and a list of business transacted. In 1660
he began a new series of minute books, three separate series which
have been maintained ever since. Under his direction the archives
of Parliament came to maturity, assuming the form which, with
minor variations, they have preserved ever since.

John Browne was a firm adherent of the parliamentary cause during the Civil War, needing the army's protection from its enemies and becoming, as the Commons observed in 1649, a great sufferer in his estate for adhering to Parliament. His sufferings were still further increased at that time by his loss of the Clerkship, as the Upper House itself was abolished and the parliamentary office with it. The Council of State, however, found Browne employment in a variety of capacities, as commissioner at home and as envoy abroad. His abilities must have been marked (indeed the records at Wesminster bear ample testimony to his assiduity and thoroughness), and in 1660, on making full protestation of his loyalty to Charles II, he was reinstated in his post as clerk, and continued to serve till his death in 1691. The plague, the great fire, the clash between King and Parliament, to all these John Browne was a witness. Did he sit in Westminster Hall taking notes when the King was tried? Did he see him on the scaffold?

John's first wife was Temperance, daughter of Sir Thomas Crewe of Steane near Brackley in Northamptonshire, who was Speaker of the House of Commons. No doubt visiting his father-in-law brought him to this part of the country for the first time. He must have liked what he saw, for he soon bought several properties in the county, among them Radstone manor which was only three miles from Steane and had extensive woodlands.

Sir Thomas Crewe acted for John Browne in this transaction. Sir William Spencer asked £10,000 for Radstone, but Crewe offered only £9,000. Reporting the deal to John, Crewe ends his letter: 'Reckoning in the £50 which Mr Prescot must have, and another £5 which one Glover, another of Sir William Spencer's servants, will expect, it will cost you near upon £9400.'

When John Browne's first wife Temperance died he married in 1636 Elizabeth Packer, aged nineteen, at St Stephen's, Walbrook, in London. Her father was Clerk to the Privy Seal. Then some time between 1650 and 1660 John Browne bought the manor of

Eydon and when they came to live here they brought their two daughters, Elizabeth and Martha, with them. The fact that both girls later married locally, together with evidence in letters that passed to and fro, make it clear that John settled down to live the life of a country gentleman, spending as much time at Eydon as he possibly could, although by virtue of his office he was provided with a house at Twickenham.

The man seems to have had any amount of money, for soon he bought the Wakelyn manor and land, and Crockwell, a 315-acre farm in the adjoining parish of Canons Ashby, for £4,000. Then he bought a small parcel of land in Moreton Pinkney parish, on the opposite side of the brook to the land he already owned. The Moreton men hated seeing Eydon men working their side of the brook, so there was trouble, for John issued a summons to a man named Maunder to appear before the commissioners at The Red Lion, Moreton Pinkney, on 22nd January 1692, to be examined on oath.

There was trouble too at Crockwell, for in the Leicester records there is an account of a to-do through a father and son overlooking the boundary stone. Probably they ploughed up a bit of Browne's land. His steward had to keep his eyes very wide open or the Eydon folk would have cheated his master: '*5th May, 1683*. Acknowledgement by Thos. Voill and Thos. Voill Jun. that a mistake was made because the boundary stones between their land in Eydon and closes belonging to John Browne called Over and Nether Crockwell in parish of Canons Ashby were overgrown, and release their claim to the freeboard to John Browne.'

A few years before, a national postal system had been in-augurated. Our carrier took letters to Banbury and posted them after paying the charge. When John Browne was at Eydon, his brother-in-law Philip Packer kept him well informed about London events, and, when John was in London, his steward wrote to him, giving all the latest news from Eydon. A letter dated 23rd May 1670 from Richard Ellis to his master, John

Browne, gives an account of what happened to the man and horse provided by John Browne at the muster of the militia. 'Almost all the young men in the town were active about the maypole, it stands by the elm tree, carts and coaches may pass by.' Evidently something went wrong that day. I read that it was always difficult, especially in peacetime, to get these men to take their duties seriously; did this man object to leaving his mates amusing themselves with the maypole and so get lost on his way to the muster? Some folk can be very stupid; maybe the Eydon fellow thought Richard Ellis ought to have sent one of the Londoners in Browne's employ. Evidently the maypole was on the small green by the stocks, but the elm tree mentioned must have been the predecessor of the elm we call the Cross Tree. Deceandolle gives the life of an elm as 335 years. I should like to think it was the present tree, for it is very aged, but I'm afraid it is not that old.

In 1666 Elizabeth Browne married Toby Chauncey of Edgcote, who must have been a little boy when his father entertained King Charles and the two princes the night before the battle of Edgehill. Alas, poor Elizabeth died within a year, leaving a small son who died the following year. Ten years later Martha Browne married Sir Roger Cave of Stanford, a little village on the edge of the county near Lutterworth.

The rector of Eydon who married Martha and Roger was John Parkes, BD, and I believe he was a good friend of the Brownes. He was not an 'ignorant Mass priest', but an educated man, and probably had some money, for he married Elizabeth Holbeach, daughter of the lord of the manor at Farnborough in Warwickshire.

Soon after Parkes came to the village he helped John Browne to face a very difficult situation. In 1654 some Banbury folk became Quakers. Banbury is ten miles away, and it would not have mattered so much if they had stayed there. But an old Eydon man went and joined them and came home and said, 'he shouldn't pay the church rate'. Being a true Quaker he didn't. They gave him quite a bit of rope; let him go on for three years, during which time I'll be bound that John Browne and the parson talked very sternly to him, reminding him he was setting a bad example, and that freeholders always had paid the church rate and so forth. But Thomas Smallbone was adamant, his 'no' was final. So in 1658, when he owed £3 5s., they took him to court and he was sent to prison for five weeks, and his goods taken to the value of 9s. It was bad enough for squire and parson to have to deal with a passive resister, but the worst aspect was that Thomas brought Quakers home and went up to Culworth and hob-nobbed with Quakers there.

I can see these two good men, John Browne and John Parkes, the rector, sitting by the manor fireside anxiously discussing the situation: it was the thin end of the wedge and the Quakers were increasing in numbers all over the land. What could they do? They must have decided to draw the attention of the House of Commons to the situation. Browne must have said: 'You write out a statement and I'll get it on the agenda at the House of Commons.' Parkes sat down and wrote:

These are to certify that there are in Northamptonshire, in ye townes of Culworth and Eydon, very greate Assembly's of Quakers and Anabaptists meetinge in greate multitudes and quite frequently, sometimes twice in a weeke, plotting, continuing, and prayinge against ye peace of ye church and state; castinge out severall scandalous papers against ministers, and theye preaching ye truth, whereby ye peace of ye county is much endangered, ministers discouraged, good people grieved, weake ones seduced and ye erronious and dissatisfyed people confirmed in theyr dangerous positions; nay, they publicly say that they hope they shall have another day to put into execution theyr wicked designes; this will be asserted by

Yr. humble servant

September   John Parkes.
ye 3. 1660.

John Browne took it to London and handed it to the Speaker
or one of his friends. After it had been read in the House of
Commons, on 3rd September 1660, he put it on his file, and it is
in the House of Lords' archives to this day. The House recom-
mended to the justices of the peace of the next assize of the county
of Northamptonshire that they should give special charge and
directions to the justices of the peace and all other officers to take
care to suppress and prevent meetings of Anabaptists and Quakers.

The statement read in the House was, I believe, written by a
good and conscientious man, truly grieved by Smallbone's
conduct and fearful of his influence in the village. It was all so
mysterious; one would have thought five weeks in prison would
have taught him a lesson, but no, he became wilder and wilder
and said the most terrible things about the Church and parsons.
If he'd been a bad lot it would have been understandable, but he
was a good honest man, paid his debts and did not blaspheme. It
was most unsettling and mysterious.

When Thomas Smallbone started being awkward, the village
was beginning to recover from a disaster. On 13th August 1651
a fire had broken out in the village which consumed twenty-six
houses, besides barns and stables, with 223 loads of corn and hay,
the damage being computed at £1,000 upwards in money of the
time. That would be about one-third of the houses in the village.
The village was so compact that in 1651, when every house was
thatched, with hay and corn ricks close to the houses, a fire
would spread like a prairie fire. Like the fire that raged in my
own lifetime, in 1905, it sounds as if this one too started near the
Wakelyn manor house and spread up the street. There are signs
that before the fire some houses on the east side were further from
the street than they are today; they were not rebuilt. I believe
after the fire John Browne set to work and did some planning to
tidy up the lower end of the street. For there till recent years
were six blocks of three cottages, all built at the same time. Look
closely at the walls and here and there you can see a reddened

stone that has been in a fire. The best of the stones were used again and mixed with newly quarried stone.

The houses give directly on to the street; you step out of your door into the street. Strangers have to be careful or they'll fall over someone's doorstep which is trespassing on the footpath. Some houses face the street and some have their backs to it: the set-up here is enough to give a town and country planning officer a nightmare, but they are solidly built.

Although John Browne's connection with the Crewe family ended with the death of his first wife Temperance, a friendship was formed with the family that endured for the rest of his life. During the last few years of John's life the rates were paid in the name of Lord Crewe, so evidently he did some secretarial work for John.

About 1681 Lord Crewe built at Hinton in the Hedges, near his home in Steane, two alms-houses for poor widows. He wanted to make some investment so that the poor widows could be paid £5 a year each. Every time he came to Eydon he passed a parcel of land, nineteen acres and a bit, that was for sale. John Browne told him it was good land, well worth the money, so Crewe bought it and it belongs to the poor widows to this day.

It was not all work for poor folk; they celebrated each year Plough Monday, May Day, Midsummer Eve and the end of harvest. Every village had a fiddler to lead the singing and dancing on those occasions. Travelling pedlars came round bringing the district news and selling ribbons, brooches, laces and pins. The carrier to Banbury brought home goods unobtainable here, and also letters. As only a few could read and write he would not have a very heavy bag. There were no daily newspapers, for the *Northampton Mercury* did not start until 1720.

By the end of the seventeenth century the parson here was an educated man with a good standard of living, second only to the squire. Changes wrought by the Reformation demanded that he should do his duty faithfully and well in the parish, be loyal to the bishop, and obey the law of the land. We can be sure that John Browne was insistent he should do his duty, for he was that sort of man. I believe in return John took steps to improve the parson's standard of living. He could help him gather in the tithes; he could buy a plot of land and give it to increase the glebe land. As John always turned out well dressed, it would not have pleased him to see the parson wearing a dirty, worn-out suit. The idea of the black-coated parson with clean hands and polished boots, more at home drinking a glass of port with the squire than working side by side with poor folk in the fields, had arrived. These ideas are borne out by the fact that Parkes was here for forty-two years and his successor, Hutchings, for thirty-seven; both died on the job. Also, Baker gives the value of the living in 1553 as £17 6s. 8d., while in 1655 it was £110 per annum. Gregory King in his estimate of average incomes in 1688 puts the lower clergy at £50 per annum and, for comparison, artisans at £38, and labourers at £15. Evidently the living here was well above the average, so Hutchings could employ a man to do the hard work on his land, as we shall see later.

Some idea of the size of the village and the sort of houses it had can be gauged by details of the new government Hearth Tax which was introduced about this time and which was based on the number of fireplaces in the houses. In 1668 John Browne's house had fifteen fireplaces, and in the village one house had eight, one seven, one five, six three, thirteen two and forty only one. This is the only indication we have of the size of the manor house; it shows how much larger it was than any other house here. During the century before John came no one seems to have lived there long; so the probability is that it was on the small side and old-fashioned. Fifteen hearths: there must have been a fireplace in several bedrooms, a luxury in those days. No doubt

John enlarged the house and modernised it, so that it was comfortable for a lady and gentleman to live in.

This tax was easy to assess at the cottages where only one small chimney was visible, but during this period farmers and tradesmen were building houses with a bedroom fireplace. Two, three or four flues could be put into the one chimney stack visible from the road. So it became necessary for the tax collector to go inside the house and upstairs, to count the fireplaces. The women complained; it was intolerable to have a man come into your house with mud on his boots, and go poking about, opening every door, they said. The wives of MPs said it was outrageous. They did not suffer in silence, or in vain. Their poor husbands when they got back to Westminster told their troubles to their friends, only to find they too had had a telling off. So they said, 'We shall have to alter the law, we can't stand this any longer.'

And so it came to pass that in 1692 the House of Commons annulled the Hearth Tax and introduced the Window Tax in its place. They said, 'There's no need for the collector to go inside a house now, he can walk round outside and count the windows.' Windows above a certain size were counted as two windows, and if a window lit two rooms it was counted as two. Cheese rooms and dairies with wood splines or iron bars were exempt, provided there was no glass. A house at a rent of under £5 yearly could have up to six windows and paid 6s. 6d. a year. In 1780 the rate for ten windows was £2 16s., for twenty £11 4s. 6d. A farmhouse in Partridge's Lane had been rebuilt in 1683; part of the old one had been demolished to make room for a new block. Another part of the old one became a stable. The farmer living there when the new tax became operative was wild; I shouldn't wonder if he swore, for no doubt the tax increased his payment. He sent for the mason and had him take the glass out of three windows on the south side, and brick up the opening between the stone mullions, and they are bricked up to this day.

Although the majority of houses here appear to have been

either built or rebuilt during the latter part of the century, I should be surprised if some of the earlier houses did not still stand in the street. The living-room in these houses was shared with a cow and a pig on the other side of a partition. It had its advantages for it helped keep the room warm in the winter. The animals were there only at night; during the day they were out on the commons looking for something to eat, so the room was aired each day. In these houses, when you went to bed you climbed a ladder to a loft.

For the rebuilding after 1651 very little material from outside the parish was needed. Stone was here and sand in abundance.

Lime was made up on Woodford Hill to mix with sand for mortar. The wood needed for timber grew in the woodlands, and straw for the roof in the fields. Glass, lead and strips of iron had to be brought from Banbury; we reckon a cart-load would have been sufficient for eight to ten cottages. The blacksmith made the window-frames, locks for the door, pot hooks for the fireplace and nails for the carpenter's use. The glazier made the lead lights and cut the glass to fit. Then the stone mason, the carpenter and the thatcher built the house.

Tradesmen's wages were 1s. 2d. a day. The mason would build the walls of a cottage for £4 and the total labour cost would be about £15. Add say £10 for stone, wood and so on and you

could have a good thatched cottage for about £25. But not if
you wanted it built all of good cut stone with gable windows
and a water table where the thatched roof meets the end walls.
My cottage was a compromise: the front is of good cut stone; it
has a gable window in the attic and the water table is quite good.
But in the back wall on the street they used any old stones that
were handy, including some burnt in the 1651 fire. We shall not
be far out if we say those blocks of three cottages cost John
Browne about £90 each, or that you could have had a six-room
house of good cut stone with all the extras built for about £150.
Judging by Gregory King's table of wages in the nineteenth
century, we here were in a very low wage area, the farm labourer
being paid only 8*d*. a day. During haytime and harvest he could
earn 1*s*. a day, though if his employer provided him with meat
and drink he got only 6*d*.

How did they live in those days, the men that built the house
I live in? Their food consisted mainly of rye and barley bread,
pease pudding, beans, butter and cheese. Many small birds were
eaten, larks being especially prized – they were sold in the towns
at 2*d*. a dozen. No doubt a rabbit often went into the pot and
sometimes a hare or partridge, though that was agin the law. The
housewife malted barley and made beer. She made her thread
from nettles, and spun and wove and made the family's clothing.
Every house had a tinder box, flint and steel. But what a performance to light a fire! I know, for I've tried to get a light with
my tinder, flint and steel. But there, if I had to do it every time
I wanted a light maybe I should become an expert at the job.
Clocks were too expensive for poor folk – their day was regulated
by the church bell. It was a job an old man could do, ring the bell
morning, noon and curfew. The bell that was hung in 1603 still
rings out on church festivals.

We know much about John Browne and Eydon in his time
but nothing about the village courts held in his day. We know
little about Sir Roger Cave but we get quite a good picture of

village life while he was here because court records are available for this period. Fortunately his eldest son William survived to sell the manor to Richard Williamson, Captain of the Northants Militia. As both families employed a Daventry attorney, the documents are in the Northamptonshire Record Office. Were these the good old days, I wonder, that the old folk had deep in their subconscious minds – the days their grandparents used to talk about when they were children? It's such a splendid idea, that twelve men good and true could have a meeting and pass a law, and fine those who disobeyed. The times I've sat on the parish council and wished we could pass a little law; yes, they were the good old days.

Where the courts were usually held I do not know. One was held at the manor, and another adjourned court was held at 'Ye signs of ye Bell alehouse'.

Three different courts were held, one to make rules and regulations, one to try offenders and another to register changes of ownership of land or house with the lord of the manor. At one court in April 1778 there were sixteen changes of ownership registered and each new purchaser did fealty to the lord of the manor and paid him a fee. The court elected its officials, who were also responsible for seeing that all fines were paid and had power to distrain goods if necessary. The court also chose a town crier to summon all householders to the courts. Considering the size and shape of the village, I reckon they paid the crier uncommonly well to give him a shilling for his services. Even if he went round twice in case anyone hadn't heard him the first time he hollered, he still wouldn't have been an hour on the job.

The court baron made the rules and regulations pertaining to the common lands. This is a sample of those made on 29th April 1699:

1. It was agreed that all commoners shall brand or mark their sheep with a sufficient publick mark whereby they may be known twice a year, first time May day and the next time Martlemas and

that every commoner shall have all his sheep and lambs together in one place the day before May day and Martlemas, if any refuse so to do they shall forfeit 1s.

2. It was agreed that the rams shall be taken up at Bartholomew and be flitt as formerly and kept tied till the 14th October, penalty 6d.

3. It was agreed that no horse tye shall be above 16 foot from his stake to the horses foot, penalty 6d.

4. It was agreed that if the hayward shall find any hogs or pigs in the field that are not ringed* the pigs being above 10 weeks old he shall have power to pound the same and to take for his pimlock 4d.

Regulations were made fixing the time when the cows should go into the cow pasture and the sheep into the cornfield. Evidently some of the commoners sold their grazing rights to farmers; this was regulated and a penalty exacted if broken. The maximum fine of 5s. was incurred if a man 'set any horse commons to any man that liveth out of towne, though he may live in the parish'. Quite right too. I should have been dead agin any Woodford man bringing his horses here to eat our grass; or any Eydon man mean enough to do such a dirty trick. The strips of arable land were divided by a grass baulk, wide enough to enable a man to walk down the strip to admire his corn or peas during the growing season. A man might carelessly turn his plough and rip up some of the turf. If he'd replaced it all would have been well, but he was in a hurry to get home so left it lying rough. 'Right ho,' his neighbour said to himself, 'you wait till the next court.' There he ventilated his grievance, and I've no doubt an interesting discussion ensued. Every man was entitled to have a say in the matter; some would treat it lightly, others would think it a very serious matter; they would discuss the pros and cons in detail,

---

* This refers to a ring put in the pig's snout, to prevent it rooting up the turf.

including the proposed fine, before they made this law at Eydon: 'It was agreed that if any man shall suffer his plow to catch any piece of a baulk and if he neglect to lay it down again, he shall forfeit and pay 6*d*.' That was passed in April and the first offender was charged in October.

Sometimes the business at court was soon over if they decided to make no changes: 'We agree to stock with all sorts of catell as we used to do till the next Court.' The men's greed for every scrap of land they could possibly claim, their personal rivalries and the ever-present feuds between individuals would add interest to the court proceedings. If I know aught of country folk, plotting and scheming would precede the great day, and no new regulation would be accepted till it had been thrashed out in a wordy battle between the interested parties. What a job the jury would have, for ten or twelve good men and true, unbiased in their judgement, would be expecting too much of this village at any period in her history.

Now we turn to the court held on 22nd October 1697, before W. Calcutt, Sir Roger Cave's steward. Not to make rules and regulations, but to administer those in force at the time:

> ... Thos. Hawe's for his yearling colt following his team among ye peas contrary to our orders, fined 6*d*.
> Thos. Smallbone for his ram going loose in ye field contrary to our orders, fined 4*d*.
> Astill Smallbone for flitting [tethering] his mare and colt contrary to orders, two defaults, 1*s*.
> Mr. Hutchings for his cart going up and down ye baulks, 6*d*.
> Astill Smallbone for keeping his sheep in ye pasture, contrary to orders, fined 3*s*. 4*d*.
> Thos. Daniel for drawing out a baulk, contrary etc. 6*d*.
> Thos. Garland for breaking ye assize of ale, 6*d*.

Garland was mine host at The Royal Oak; and Smallbone was a Quaker, so it is likely they did not go to the courts to help make the rules and regulations or keep those that were made. Maybe that is why they fined Astill Smallbone 3s. 4d. for a sheep offence, the heaviest fine in the records. Mr Hutchings was the rector. I should have thought he would have impressed on his man the necessity of setting a good example in the village. But no, he was frequently charged, and it looks as if his man thought he could do just what he liked in the parish. This was a serious offence for which he was fined 6d. 'We present Mr. Hutchings for his servants casting up and down ye baulks in ye corn.' Another offence cost Mr Hutchings 1s. because his man tethered a mare and colt within forty yards of 'ye corn'. And so the courts not only tried to keep the poor people in order, but also the good: parson and Quakers along with the publican had to keep the law or pay a fine. I'm sure the constable here was a man who did his duty; he'd go to the rectory as bold as brass to collect the fine. The more I think about these proceedings the more convinced I am that these were the good old days.

Horses and cows could be tethered to graze in the fields, but not pigs; someone had to keep an eye on them or they'd roam and soon do damage. Children would act as shepherds while father got on with his work; it was too slow a job for him watching pigs for long hours while they found something to eat. It was a monotonous job: the children found something more interesting in the field, and forgot the pigs, so 'Ed Prestidge was fined 6d. for his children loosing a sow and piggs in ye cow pasture.'

An important item in the village set-up was the pound, a walled enclosure at the corner of the Byfield road. It was the duty of the 'thirdborough', a court official, to drive any animal found loose in the fields to the pound and keep it there till a fine was paid. Easier said than done. The poor man had other work to do and it was tiresome to wait there for old Bob to come and pay 3d. and take his pig home. Had he gone for his dinner that day in October 1706 when John Smallbone fetched his cow out of the pound and took her home, without paying the third-borough? It was a very serious offence, the court decided, for they fined him 3s. 4d. Or was that heavy fine inflicted because John was a Quaker?

Another time it is evident that the court did not know who the actual culprit was: 'We present all people for leaving the pound gate open and propping it open, fine 6d.'

The court that dealt with changes in ownership of property was a stern reminder to every freeholder that he held his property by favour of the lord of the manor, and a small annual payment was made in acknowledgement of the same. With the exception of these, the lord claimed ownership of every scrap of land in the parish except the roads and footpaths. Strips of grass that grew in the street and the lanes, corners here and there and the roadside verges in the village, all were called 'The Lord's Waste'. Many cottages had no garden, only small backyards in which animals were housed, so there was no room for a stack of firewood. They did not burn logs as we do, for wood was too precious; they burnt the brushwood. It made a cheerful blaze, but soon burned away. They did not sit up dark nights round a cheerful fire while mother told the youngsters tales; when the pot had been boiled and the contents eaten all went to bed. So if father brought a bundle of wood home and dropped it on the grass by the door till the morning he had committed an offence. If mother cleaned the pigsty and there was no room to put the muck in the yard, out in the street it went till father could cart it away. At the court held in October 1753 there were twenty-seven various offences recorded, including eighteen charges of laying wood or dung on the lord's waste. Two got off very lightly with a fine of 1d., while the others paid 2d. Edward Clanvill was charged with a 'publick nuisance in emptying a bogg house [privy] in the street'. I'm surprised they let him off with a 2d. fine. Most respectable people appeared at this court. Alice Ansley of The Royal Oak put dung on the lord's waste, and folk like Smallbone, Brightwell, Dodd and Prestidge were unable to keep this law. Maybe the fine was so small it was worth it for the convenience.

That day they started off as a token of respect with the rector, the Rev. John Spencer, or his tenant J. Allit, for enclosing a plot of ground upon the common and building on the same, fined 6*d*. The stone pits up the Byfield road brought business to this court, for Stephen Chiles was charged with 'a publick nuisance in not mounding and guarding his stone pits near the Kings highway to the great danger of the lives of the inhabitants'. George and William Tew were charged with a similar offence, each being fined 4*d*. The same day Stephen Chiles had to pay 2*s*. 6*d*. for 'trespassing with his team in the fields of Eydon where there is no legal highway'. That was one of the most common offences for, with very few hedges, in the dry periods a man with a horse and cart cut across country to save time and mileage.

The eighteen householders charged with a trespass on the lord's waste paid their fines that day, and did the same thing time and time again. So it is evident they thought it a pretty rotten law, and as there were so many offenders it was no disgrace to have to go to court. They must have provided endless amusement for the poor folk and when the constable collected the fines that day he handed the steward 5*s*. 8*d*., less expenses. The poor lord of the manor was losing money.

Chapter 2

Enclosures, 1762

During the latter half of the eighteenth century the birth-rate in the country was going up and the death-rate down, with the result that the number of mouths to be fed was increasing, while production of foodstuffs was stationary. Pioneers in agriculture were introducing new systems of drainage, improving the yields of corn and the breeding and feeding of cattle and sheep. The new husbandry could do nothing to help men on the common lands; enclosed fields were absolutely necessary if the maximum amount of produce was to be obtained. The common pasture and the strips of arable that changed hands annually were terribly wasteful; the only good thing one can say about them is that they gave a man a measure of independence.

Enclosing was the act of enclosing land by fencing: after this had been done it became an enclosure. It was a sorry business but there was no other way if all the babies being born were to survive and grow into men and women. Birth control had not been invented in 1750. About that date, as far as I can learn, roughly a third of the parish was common land (550 acres), the remaining 1,125 being held by freehold farmers and the rector; Williamson, the lord of the manor, had the largest amount. The west field was mainly common pasture and the arable land lay in the north and east fields. A few fields have escaped the plough during the last fifty years, so you can still see the strips the men drew lots for at the annual court.

The neighbouring parish of Woodford Halse had had their common fields enclosed in 1734, so the men here knew all that was involved: how if you were fortunate and were granted three acres, you had to plant a hedge and dig a ditch on two sides, or maybe three. Then you had to protect the quickthorn you had planted for some years or your cow would eat it; and if she did not eat it she'd pull it out of the ground for devilment. The farmers here went to market and heard tales of happenings in villages after enclosure and came back and told tales of woe. Oh, it was a to-do. And they frightened the little men, men with grazing rights and a couple of strips in the arable fields. The farmers were getting the men just where they wanted, with the result that many sold their rights to freeholders long before the Enclosure Act became law. They also realised the many disadvantages under which they worked their strips situated in two or three common fields, or maybe several acres together which they were unable to enclose in a ring fence. They must have looked enviously at two large barns in the parish: one on Wilbraham's ancient enclosure and the other on the lord's enclosed fields. There corn could be stacked in the dry and threshed when convenient; the straw could be fed to cattle during the winter and the manure was in the field when the time came to spread it. At home the farmer was cramped for room, with only a narrow strip from his back door to the Back. One man was evidently able to buy his neighbour's strip and build a barn like the lord's; but he still had to cart his corn to the barn and when the manure was made it had to be taken to his arable land.

So when Captain Williamson suggested enclosure like other parishes around he had the backing of many influential people in the village. The business began when he sent a petition to Parliament, which led to an Act being presented to the House of Commons. At the time we were represented in the House by

Sir Justinian Isham and William Cartwright of Aynho, the two members elected to represent the whole county of Northampton. No doubt Cartwright saw the bill through the House, after he'd been given all the details by Captain Williamson.

Williamson was evidently a keen man with money, for documents at the Record Office show that he was slow in making his wife a marriage settlement so that her trustees, through the Court of Chancery, had to bring him up to scratch and he settled £6,000 upon her. Jane was a Knightley of Fawsley, one of the old county families who were staunch Puritans in the seventeenth century. At the time of the enclosures they had a reputation for being a very tight-fisted lot. There is a story of the Knightleys' attitude towards poor folk which may be a fable, but it reflects the way they were thought of in the district. Badby village was part of the Knightley estate and the story goes that when the enclosure was made there, a field was allocated to the cottagers of the village. Valentine Knightley persuaded the commissioners to allow him to grow one more crop on the land, before it was made over to the village. He planted trees – oak, ash and elm. You may have your doubts and so may I, but Badby folk have heard this tale so many times they've no doubts about its truth.

After the Enclosure Act had become law, the next stage took place in the village. The commissioners may have been named in the Act, or they may have been nominated by the lord of the manor, the parson and the chief landowners in the village. These were the men that met here to see the business through: Francis Burton, Aynho; Job Bazeby, Priors Marston; Clement Wilson, Watford; Thomas Prestidge, Culworth; all gentlemen. Thomas Price of Greens Norton acted as clerk. Two surveyors were employed, R. Liddington and Rob Weston. Their first meeting was on 26th March 1761 at the house of Alice Ansley, known by the sign of The Royal Oak. What a pity they did not leave us the minutes of that meeting, the most momentous of all meetings ever held in the village. Such a meeting had never been held before, or can ever be held in the future. The business was to divide several hundred acres of good land free of encumbrances among thirty to forty men.

At an auction sale the highest bidder wins, but there was no bidding at this meeting. The only man who could assert his right to a portion was the parson; he could demand so much in lieu of tithes, great and small. The other men had to prove to the commissioners' satisfaction their right to a portion, either by freehold ownership or ancient rights in the common fields. During the centuries these rights had been slowly but surely diminishing, so that many had become vague and ill-defined. We can be sure Captain Williamson was there with his steward, and the parson would ride over from Fritwell, for this was business he could not leave to the curate; he earned his money at church. The farmers would all be there, some sure of getting a share of the loot, and some hopeful they'd come in for a few acres. Poor men were dressed in their Sunday clothes, a bit nervous among all the gentry but determined to assert their rights in the share-out.

After hearing the claims of all and sundry, the meeting adjourned, for the commissioners would have to walk round the parish and see the land, the roads and paths, and old enclosures. The surveyors' first task would be to make a plan of the three fields, to help the commissioners adjudicate at the next meeting. Several meetings would be necessary, for there were so many details to be taken into consideration and so many claims and counter-claims put forward by the interested parties. The land near the village would be in great demand, but that near Warden Brook was up another street. The hill makes it a hard pull for horses with a heavy load, and that was a consideration every farmer would bear in mind. The squire, the parson and the village men were united in one factor only: every man tried his level best to get as much land as he possibly could. They'd plot, they'd scheme, and they'd argue at the meetings. My word, the commissioners had a tough job on hand.

Although I hate the sorry business, I must give the gentlemen credit for the meticulous care taken for the general well-being of the village, and the preservation of ancient rights of way. Footpaths were such a boon to poor folk who used Shanks' pony, but a bugbear to farmers. We can be very sure that if the favoured thirty-seven had had their way, we should have no paths through the fields today.

When the commissioners had completed their enquiries and the Act had been made law at Westminster two copies were made, each signed and sealed by the commissioners, one for the County Clerk of the Peace and one for the parish. The heading is:

> Award or instrument in writing of the Commissioners appointed in and by an Act of Parliament made and passed in the first year of the Reign of His Majesty King George the third, instituted An Act for dividing and inclosing the Common fields, Common pastures, Common meadows, Grange lands and Waste grounds of and in the Manor and Parish of Eydon in the County of Northampton, which award bears date 9th day of January, 1762.

It is far too long to quote in full, but if you will come with me to the top of School Lane and stand at the corner we'll take a sample road or two:

> ... That the ground now measured and set out being of the breadth of forty feet from the gate going into Richard Williamson's old enclosure called High Fields at or near the North West Churchyard gate and thence going Northwards and leading on the East ends of the several allotments of the said James Stopes, John Watts, Clarke Adams, Joseph Ashby, Ann Banwell and on part of the North West and North end of the said allotment of the said John Daniel shall be and remain at all times hereinafter a publick road or highway for the passage and conveyance of persons, horses, cattle and carriages and shall be deemed as part of the public highway between Eydon and Preston Capes.

A gate was to be set up at the pound, the corner of the Byfield road; and another at the west end of the town for the Preston road, at or near the north-eastern corner of the dwelling house of John Thackhall. The proprietors of land were to pay for their maintenance, James Stopes and his successors excepted. The road believed to be the Roman road to Trafford was to be a bridle road twenty foot wide for all persons to pass and repass on foot and horseback between Eydon and Banbury. Out of this road a three-foot-wide path led in a 'straight line to a certain spring called New Well and going over part of the said allotments of the said James Stopes for his great and small Tythes of the said fields at Eydon, shall at all times remain a public footway for all persons to and from the said Spring called New Well. . . .' We know it as the Red Well, and it was very important in those days, for it is a chalybeate spring. Up to recent years it was considered very good for bathing weak eyes, and we all agree it is much nicer water to drink than our tap water.

Provision was made for the upkeep of the roads: '. . . There shall be a convenient cart road 20 feet wide to $\frac{1}{2}$ acre sand pit lying on the west side of Stanhill furlong in the East field on land alloted to Thos. Short Harris and Margaret, his wife, for a public gravel pit for the repair of roads within the Manor of Eydon.' That is down the Preston road in the gravel pit field. A shallow depression in an otherwise level field shows where the half-acre was situated; very little can have been dug, so Thomas Short came in for an extra half-acre above his ration.

Stone for the repair of the roads was to come from a public stone pit of half an acre, near the road to Chipping Warden. That is the top of Bufton, and appears to have been worked for the small stone near the surface of the ground, not the building stone that lies deeper.

The two brooks on the parish boundary were to be scoured and cleaned by the proprietors of the adjoining land, as had been done in past years.

The allocation of the common lands appears to have been mainly the surrendering of freehold land in one field for a larger area in another part of the parish. Thomas Esom for one yard of land and one half part of Grange land, received 55 acres 1 rood in the west field. Richard Hutchings, DD, for one quarter and half quarter yard of land in the west field, was given 13 acres 1 rood by the brook near Trafford. He was responsible for the fencing on the east side, the west and the north-west.

The Rev. J. Stopes was awarded 231½ acres in lieu of tithes, great and small. Everyone else had to pay a share of the expenses, but not him. Everyone allotted land in the award appears to have been an actual owner, though some evidently owned very small plots. John Daniel, having previously owned 20 acres, received 32 acres 2 roods in the east field. Edward Bull, the younger, in lieu of his odd lands and meadowing ground, received 1 acre 23 perches, also in the east field. Robert Gardner for his piece in the fields was allocated 1 rood, 5 perches in the west field. He had to plant a hedge on the east and south sides of his tiny field, and to pay 2s. 7d. towards the expenses of the business. When William Tew was allocated 32 acres 3 roods up the Byfield road, part of the land he already held was one quarter of a yard land lately purchased from John Smallbone. I expect he was the last member of the old Quaker family to live here. In the Land Tax return for 1800, a Smallbone owned property here, but lived at Woodend.

The total cost of the whole business was £773 10s. The award says it shall be paid by a pound rate, payable to Thomas Freeman of Daventry, Williamson's steward. He paid £85, John Wigson, £22 5s., Edward Esom, £7 19s. and Rich. Hutchings, DD, £11 11s. The amounts they paid work out at 17s. 6d. an acre. At that rate the land enclosed was 884 acres, nearly half the land in the parish. It included land owned by freeholders; the Act gave them the right to enclose. That was the extent of the common fields. As many strips and plots were already privately owned, it appears to me that those owners shared the remainder of the land between themselves. In this district hedges were to be of quickthorn with a four-foot ditch; sheep and lambs were barred for several years lest they damage the hedge in its early growth.

In the Stone Pits here lay a lot of loose stone, which was used along the back of the village for a wall, and around the pits. Another temporary fence that would be used as a shield while the newly planted hedge was growing was the dead hedge. I remember one down the Warden road on John Henry Ivens's land. It was a row of upright branches of thorn, kept upright, I expect, by a few posts and bound horizontally by withies. Probably furze could be used for the job, but I imagine the life of this sort of hedge would be only three or four years. It is a job requiring patience, growing a thorn hedge big and strong enough to withstand a bullock when he wants a bite of the nice grass on the other side. Judging by the rate the hedges grew by the side of the Great Central Railway, twenty years must pass before horses and strong bullocks know it's their master. To the big farmer the obligation of fencing was no hardship, but to a man getting on in life, the owner of a few acres, it was a terrible hardship. The cost of planting a hedge and the years it restricted the use to which the land was put were indeed a burden on the small man. We can be sure his neighbours were not helpful. They'd keep him up to scratch, for big fish live on little fish on land as well as in the sea. And so it was that in many cases the men that were allotted only an acre or two sold out to one of their neighbours. What else could Robert Gardner do with his plot in the west field, the size of a site for a house today, with the obligation to plant hedges? John Wigson was allocated 29 acres in the east field, bounded on the east by Rich. Williamson, north by W. Brooks, south-east by Edward Esom. This was bought the following year by Richard Williamson for £455. Edward Esom, Wigson's neighbour, came in for 10 acres 1 rood; this also was bought by Williamson for £156. Good land for a trifle over £15 an acre in 1763.

The following is the only scrap of information of the enclosure period I've obtained by oral tradition. It shows how history has been passed down from one generation to another for nearly two centuries. Years ago Farmer Lines told me that Williamson and the parson exchanged land up the Byfield road for some adjoining Bufton. In 1966 I found among the documents at the Record Office a memo recording the exchange. Farmer Lines never saw the memo; he was always too busy on his farm to waste precious time, as I've done, looking at bits of paper. But he'd a good memory, a veritable storehouse of country lore.

The enclosure of the common fields was not the end of the land grab by a long way. The lord of the manor, the parson and farmers had shown what could be done; now the smaller fry got busy. Two houses in the street have four-foot-wide bays encroaching on the footpaths, to keep pedestrians a respectable distance from windows. I doubt if they were charged at the Court Leet, but others were:

> ... 12th October, 1763 – George Rainbow, labourer for a publick nuisance in making a ditch and planting trees on the King's highway to the narrowing and straightening of the same to the annoyance of the inhabitants and passengers, fined 1s. ...

William Prestidge, at the same court, paid 1s. for a shop on the waste, six years' rent. John Thackwell paid 6d. for a wash-house on the waste for six years' rent. Now 2d. a year for a shop, 1d. yearly for a wash-house, you can't call that dear! Evidently John Thackwell paid up, for on 20th October 1764 he was fined 1d. for an encroachment on the waste, building a wash-house on the same. As fines were no deterrent they became an annual rent, and the lord of the manor kept these courts going till the time came when the fines no longer paid the expense of the court.

Now we will leave the village and go up the Byfield road to

the junction with the Woodford road. Between the two roads is a three-cornered field; the roadside fence is a post and wire fence. The blighter that was allocated this field failed to keep his part of the bargain, to plant a hedge. Probably it was left unfenced for years and when it was fenced it was a post-and-rail affair. I raise no objection to the type of fence, but what makes me angry is that he robbed us of the forty-foot-wide road to Woodford, so that that part is the narrowest road in the parish. The road has been widened so that it is now very close to the fence and the hedge on the other side of the road. Still it is not wide enough for modern traffic. I hope this will be borne in mind if in the future the County Council decide to widen it. If I should be here, I'll kick up such a hullabaloo if they propose paying the owner of the field for the strip of land necessary. I'll write to our MP, I'll enlist the help of the *Daily Express*, oh, I'll make such a shindy if they propose paying ratepayers' money for stolen property. You can't get away from it. There it is in black and white for anyone to read in the 1762 Award:* the road to Woodford shall be forty feet wide, and it is not; all because years before Wilbraham had enclosed fourteen acres on the other side of the road. Not that it was worse here than in other villages. At Moreton Pinkney it was dreadful. There they had two nice greens in the village, but both were spoilt by land grabbers in the post-enclosure years.

The abominable part of the enclosure was not the Act of Parliament but the way many of its wise and good provisions for the welfare of the village were absolutely ignored. I doubt if the gates were ever set up at the entrances to the village, but that was no vital matter. The shameful thing was that many farmers failed to do what the Act said they must do, put fences round their land. To save a fence some put gates across the road to plague the traveller by day and by night. Oh, the bad language those five-barred gates must have caused through the years. It's only we folk

* The document citing the commissioners' allocation of land, siting of roads, footpaths and so on is called 'The Parish Award'.

that have driven a horse and trap that know the bugbear they were.

I'm grateful to the motorists in the 1920s who bumped into them, and it was the gates that suffered; so the motor has done one good thing for the traveller. Then the right to dig stone and gravel for the parish was allowed to lapse, and in a few years the ratepayers were buying stone to put on the roads. It was shameful the way the farmers quietly took over land to which they had no legal right; and did nothing for the village in return. They had it all their own way for a few years after enclosure, for Captain Williamson died soon after the Act was passed and for some years his estate was in the hands of his executors. They had no interest in the welfare of the village folk, and the same must be said of the rector. He lived fifteen miles away and his interest in the parish was how much money he could take out of the living, and leave enough for the poor curate to live on and have a new suit sometimes, so that he looked fairly respectable. Now if John Browne had been lord of the manor it would have been a very different story; he would have kept the farmers up to scratch and we should have had no gates across the world. He would have fetched the award out of the chest in church and would have read it to them; and they would have done what it told them to do, for John believed in law and order.

One surprise in the award is the number of field names that have vanished; so our map of field names is very little help in tracing the allocation to the new owners. The names used in the award were names of areas of land that during the next few years were divided into fields. Probably a generation passed before the fields took shape as we know them today. Many names were soon forgotten, and Runwell Furlong, Benson Leys, Penny Ham are quite foreign to us. As new fields were made new names were given them for the convenience of the farmers and the men, women and children that worked in them. Cooks Ground, Hunts Meadow, Ashbys Hill and Harris Close remind us of men that once lived here. Men working the fields often talked of the overseas colonies, men who were fully aware of the fact that the penalty for wrongdoers was often transportation. So we have Botany Bay, Manitoba, New Zealand and Van Damens land as names for fields.

We have already seen that Williamson began buying out the small man almost before the ink was dry on the award. He died in 1768, and twenty years later his successor, Francis Annesley, began buying as soon as he owned the manor, before the Hall was built. Williamson bought at about £15 an acre, but a few years later Annesley paid up to £30 an acre for some of his purchases. These two men with some outside help reduced the number of landowners in the parish from thirty-five to seventeen in twenty-seven years.

The Land Tax return for 1789 shows that there were six tenant farmers here with over a hundred acres, and four men rented from fifty to ten acres each. Some of these would be tradesmen who kept a horse or two for business purposes. In a very few years the land in the parish had got into the hands of a few men; the tenant farmer and the absentee landlord arrived on the scene at the same time. These men owned land here in 1789: Horn, Adams, Henson and Russell – strange names that occur only in those returns. Were they prosperous tradesmen in the nearby towns, I wonder?

Chapter 3

The Rev. Francis Annesley

With the enclosure of the common lands the lord of the manor courts faded out, but the need for a court for the good government of the parish remained. Someone had to collect rates and taxes and keep order in the village. A court was instituted consisting of the larger landowners and those who held property above a certain value. They elected the overseers of the poor, the constable and a 'waywarden' in charge of the roads, and someone to collect rates and taxes. As they met in the church vestry, this court is usually referred to as 'the Vestry'.

For a few years after the enclosure there would be work in the parish for every able-bodied man, for the farmers had long been waiting for the day to dawn on which they could start operations. They'd watched the Woodford farmers at work, and taken stock of how they laid out their fields; so they had plans already made in their minds. It was a big job that had to be done in addition to the ploughing, sowing and reaping and care of the livestock. Hedges had to be planted, ditches dug, gates made and hung, all work that entailed extra labour. Some of the men who had been their own master would be very sorry for themselves, having to work hard six days a week, but it's probable their wives thought otherwise. They'd find 8s. a week very nice after years of hand-to-mouth living; it was a small wage but it just enabled a frugal housewife to pay her way.

I think the one thing the women would miss most was the right to gather firewood. There are two areas in the parish to the west and north-west where furze and bracken still grow; I believe they were the places where bushes and scrub provided the poor folk with the firewood that they carried home and dumped on the lord's waste. After the award these scrub areas became private property and the women were trespassers if they went to gather firewood as their mothers and grandmothers had done in their day. We can be very sure that this aspect of the new order was impressed on the people by the farmers.

The first chance the people had to buy coal easily for their fires would have been in 1778 when the Oxford canal brought coal within seven miles of the village, and the first coal merchants came on the scene. It cost about 1s. a hundredweight here, or less if you fetched it from the wharf at Cropredy or Marston Dales. What a treat it must have been, to sit by a coal fire for the first time, a fire that burned for hours; not like the brushwood that burned away so quickly. It would have to be used very sparingly

for some years to come, for a man had to work a whole day to earn a hundredweight of coal. So the age-old motto 'Early to bed, early to rise' remained in vogue: no sitting up at night by a nice fire yet awhile for poor folk.

For most of the children born the year the canal was opened life was a grim struggle for existence, a matter of keeping body and soul together. Very little better than in the village six hundred years ago, and a dreadful setback from the preceding century. The Industrial Revolution and war with France (1773–1815) came at a time when the population of Britain was increasing by leaps and bounds. To encourage farmers to grow more corn Parliament passed a law restricting the import of corn from Europe till the price here had reached a certain level. During the years 1786–90 wheat averaged 46s. 2d. a quarter; by 1811–15 it had risen to 83s. 3d. for the five-year period. These figures are given in *The Common People 1746–1946* by G. D. H. Cole and Raymond Postgate. There was a temporary slump in the price after 1815, then it rose and remained high till the 1840s. These authors estimate that a labourer's wage in the west country rose from 9s. to 13s. a week during this period. I believe we were in a lower wage area than any that they investigated when they made their survey. For when they quote building workers in the west country earning 2s. a day, in the same area farm labourers earned only 1s. 3d. I have a bill for work done to a house at Moreton Pinkney in 1783. The mason and carpenter were paid 1s. 8d. daily. If they had to work a week to earn 10s. we may be sure no labourer earned more than 7s. for a week's work. Although I cannot quote chapter and verse, I believe the farm worker's ordinary wage was 9s. a week during the first half of the nineteenth century in this area. That was what I was told many years ago, and I've found no figures to disprove its accuracy. Shepherds and cowmen who worked seven days a week earned more for the extra day, and the responsibility of this work was rewarded by a higher wage.

Wages rose very slowly, while prices of foodstuffs rose rapidly, with the result that farm workers got poorer and poorer during this period. And the poorer they became, the larger their families grew. Some of the pleasures of this life are cheap at the time, but you pay for them afterwards. Bread, the staple food of the folk, cost 1s. 9d. for a loaf about 4 lbs in weight, cheese 7d. per lb, butter 9d., bacon 3d., sugar 9d. and tea 3s. per lb. Poor people did not drink tea in those days. Potatoes were not cheap, so if poor folk grew them I think the yield must have been very low, compared to the weight our modern varieties produce. Tea-kettle broth was invented at this time. In case you do not know the recipe, this is how to make it: break up some bread in a basin, place on it a noggin of dripping or lard, fill up with very hot water and it is ready to eat.

The population here in 1801 was 484; in 1831, 630; in 1841, 647. Then a decrease set in, and it was down to 500 in 1878; this continued with temporary rises and falls; in 1961 we numbered 335 men, women and children. Cottages here were grossly overcrowded, so poor little cottages were built in back gardens and any odd corner. A brickyard on Barnetts Hill made bricks and drainpipes for land draining, so several small cottages of brick were built. Bricks cost in the region of 30s. per thousand. There was plenty of rough stone lying about, but to build in stone took much longer than brickwork. Adjoining my cottage was a stable or cowshed. The thatched roof was taken off, the walls raised and a roof of slate put on. Then it was divided by a 4½-inch wall to make two cottages, each with three rooms, a living-room and two bedrooms. All the rooms were under eight foot wide. The village was not allowed to spread, since agricultural land was too valuable for housing poor folk. Not that the Rev. Francis Annesley or any of the farmers were asked to sell land at a good figure for housing; they did nothing to help house the young folk that married at this time. It was the small property owners who tried to meet the urgent need, and when all is said and done a little house on your own is better than living with your mother-in-law.

Annesley may not have done much building for others but he did plenty for himself, and so provided work for the able-bodied men of the village. This helped to stave off the worst after-effects of the enclosures, so that I believe that they were not hit hard here in Eydon until after England was at war with France in 1793.

The Rev. Francis Annesley was rector of Chedzoy in Somerset and when Captain Williamson died his executor sold the estate to him in 1788. Did he marry money, I wonder, when he married Mary, daughter of John Walker of Bicester; or did it come from his mother, the heiress of James Earl of Anglesey, her grandfather? This Francis was a shrewd customer if ever there was one: with all his money he went into the Church and became rector of Chedzoy. Then he played the game so many clergymen played in those days. He had the belly-ache and sent for the doctor. He knew very well what he was expected to say, so he said it: 'You will never be well here, the place don't suit you.' Here it is in black and white: 'Rector of Chedzoy Somerset. The place did not agree with Mr. Annesley. Richard Cross was appointed Curate by the Bishop of Bath and Wells by the desire of the parish at a salary of £60 with a house worth £20. W. Conray. Patron.'*

If the living brought in £160 per annum, that left a clear £100 for the absentee rector. It is evident that he had a farm in the village and one of his letters is headed Chedzoy, though for the next three years he appears to have lived at Bath, Sidmouth and Balscote near Banbury. During those years his letters to W. Walford, a Banbury attorney, have enabled me to trace the course of events. In January 1788 he agreed to buy the mansion house, land and timber for £6,600. The house, dog-kennel,

* This and the following quotations are from documents in the North-amptonshire Record Office.

fish-pond, court-garden and outbuildings occupied about three acres. Then there were three houses, three cottages, six gardens, six orchards, ten acres of wood and three hundred acres of pasture and meadow land.

No time was lost, for although the legal transfer had not taken place Annesley had taken over the land and growing crops in March, when he wrote: 'Mr. Williamson has given me leave to pull down the old house and begin building. I wish Mr. Davis would order one of the labourers to look after my horses, for Stroud has sent three mares, and I have ordered two horses from Balscote to assist in taking the rubbish and getting together some materials for building.' John Browne's manor house, stables and outbuildings were completely demolished, and all that remains today is the pillars of a gateway in the pleasure gardens in front of the house.

The new mansion designed by James Lewis, a four-storey building, took longer to build than Annesley had anticipated, for in September 1790 he wrote, 'I expected Harringham by this time to have got the building forwarder than the middle of the second storey, but the freestone, I believe, has been some impediment to the business.' The usual practice then was to employ what we now term 'direct labour'. The owner bought the stone and the mason built the walls for so much, the carpenter then did his work, and so on through all the construction of the building. When Edgecote House was built in 1755, stone was quarried a few hundred yards away from the house. There is any amount of good building stone on this hill, but to get it out of the ground and cut it so finely that there is only a quarter of an inch of mortar between the blocks was a very big job in those days – no crane to lift them out of the quarry, no mechanical saw to cut them to the right size. It all had to be done by men's strong arms, toil and sweat. They dug a pit near the house, for it would have been nice for Annesley if he could get the stone on his own ground. It is there today, and as it was not extended either the stone was not good enough or it lay too deep to be a payable proposition. So they had to go to the owner of the main quarry here, William Tew.

Now Mr Tew knew all about the trial hole that Annesley's foreman, Harringham, had dug, and he knew Annesley had money, so he grinned up his sleeve and waited. He was not surprised when Harringham went to see him; he wanted a lot of stone and he wanted it in a hurry. Mr Tew would say he was busy, folk all over the place were wanting stone; and he could not get it out of the ground fast enough to satisfy his customers. There was only one thing Harringham could do: offer him such a tempting price that he set on a number of extra men to quarry and cut the stone.

While the mansion was being built Annesley was buying any land he could in the parish. He wrote, 'I shall have no objection to purchase any estate that will pay 4% clear of all deductions of rates and tax's.' Altogether he bought about a hundred acres in the parish at about £14 an acre, and some in the adjoining parish of Moreton Pinkney that later caused trouble.

These letters give us a glimpse of a man and boy who may never previously have gone farther than two or three miles from Chedzoy being sent on the long trek of a hundred miles, on unknown roads with no signposts, to this remote village:

May 6th 1788.

I should think Mr. Davis might do without any more mares, as six oxen and one mare will be sent from Somersetshire to Eydon the first or second week in May and will make two teams or one very strong team. The great price that Stroud charges for the mares is my principle objection and to obviate his exorbitant price I will have two mares or another yoke of oxen if Mr. Davis thinks sufficient and if Mr. Williamson should want the money for the hay and corn I will send a draft.

Four days later he wrote:

I am glad another mare is bought if it was deemed necessary. I have upon the road ten working oxen and one mare, they will pass through your town on Thursday or Friday on their way to Eydon with a man and a boy, to do what business Mr. Davis thinks proper. He is a good ploughman and labourer and will stay till harvest is got together.

On May 13th he writes:

... should you hear or see my people with the oxen, give them some directions about the road to Eydon, and there will be some chains wanted. Mr. Wheatley may get by seeing those in my cart as it passes through Banbury. Mr. Davis has bought me a flock of sheep and if he will let me know the money he has deposited a day or two before he draws upon me at Messrs Hoare, I will give them an order to pay. The oxen will not be able to work for some days after their journey.

Let us hope they arrived safe and sound, and that Mr Davis gave the poor beasts a good rest after walking twenty miles a day for five days.

The mansion was built about two hundred yards further from the village than the old house, in the best position for the charming and extensive view of the Cherwell Valley. The south side has a fine flight of steps leading to a portico supported by four Ionic columns with decorated pediments. Adjoining the house is a conservatory in which flourished orange trees and palms until recent times. The nearby stable block is surmounted by a turret with a striking clock. Two lodges were built at the park entrances, the picturesque one in the village having a square tower complete with a fire bell. Over the doorway is a carving in local stone of the Black Moor that surmounts the shield forming the Annesley coat of arms. We used to call it 'the black man's head', for it depicts a Negro. A path was made from the mansion to the church, and at the entrance to the churchyard a fine stone gateway was built. Being a religious man Annesley had tablets inscribed and fixed to remind all that entered that way to 'Enter into His gates with thanksgiving and Come into His courts with praise.' Above the gate is the shield of the family arms, so if you take the Black Moor's head from the lodge and place it above the shield on the gate you will then have the Annesley arms complete.

A kitchen garden was made by enclosing one and a half acres with a nine- to twelve-foot-high brick wall complete with glasshouses and a bothy for the gardener. In the greenhouses there were till recently peach and nectarine trees bearing lead labels stamped on one side '1791' and on the reverse '1861'. Evidently the original trees were replaced at the later date. In the Rookery among the trees an underground icehouse was made so that when the pool was frozen in the winter ice could be cut and stored for summer use.

Everything possible was done for the gracious living of the

gentry who dwelt on the ground floor and first floor of the mansion. The servants in the house worked chiefly in the basement and slept, when the day's work was done, on the second floor, except for the footman who had a bed in the pantry, where the silver was kept.

Around the mansion are several trees that were obviously mature long before Annesley came on the scene – a cedar and several oak trees are very aged, and some huge old trees in the Hopyard went the way of all flesh half a century ago. Whether he planted the redwood that by Californian standards is still a baby is a query that only an expert can answer. He planted the plantation to screen the house from the road, and a splendid variety of our native trees make the park a real beauty spot. I believe we owe to Annesley the lime trees in the village and churchyard. Part of the latter were carefully trained to form a pergola.

A work of this magnitude with no labour-saving machinery must have produced an upheaval comparable with the building of the Great Central Railway. I can see men from all the surrounding villages walking here day by day to earn some of the good money Annesley was spending. The making of bricks for the kitchen garden wall would keep the Barnetts Hill brickyard busy for some time, for every brick was made by hand. Probably stone from the old house and buildings was used for the lodges and walls, but the stone for the mansion and stables was freshly dug and sawn to size.

Annesley's letters show that he was fond of his gun and looking forward to some sport at Eydon. He mentions hares, and there were also a few pheasants, partridges and numerous rabbits on the estate. Only thirty years had passed since the common fields were enclosed, so that large areas in the parish were now out of bounds for men who had roamed them night or day all their lives. A skilful man and dog could often take home a hare or rabbit for the family dinner – if caught in the common field he was within his rights. Now if he left the public right of way he was a trespasser and every bird or animal belonged to the squire or a farmer. Many a man had lost the right to keep a cow or a sheep because he had not been able to prove his right to the satisfaction of the commissioners who allocated the land enclosed by Act of Parliament. He had also lost the right to gather wood from the wastes to keep his fire burning in the winter and to cook his scanty meals. While Annesley was building his mansion and living on the fat of the land, the poor folk in the village were sinking lower and lower into abject poverty. So that Annesley, when he went shooting, should have sport and game to hang in the chamber near the kitchen until properly ripened, a gamekeeper was necessary – absolutely necessary, for folk were half starved and men were desperate although they knew the cruel sentence awaiting them if they were caught poaching. So Annesley engaged a gamekeeper. (Terms: 8s. weekly board wages; £15 15s. yearly wage; a coat and pair of buckskin breeches each year.)

Evidently they soon fell out, and Gregory charged Annesley with withholding his son's wages of £15. Annesley said they were not laid down in their agreement when he wrote to Walford, his attorney, and said, 'I think there are not many such knaves in the kingdom as many gentlemen would be subject to the same imposition; none can be safe without a written agreement, and it is my determination that if there is any reason or equity in the Law, I will not submit to such a fraudulent demand before it is decided in a Court.'

Probably suspecting Gregory, Annesley had a poster printed and posted up in the district. It read:

January 15th 1801. Whereas an Anonymous letter was a few days since received by Rev. F. Annesley of Eydon Lodge in the County of Northampton intimating a combination of persons had designed to Assassinate him. Any person except the writer of the letter will make a discovery thereof to the said Mr. Annesley, such person shall receive a reward of £50.

Writing to Walford he said, 'I have had my hares destroyed, and would not grudge parting with some money to find out the people. I think there is sufficient reason to suspect the man that was my gamekeeper last year.'

Another row blew up that gave untold pleasure to Eydon folk, for we do love to see a David stand up to a Goliath. Annesley bought land the other side of the brook in Moreton Pinkney parish. If he'd let it to a Moreton man there would have been no trouble, but he farmed it himself and the Moreton men hated to see Eydon men working their side of the brook. A certain W. Howard made a statement:

> ... I was at the Dun Cow at Moreton (Mr. Brooks) and Daniel Wilson Jun. was there, and he said he was in his father's ground and let a gun off and Annesley sent his groom to see what he had shot at; dam Annesley, great chub head. Why did he not come himself and if he had I'd have blacked his eyes and dam him I'd have sent him home with a broken head if he had come and he said if he could catch Annesley by the brookside he would unhorse him.
> I am your humble servant ...

The Wilsons' hatred of Annesley did not deter them from coming to Eydon for another type of sport, as is shown by the final note of the series, dated 22nd December 1801, which states:

> ... that at Cockfighting at the Royal Oak, Thomas and Daniel Wilson of Moreton Pinkney threatened Ward, Annesley's gamekeeper that they would throw him in the brook if found on the Moreton side and drown him. Annesley may whip me, then I'll black his eye.
> Witness a butcher, said he heard Dan Wilson say how he would serve him if he got him by the brookside and how he would mash his bones.

The rumpus died down in due course, no blood was shed and the £50 reward was never claimed. I'll be bound it gave the people here and at Moreton a lot to talk about at the time and amusement that cheered them up considerably.

When Annesley had completed his mansion he had a clock put in the turret over the old stables. Years ago they used to say that it was made by William Prestidge, a local craftsman famous for

his grandfather clocks, because he had installed it and started it working, but it was in fact made by Aynsworth and Thwaites of Clerkenwell, London, and the bell bears the date 1791. Fixing up the clock must have been a big thing for William Prestidge, for no country clockmaker was likely to install more than two or three turret clocks in his lifetime. What a red-letter day it was when the clock started working. In the confined space behind the works crouched William. He'd carefully adjusted the face in the turret and the long pendulum and hung the massive weights. Then he wound her up and started the pendulum swinging. A craftsman himself, he could appreciate the work of the London clock-makers. He'd watch the wheels slowly revolve, and wait anxiously to see if the striking apparatus worked properly. Yes, there was a whirr and a clatter as the hammer hit the bell so hard that it was heard in the village. I'll be bound Annesley stood in the yard below looking up at the clock face as the minute-hand neared the hour. He'd say to himself when she struck, 'Now the men will have no excuse for being late in the morning, or be able to slip off before time at night.' The cooks could see the time from the kitchen window; now he could insist on lunch being served on time, and dinner at the exact time ordered. What an asset the clock would be in keeping his inside and outside servants up to scratch! He would have a gold watch in his pocket, and a clock stood in the front hall for the convenience of Mrs Annesley, but it's doubtful if there were more than two or three clocks in the village in 1791. Clocks and watches had been made for over a century but they were very expensive. The old-fashioned folk would look on them as a luxury rather than a necessity of life. 'Us ah done werry well without em', the old boys would say.

I read that in earlier times the church bell was rung at frequent intervals, from sunrise to curfew at night. But what I want to know, and what no historians can tell me is, how did the bloke who rang the bell know the right time to ring it? There were days when a sundial would help, but they were few and far between. Some days the rising of the sun would give him the tip, but I can't see old Ben getting out of bed and standing in his nightshirt waiting for the sun to come over Ashby church, then tearing down to pull the rope. It seems to me that if he could get the first ring he might be able to space out subsequent rings with the help of an hour-glass, just as the parson used to time his sermons. I can't reckon out how Ben knew the time to ring, unless he'd a sort of radar apparatus that has been eliminated in me by clocks and watches. I can't imagine that in 1750 the overseers here would go to the expense of buying old Ben a clock, so that the bell should be rung at the exact time each day. No, it's a complete mystery. The public need of that regular bell rung here ended the day the Hall clock first struck the hour; Annesley and Prestidge soon made old Ben's job redundant.

Besides being a clockmaker, William Prestidge was owner of The Royal Oak public house, which he had acquired in 1791. He clearly needed his clockmaking to make ends meet for when I looked at sundry documents relating to our public house, I found it was generally in debt or not making much money. For nearly two centuries there were two pubs here, and when the Black Moor's Head was closed in 1877 The Royal Oak still had to meet the competition of the two off-licences held by Raymond Gostick and Thomas Inge. Bearing in mind the fact that a century ago the squire and most farmers brewed their own beer, one can see that keeping a pub was not the quickest way to make money. A capable housewife with the knack of making a good brew would be an asset at The Royal Oak; even so, there was no living for a family there selling strong drink, as my father dubbed the publican's wares.

The house was evidently an old establishment when Thomas Garland made his will in 1725. He left the premises to his cousin Richard Ansley, son of William Ansley of Banbury, a butcher, subject to the conditions that he paid 'my sister, Elizabeth Prestidge, 30s. per annum for her life and £30 to her children'. Richard made a will in 1750. I like the way he starts off: '. . . In the name of God, Amen. I Richard Ansley of Eydon (mason) being of sound and disposing mind, memory and understanding, thanks to Almighty God for the same. . . .' He left the property to his wife Alice for her lifetime, then to his son Thomas. Should Thomas die before reaching the age of twenty-one, it was to go to his daughters, Mary, Elizabeth, Alice and Hannah. Thomas did not die before twenty-one, for in 1765 he mortgaged the property to William Hines, butcher, for £20. Three years later, Hines made it £40 at five per cent but this time to Mrs Susannah Ansley. Thomas must have died and his sister Hannah was now called Susannah. For in 1769 Hines took over the property for

£93 13s. from Susannah Ansley, spinster, sister of Thomas (stonecutter), son and heir of Richard Ansley. The contents of the house to be valued are listed:

In the kitchen – 9 pewter plates, 9 pewter dishes,
                        1 spit mortar, 1 dripping pan, 1 spit,
                        1 fork, table and 6 chairs.
In the parlour – 5 tables, 6 chairs, a clock and a case.
In the entry   – 3 kettles, 3 pottage potts, 1 boiler.
Brewhouse   – 9 tubes, 1 cooker and a furnace.
Cellar   – 10 barrels.
Three chambers contained beds, bedding etc.
Included in the deal were two sittings in the parish church.

Hines sold the property to Richard Sewell, and in 1784 he sold it to John Harris for £126. Apparently a member of the Garland and Ansley family repurchased it, for in 1791 William Prestidge mortgaged it to William Moor for £80. The first mention I can find of Thomas Garland is in a court roll of 1697, when he was fined 6d. for breaking 'ye assize of ale'. As they sold ale at The Royal Oak, we can now say that the publicans from 1697 to 1836 were Garlands, Ansleys and Prestidges. William Prestidge died in 1836, and his widow Doreas and son Daniel (a clockmaker) sold the property to Robert Taylor, a blacksmith. We are not told the price he paid, but we know he mortgaged it to a Mrs Peebles for £50 in 1845. Evidently that was not enough, for in 1853 the mortgage was £220 of Thomas Douglas of Edgcote. In 1855 the mortgage was held by Douglas, Henry Bennett of Epwell and Alfred Hopcroft, Brewer, of Brackley. When Robert Taylor died in 1878 the mortgagees took over the property, so evidently no one was prepared to pay more than £220 for it. So they let it on a lease to William Herbert, a Banbury man who had married Taylor's daughter. In 1893 the three original mortgagees were all dead, and after forty years the mortgage still stood at £220. It was now in the hands of Antony

Vitty, George Smith and Alfred and Ernest Hopcroft. That year the Rev. John Taylor, clerk in Holy Orders of Tunbridge Wells, paid £220 for Vitty's and Smith's share of the mortgage. As he was the old blacksmith's son and brother of Mrs Herbert, I thought it very kind of him to want to secure a home over her head. But I was wrong, for on 30th January 1896 Hopcroft and Norris paid him £220 and became the sole owners of the property.

At that time there was a boom in property values in this district, as the Great Central Railway was being constructed. Any house with a licence to sell strong drink was worth big money, for the brewers were competing to buy them along the route of the railway. Two years later Phipps, the Northampton brewers, paid Raymond Gostick £1,000 for his house, shop, bakehouse and off-licence. Without the licence it would not have made half that money.

Cheeky servants and cunning poachers ceased to annoy the Rev. Francis in 1811, for that year he came to the end of the road. His wife Mary died on 16th January, and Francis on 28th February. As they were childless the estate passed to a nephew, the Rev. Francis Annesley, BD, sometime rector of Sawtrey St Andrew, Hants, and Fellow of All Souls, Oxford. He placed in the church a marble tablet in memory of his uncle, 'with pious and unfeigned gratitude'. I should jolly well think he did, bearing in mind that he had inherited the new mansion and estate, free of encumbrance. He reigned here for twenty years and died at his London home in Eaton Square on 13th December 1831, aged sixty-eight.

As Annesley never married the estate passed to a nephew who had closely followed in his footsteps as Fellow of All Souls and rector of Sawtrey St Andrew, so the third parson came to reside in the mansion. This was the Rev. Charles Francis Annesley, MA, FSA, FHS. The second Annesley's elder brother was Arthur, Viscount Valentia of Bletchingdon, who had married Catherine, daughter and heiress of Sir Charles Hardy. The third Annesley here was their second son. I believe he was another bachelor, and that may be the reason why his mother came to reside with him for the evening of her days. A tablet in the church records shows that she died at Eydon on 1st November 1848 and that her father was Admiral of the Fleet and Governor of Greenwich Hospital. Surely he was the Hardy who Southey immortalised in his account of the death of Nelson on the *Victory* at the battle of Trafalgar – a story that will never die while Britishers leave this island and sail the seas? The Rev. C. F. Annesley died here on 26th September 1863, and again the estate passed to a nephew, Arthur Annesley of Bletchingdon, later Viscount Valentia. As he owned several houses he let the Hall on lease to Colonel Cartwright.

I remember seeing Viscount Valentia, who was the last member of the Annesley family to have connections with Eydon, when he came to open the village hall. He was then a virile old gentleman of eighty-three and a fine specimen. He'd served in the South African War, been MP for Oxford and Master of the Bicester Hounds. But he had to sell his estate after Lloyd George's famous budget of 1910. They'd had a good innings though, the Annesley family, holding the same estate at Eydon from 1788 until 1910.

Part Two

The nineteenth century

Chapter 4

The hungry years

The first Annesley died in 1811 and a tough, hard nut he was too. He did a great deal here but it was all for his own comfort and that of his wife. His nephew, another Annesley, succeeded him and gave a gallery to the west end of the church. When he died in 1831 his nephew succeeded him in his turn: the Rev. Charles Francis Annesley, who lived here from 1831 to 1863. It was in his time that a new rectory was built, and a new school; but it was also a time of great hardship, known as the 'hungry forties', when food was scarce, unemployment was rife and many had to leave the village to seek work elsewhere, even as far afield as Canada and Australia.

I do not know whether it is better to write about all that occurred in Eydon in these middle years of the nineteenth century when Queen Victoria was on the throne or to follow a few selected incidents through from their beginnings at this time to the present day. I think, however, I shall try to show what a busy time this was in village life and will pick up some of the strands again later on in the part of this book devoted to my own family. But these thirty-odd years from 1830 to 1860 were a curious time, with so much that was new running side by side with the old, such as stocks on the village green, men poaching for much-needed food, and riots against the new-fangled machinery.

When the Rev. Charles Francis Annesley was at the manor, the Rev. Francis Clerke was rector. I like to think that they were friends. Both were Oxford men, both away from their ancestral homes, Clerke a bachelor, Annesley married but childless. Neither were hunting men, and it is very unlikely that either took a very active part in the social life of the local gentry. It appears to me that it would be little short of a miracle if they did not become close personal friends. I see them coming out of the church together after evensong one autumn evening in the year 1852. Talking quietly, they slowly walk through the park to the Hall, for tonight Clerke is having dinner with Annesley. Later they sit comfortably by a blazing log fire in the drawing-room talking of their years at Oxford, the men they've known and how they've fared in subsequent years. They talk of Parliament, of the new railways and the revolutionary ideas of the times, for their world is being shaken to its very foundations much as ours is today. Inevitably the conversation would sooner or later get round to village affairs. They'd agree that the poverty and squalor was still very bad. They'd ask: 'Can we do any more to help? We are already employing far more men than we need.' I think Clerke might have said: 'The school is terribly over-crowded, we do need a larger building.' Then Annesley would have an idea: 'If I built a school it would make a lot of work for the unskilled men in the village, and it would get some of the youngsters off the street.' And I am quite sure these two men would cogitate on the real problem of those days – the poorer people were, the more children they brought into this world.

Quite a considerable number must have left the village in the forties for the population decreased during the next ten years, although the birth-rate remained high. Many must have gone to the towns to work in the factories that sprang up like mushrooms, and to help build the houses to accommodate the workers. The making of the Great Western Railway in the late forties made work for men willing to walk the seven miles to Cropredy and

Claydon to earn 2*s*. 6*d*. a day – one man worked on it for several years.

Across the seas the United States, Canada and Australia were crying out for workers, and in England the authorities set out to encourage men to emigrate. In 1835 an Act was passed '. . . for the amendment and better administration of the Law in relation to the poor in England and Wales'. This gave parish overseers authority to borrow up to £100, to be deposited with the treasurer of the local union. They could expend not more than 3*d*. a mile on each adult, to take emigrants to the port of embarkation. £1 could be spent on clothing and 10*s*. on bedding and utensils for each adult to fit them out for the journey. This scale applied 'For Eastward of the Cape of Good Hope'. For Australia the scale was higher. A handbill issued by John Marshall & Co., emigration agents, refers to 'free emigrants' being sent out at the expense of the Australian colonies, but no mention is made of free passages to Canada. This Act is in the parish chest, so we know the parish authorities were aware of the government scheme; if they had adopted it, the repayment would have been a charge on the rates and each ratepayer would have paid his quota. But strange to relate they borrowed £75 from Gillet and Tawney, the Banbury bankers, giving an IOU signed by thirteen parishioners. Annesley and Parson Clerke did not sign; probably they would have preferred the government scheme. Why did the village fathers formulate a scheme of their own? My guess is they thought it extravagant: they thought they could do it more cheaply. We may be sure they counted the miles to Southampton and the 30*s*. outfit for each adult and it came to a dreadful lot of money. So the money was raised by a voluntary rate, but later this gave them another headache.

Evidently Eydon folk made a move in 1845, for a memo states that four men and four women, eight children under seven, and seven aged seven to fourteen left for Canada on the *Canton* on 26th March 1845. That looks like four families. Another family here at the time was a headache to the overseers. Evidently the husband had gone to Canada and left his family to the tender mercies of the overseers and the Poor Law. A memo reads: 'To keep Ann Willoughby and her 7 children in the Workhouse for a year would cost the Parish £41 13s. 4d. To send them to Canada would cost £62 10s. 0d. If it should be agreed that they should be sent and the money be borrowed and paid off in four years, it would raise each ratepayer's voluntary rate 7½d. in the £.' That was the problem, and this was the decision: 'Agreed to raise money to enable Ann to emigrate and join her husband in Canada, the money to be borrowed and paid off in two years with interest at 5%.' The £62 10s. had to cover the journey to Southampton, provide them with bedding and eating and drinking utensils as well as the fares on the boat. They left old England on the *William Braham* on 10th May 1845. The shipping company agreed to provide on the journey for each person over fourteen years of age (and half the amount for children under fourteen) the following:

½ lb. preserved meat, pork or beef, six days each week (no meat on Fridays); 1 lb. potatoes; ½lb. bread; ¼ oz. tea daily and 3 quarts water; 1 lb. rice weekly; split peas, suet, sugar, oatmeal and vinegar issued weekly.

I sincerely hope Ann wasn't too seasick on the boat to enjoy the abundant fare, for never in all her life had she had so much meat on the table to share with the youngsters. As the eldest was eighteen, she'd have help in caring for the little ones on the journey. What an undertaking it was for a poor woman – a long tiring journey to Southampton, then three weeks to a month on a small sailing ship of only 452 tons with such a family. Ann was forty-eight years of age, Urania eighteen, Sophia seventeen, George thirteen, Sarah ten, Martin seven, Susannah five and Noel three.

It was a long time before the authorities here forgot the

'emigrants of '45' – they departed, but the repayment of the debt hung fire. If all had gone well it should have been cleared off in four years, but in 1850 a considerable sum was evidently still owing. A memo reads: 'Agreed in Vestry, that a subscription of 2½d. in the £ be collected for the purpose of paying off part of the Emigration loan etc.' This subscription raised £26 14s. 2d., but we are not told if that cleared the debt.

In spite of this discouraging experience in 1850, '... it was agreed in Vestry that a subscription of five farthings in the £ be collected for the purpose of assisting Isaac and George Jeffs and their families to emigrate to North America.' The rate produced £13 8s. 0¾d., and £1 18s. 5¾d. was collected. I regret leaving this story unfinished, but I've come to the end of the memos dealing with the praiseworthy emigration scheme.

Has it any bearing on letters that come to the village occasion-ally from America, from people trying to trace their ancestors? Usually the ancestor had been done out of some land, and this may be an echo of pre-enclosure days, when poor men were done out of their land by crafty neighbours. One American wrote that he understood that his mother's grandfather at Eydon was a Sir William Ashby, and that his family had been done out of land. I wrote to him and gave all the information I could of the family, and I was very sorry to have to squash his hopes of having had a titled ancestor here once upon a time.

Farmers who have lost money year by year and have seen bankruptcy staring them in the face unless the economic wind should change, men and lads who drew the dole in the 1920s and 1930s can fully appreciate the heartbreak of the years when the ratepayers here sent men and women to seek a new life in Canada. So great was the misery of unemployment that the government finally made a payment sufficient to keep a man alive if he would work. If a man would not work he could starve.

The magistrates of Speenhamland met in 1795 to introduce a scheme fixing a minimum wage for the poor of Berkshire which was related to the price of bread. Unfortunately they were persuaded to pay the extra money out of the parish rates instead of forcing employers to increase the minimum wage. This system was widely copied and each county drew up a scale by which every poor person received so much extra money each week depending on the price of a loaf of bread. As the loaf cost more, so the money given out increased. It was a parish handout to labourers based on the local price of bread.

It was the parish overseers' duty to see that every family received the stipulated amount each week. The farmers were bound to find work for the men; a small farmer had to employ one or two men, a big farmer more. The number on the parish naturally varied according to the season of the year. At Maids Moreton the farmers paid the men 6d. a day and the parish made it up to 1s. or 1s. 3d. This would mean that exclusive of rent a man and his wife at this time were bound to receive a minimum of 6s. a week even if the man's industry could not earn him that much. A shilling a week for each child in the family was probably added.

At Moreton Pinkney the farmers met each month at one of the pubs to allocate the men to their employers. Mozely says: '. . . the men assembled at the bar, or in the yard behind to hear their fate for the ensuing month. The appropriation was sometimes equally disagreeable to the master and to the man; it was no uncommon thing for master and man to begin or terminate a month's association with a fight on the green. . . .'

In one place it is likely that the allocation of master to man was decided by drawing lots; in another the men went from one farmer to another till they had been to each employer in the parish. For a memo states that 'every roundsman on going to a fresh place, is to let his master know the preceding evening.'

We were in the Brackley union, and the Poor Law assessment of the parish in 1835 was £64. That year in a six-week period Annesley employed sixteen men and boys; Ivens and Sons employed seventeen, and Parson Clerke six. Working for Annesley, Thomas Willoughby did thirty-three days' work, Jos. Dodd thirty-six, M. Eagle thirty-six, Thos. Wills jun. three; all at 10*d.* a day. James Ward did thirty-six days' work at 4*d.* a day, and William Hinton thirty-six at 3*d.*; presumably these were lads. Annesley's total wage bill for six weeks was therefore £5 11*s.*, to which the parish added £2 12*s. 6d.* That brought each man up to the standard fixed according to his dependants. It is easy to see how Annesley and Ivens could find some useful work for all this extra labour. They could set them to pick up stones on the arable land, or in the summer to hoe corn and roots or spread clots of muck on the grassland. Annesley could set them at work weeding the drive and gravel paths in the gardens. But what on earth did Parson Clerke find for them to do? He had no drive to his house and only a small garden that his groom-gardener would have plenty of time to keep in apple-pie order.

That question I cannot answer, but it rang a bell that revived a memory. When I was driving into Sulgrave with Father once long ago, he pointed out a big mound of earth in the rectory grounds, quite close to the road. He told me that in the old days a lot of men in the village were out of work. Parson Harding had a number of them wheel the earth to its present site, then they were to take it back where it came from. But the men found other employment so the mound is there to this day. Well, everyone knew the Hardings were a bit queer, so we assumed it was just another of their eccentricities. Did Clerke set those he employed useless tasks in order that they should do some work for the money they were paid?

The situation in 1845 was slightly better than in 1835, for only twelve married and eight single men were not in regular employment. The rateable value of the parish in 1848 was £2,902; a half-year rate of 5*d.* brought in £60 8*s.* The union contribution was £160, and this did not change for some years. In 1849 it cost £1 to send two families to the workhouse, and provision for a Widow Brightwell cost 1s. 4½d. They paid the Rugby overseers £1 2s. 9d. for the maintenance of Sarah Rawlings and her four children while under order of removal to the workhouse. In 1852 a coffin for a pauper cost 12s., and this was disallowed by the auditor. I'll be bound the overseers went in fear and trembling of that gentleman when he studied their accounts, for in 1866 Martin Ivens and Cresens Stuchfield were surcharged £5 5s. by A. Hayward, auditor.

Twenty-nine were on the paupers' list in 1852, the reasons stated being debility, paralysis and age; four were inmates at Brackley workhouse. That must have been a bad year, for the parish paid the union £220, whereas in 1849 they paid £180. During a half-year in 1852 Ann Rainbow was paid £2 14s. in money and 19s. 8d. in kind. In 1856 relief was given to John Eyles of Bermondsey to the tune of 12s.; it is to be hoped Bermondsey paid up. Able-bodied sons were compelled to contribute to the cost of maintaining aged parents, but often it was a costly business getting the money. In 1866 Mr Weston at Middleton Cheney Petty Sessions was paid 9s. 6d. for preparing notices to Richard Wills for the maintenance of his father and mother. Dan Curtis went twice to Banbury to prove the chargeability of John Wills for the maintenance of his parents. The overseers also went twice – another 10s. Richard and John each paid 1s. weekly during the ensuing year, so the overseers had their reward. In 1855 a warrant to apprehend Josh. Bush cost 2s. 6d., the expense of obtaining same 4s. and Mr Weston's bill came to £2 6s. 2d. That same year a new key for a pair of handcuffs cost 1s. Any connection between these two items, I wonder? Josh must have done something serious for the indictment to cost over £2.

How tantalising these records are, how many tales could be told if only one knew all the facts! All I can do is give a few snippets which do not even provide a full year's expenditure on the relief of the poor. There were many aged and sick folk who were beyond work to be relieved: in 1835 there were six single women, fifteen widows without families and three with families, five widowers without and three with, five married men without families and two with. At least twenty-five per cent of the people living here were on the Poor Law for some years. In 1825 the rent was being paid for thirteen cottages: Howard's rent alone was £5 per annum, which was a dreadful burden on the rates, although somewhat relieved by seven rents which were under £2 and three at 26s. yearly. The cottages had to be kept in repair, so Wm. Bush was paid 19s. 4d. for thatching and John Coy 3s. for mending Hunt's stable door. That is the only item I can identify, for I knew that stable door very well years ago. Alas, like all these poor people it has gone beyond recall, for Kenches knocked both stable and cottage down in the 1920s. Hunts were carriers to Banbury for generations, and evidently trade was so bad they qualified for poor relief.

Make no mistake, if an artful dodger tried to swing the lead, he'd soon be weighed up; the authorities here were ruthless. Some jobs appear to have been done uncommonly cheaply, for Edwin Coy was paid 1s. 9d. for timbering a privy, which I assume includes wood and labour. If there had been any sawn wood it would have cost much more. It could only have been made of straight ash poles nailed together to form a roof on which the thatcher could lay his straw, and it was not a very large building, probably a single-seater. No doubt John did it as cheaply as he could. Some of the people were given coal, but as I've found no complete list, I think it can have been given only in special cases.

In 1823 a Dr Garrett living in the village was paid £12 19s. 6d. for attendance on the poor. Evidently early in the century expenditure exceeded the rates for some years, for the rector, Matthew Lamb, lent £65, for which he was paid £3 5s. interest each year. Thos. Ivens lent some too. In 1823 rates brought in £228 18s. 6d. and £210 16s. was paid out, so that year the balance was on the right side. It was good of the rector to lend that £65. It shows he did what he could to help the poor folk, and it also shows how desperate the situation had become. Good, honest men were made paupers, men who would have been in regular employment if it had not been for the system.

The system meant that the large farmer need not pay a living wage to those he employed, yet the small independent man had to pay his share of the poor rates. This share really went to bolster up the miserable wages the large farmer paid, so that in a sense the poor, small, independent man was subsidising the richer farmer and at the end of it all the labourer starved even when doing a full day's work every day.

A shilling a day, and a shilling for a loaf of bread! Those years were a terrible blot on 'England's green and pleasant land' – a blot it took a century to erase. It is a story that has been told time and again, but no historian can ignore this period; it is too well documented by contemporary writers.

In my early life the politicians used the aftermath of this grim struggle for existence to lay the foundation of the Welfare State in which we live today. It is a period we should all remember, and remembering should make us very thankful for the elementary blessings of life we all, from the oldest to the youngest, enjoy. When we get a spell of frost and snow in the winter I think of ill-shod, poorly clothed men shuffling off to work, chilblains on their feet and chapped hands; men with half-filled bellies who had to pretend to work in the fields for eight or nine hours at a stretch; mothers who kept the little ones in bed as long as they could because they were warmer there, and did not need as much food as they did when running about. I imagine their agony at having to ration bread, and to see little ones die because the only milk they could afford was skimmed. The cream was made into butter that went to market; poor people and the farmers' pigs consumed the skimmed milk. The pigs got fat on it, but they had plenty of corn as well, whereas the poor man's corn was rationed. The shepherd tended his master's flock of sheep, but he seldom tasted a bit of mutton. If a sheep drowned in the brook or died in a field, the poor folk had a treat for once; they were thankful to get a bacon dinner once or twice a week.

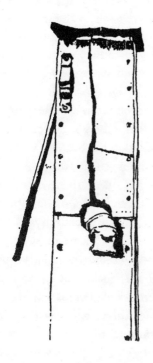

Thinking of these times I am astonished that the relationship of farmer and labourer was so good here sixty years ago. One would have thought these bitter years would have left anger and resentment in men's minds that it would have taken a good century to erase. Yet the labourers I first knew were children brought up on skimmed milk, potatoes and scraps of bread, and they showed no resentment whatever for their lean childhood. Like old Sally, they were devoutly thankful that in their old age they'd plenty to eat and a bit of meat every day. Sunday was a feast day, Yorkshire pudding, a joint of meat and vegetables: what more could a man want? The labourer went to work in watertight boots, and ample clothing: cheap ready-mades that always seemed too big for their lean frames, but they did keep out the cold. The children's clothes as far as I can remember were always on the big side, usually someone's cast-offs. Most of the women were big, buxom dames who filled their frocks so well it looked as if the buttons would fly off if they did not walk very sedately. The thin women wore shawls, so I've no idea whether their frocks were too big or too small. These simple honest men and women were the children of the paupers who went the round, and counted themselves very fortunate when they went to work for Parson Clerke. I'm sure he would treat them as men and give them something to eat and drink in the kitchen while he was wondering what on earth he could set them to do. He would not dare send them home, or he'd be in trouble with the farmers; so it's quite likely the churchyard was more spick and span in those days than at any time in, say, a thousand years.

Men doing piece-work in the fields during haytime and harvest could earn £1 a week. But to do this they would need more food than their usual diet of bread and lard, water and vegetables. So much of this hard-earned money must have gone on extra beer and mutton to keep up their strength. Three or four men working together agreed with a farmer to mow the hay and cut and bind the corn in sheaves at so much an acre. When the hay and corn were ripe, and the weather settled, the farmers wanted the job done quickly and this was the best way to get it done. The men started work at dawn, and in the cool of the morning had made a good mark by midday. Then they had a meal, lay down and made themselves comfortable for a sleep. Three hours later, refreshed and rested, they set to and worked on till dusk. No weaklings got into these gangs; the men saw to it that they were well matched physically so that both work and money were fairly shared. At Edgcote a field used to be called

'Twenty-man Field'. It was twenty acres in area and the name came from a wager between two farmers, one of whom bet he could have it mown in a day. He gathered twenty expert mowers together and set them to work early in the morning, and by night the field was mown by the men's scythes. An acre a day was good going.

I'm sure it was not all gloom in those hard times. There were sure to be some men who could tell a tale well and always raise a laugh. Sam Maubey was one. He got drunk one night and was swearing and carrying on in the street, so the constable told him to be quiet and go home. As he took no notice but kept on swearing, the constable took him to Ivens's stable and locked him up. Sam was a big strong man and he was able to break open the door and damage it. So poor old Sam went to court. There he told the magistrates in a loud voice, 'I 'ad to, I were that thirsty.' He carried on about the constable and made a proper to-do in court, told them 'they thought he was a fool, because he had no sense, but he knew how to speak like a gentleman, though he was a poor chap'. The fine and costs amounted to £2 7s. 6d. or three months. At Northampton Jail poor old Sam, no matter how thirsty, couldn't break the door down as he had in Ivens's stable. There must have been many exciting times in the village when the folk were not as tame and law-abiding as we are in these days!

It is during the time of the Revs. Annesley and Clerke that the first documentary evidence of any sort of school occurs – the name 'Thomas Horn, schoolmaster' in the voters' list for 1831. Maybe Clerke started some form of instruction class soon after he came to Eydon in 1825. It was probably run on his responsibility with some help from the parish and from the parents. But I am pretty sure most of the cost came out of his own pocket, for the farmers in those days were quite indifferent to the need to educate poor children; they wanted their own youngsters to be scholars but thought education wasted on ploughmen and dairy-maids.

A proper school was not built until 1854. The land was provided by John Ivens on condition that if it ever ceased to be a school it would revert to his descendants. The plans appear to have been drawn up by Sir Henry Dryden of Canons Ashby, for they bear his hallmark. He built a school at Adstone and another at Woodford Halse. Ours follows the same pattern: the same steep roof, the same arch-braced timbers, resting on corbels along the walls. They put a large fireplace at one end of the school which the children must have been glad to gather round in the winter months. At least they were dry and warm in school for a few hours.

Clerke did not live to see the school completed, for his health failed him; they sent him to Italy to see if a warmer climate would assist in his recovery but he died in Nice in 1853. However he must have seen the stone quarry opened and much of the stone cut. He probably even saw the walls rise, for it was completed and opened only a year after he died.

Clerke may not have seen the school finished in his lifetime but he certainly saw a new set of stocks arrive in Eydon, for they were set up on the green in 1828 at a cost of £6 15s. 6d. They are made to accommodate two persons side by side, and on the tall end are bracelets to hold a person standing facing the post, ready to be whipped. They have been repaired twice, but they are still there today, I'm glad to say. Surely at that time every village had a set, for it was an indispensable instrument in keeping law and order, and a very sensible way of punishing wrong-doers. It seems to me very remarkable that in these days so little is known and so little written by historians on the subject. In most villages they vanished long ago, and in many no one remembers where they stood. Mary Kench remembers her father saying the last man to be put in our stocks was put there for beating his wife. That would probably be in the 1850s, for my father came in 1866, and if it had been in his time I'm sure I should have heard all about it.

This is some information I have been able to gather from the *Northampton Mercury* on the subject. In 1819 at Maidford four youths were put in the stocks for three hours for playing football in the streets on Sunday. In 1858, at Kings Sutton, Jas. Meadows was put in at 11 p.m. and kept there till 11 a.m., guarded by two constables for being drunk and disorderly. Here in 1823 three constables were paid £7 6s. 10d., £7 9s. 4d. and £5 0s. 10d. That was a dreadful lot of money to pay spare-time men, more than a labourer earned in a year. Well, if Kings Sutton folk paid those two constables for thirteen hours each, that came to a tidy sum of money, though I doubt if they had any extra for night duty. Come to think of it, no one man could put a drunken man in the stocks without help, and it wasn't a job any man would tackle. So I'm very sure the stocks here were frequently tenanted. What a sight it must have been, three burly men dragging a drunken man to the stocks, getting his legs arranged properly, then clamping down the top bar and locking it. Did they put men in when they were properly drunk, or was it done in cold blood the next day, I wonder? Oh, the swearing there would be! I cannot imagine a more uncomfortable posture; the victim couldn't sit up, he'd have to lie on the ground with his feet raised, thus ensuring his maximum discomfort. The crowd that would gather round to enjoy the spectacle, the gibes and the jokes that would be made to taunt the tenant of the stocks! The joy it gave some of the men and women to see their enemy suffer the penalty of his wrong-doing! Very respectable mothers kept their children at home at such times because of the swearing that went on at the stocks. But they were the minority; the great majority were there for entertainment on the cheap and a good laugh. There's a lot to be said for the stocks, and I cannot imagine a more sure deterrent for wrong-doers.

Whether in or out of the stocks, life was hard in those tough times, and, as we have seen, men often went hungry. However, there was always the possibility of picking up a dinner unexpectedly whilst working in the fields, as John Tomlin did once. He and my father were walking across a field when John said, 'Stan' still Joe, there's a rabbit there', and he pointed to a patch of rough grass. Very quietly he walked to the spot, bent down and picked up a kicking rabbit. I have seen a hare picked up in the same way, with several dogs roaming in the field so that the hare appeared to be paralysed.

How galling it must have been to young men to be looked on as trespassers on the land where their grandfathers had tethered cows and planted corn. Poaching was one way of getting their own back, a battle of wits in which every faculty was used to the uttermost. No dinner would be quite so appetising as one picked up in a night foray, when the keeper was busy in another part of the woods. In spite of the poverty of those days, we can be sure they had a measure of enjoyment.

For the men and boys there was plenty of sport and something for the pot, free from fear of the consequences. There were, and I expect still are, perch and roach in the brooks. It's years since I heard of one being caught, but that's not surprising, as no one fishes there now, not even the boys. On the brook the humble moorhen abounds and I'm told they make fair eating. Larks flourish on the hilltop, and are reckoned quite a delicacy. As late as 1890 Dr Fowke of Byfield would buy three or four larks any time. The fact that a bird was a fine songster did not make an atom of difference; it was slaughtered indiscriminately. Larks, blackbirds, thrushes, linnets and fieldfares helped to satisfy the hunger for meat. How they caught larks I do not know, but they were caught and sold in the shops. I think snares, traps and birdlime were used, and it may be that the catapult in the hands of a skilful man brought many a bird to the ground. I learnt as a boy to make a sparrow trap with four bricks and two pieces of stick, and I'm sure they had many tricks of which we know nothing in these days. It was sport and it gave the law-abiding men pleasure. It's likely that in the 1840s the farmers began giving the men a harvest home supper, and the church Sunday School children's treats started. Grace would be said at both events, but it would not be the one Joseph Arch quoted in 1872. He pictured the poor labourer saying before he ate his bread and onions:

> Oh Heavenly Father help us
> And keep us all alive
> Around the table nine of us
> And only food for five.

Not all the labourers were as patient and law-abiding as the men in this district, for in the southern and eastern counties riots had taken place, corn ricks been burnt and threshing machines destroyed. Nine men were hanged and many transported for having taken part; but the authorities had seen the red light. They had not forgotten the recent revolution in France, so near to our shores. Also, thank God, many men in the upper classes could see that the poverty and degradation of men and women was an evil that could and should be overcome. The first shots in the battle for reform were fired in the General Election in 1831, when bribery and corruption was rampant. A man could sell his vote to the highest bidder, and everyone knew how everyone else had voted.

One result of the small number of landowners in the village was to reduce the voters at parliamentary elections. In 1702 there were forty-seven voters, in 1831 only fourteen. Evidently the political battle began when the voters' list was being prepared, the Reds objecting to John Bull's right to vote if they suspected he was Blue. Until the query had been settled, John could not vote. A memo in the poll book reads:

... That some names of freeholders are not inserted at all is accounted for by the circumstances of so large a number remaining before the Assessor undecided at the close of the Poll. And here it may be proper to observe by way of explanation as to so great a proportion; at least one third of the freeholders votes having been objected to, that it was chiefly owing to the numerous omissions and incorrect entries on the Land Tax assessments, whereby much trouble and inconvenience were occasioned, the votes therefore of many respectable freeholders were rejected and their names consequently could not be recorded upon the poll.

At the 1831 election the Rev. F. Clerke and Martin Ivens were appointed 'to assist in canvassing'. Each voter voted for two candidates. These were the candidates and the votes they received here at Eydon: Viscount Althorp, four; Viscount Milton, three; Wm. R. Cartwright, eleven; and Sir Charles Knightley, eight. Althorp and Milton were voted for by three absentee landlords: John Constable of Marylebone, the Rev. Wm. Bull of Oxford – dissenting minister – and Rich. Henson of Slapton. Althorp was also voted for by Richard Garrett, surgeon. The squire, parson and farmers were all Tory. Althorp and Milton were called Whigs.

In spite of our Tory farmers Althorp won the election. He was Chancellor of the Exchequer at the time, a strong advocate of parliamentary reform and a considerate and good landlord. In 1848 he built at Wormleighton the first model cottages for labourers in the district: well-built cottages in pairs set in large gardens; communal wash-houses and bread ovens; and a pigsty for each house at the end of the gardens – the best labourers' cottages this end of the county.

After he had been elected, Viscount Althorp (Earl Spencer's eldest son) made a speech in which he said that he stood for peace, reform and economy, and reform in Parliament. 'We shall remedy as far as we can the evils which the former administration has brought upon us.' He could not but address himself to the labouring classes, who he was sure knew he had always been their friend and to beg them to consider that by destroying the property

of their employers they destroyed the means of their employment.
The folly of destroying ricks was still greater, as it destroyed
their own food. He asked the farmers if their farms were all in
such complete order that they could not employ some additional
hands during the winter months and whether they did not think
this must be more advantageous than setting able-bodied men to
work upon the roads at starvation wages. When he talked about
destroying property he meant the breaking up and burning of
new threshing-machines. I've heard of no agitation against the
threshing-machine here but the farmers were very apprehensive,
for the labourers hated like poison the first labour-saving devices
used on the farms. The first new models were powered by a
horse walking round and round outside a barn. This operated a
geared shaft that worked the machine inside the barn. With the
old way, men threshing the corn with flails provided several with
winter work. By doing piecework for long hours they had been
able to earn money at a time when outside work on the farms
was limited owing to the state of the weather.

This Whig government of 1831 was the first to recognise that
children needed schooling, by making grants towards the
building of schools, and in 1834 Lord Althorp piloted through
Parliament the first Factory Act, to limit the hours worked by
children and young people. The parson's right to one-tenth of all
farmers' and cottagers' hay, corn and roots, was commuted in
1836 to a rent charge on land.

Another good thing this Parliament gave us was penny postage.
As Earl Spencer died in 1834, Althorp ceased to be our member
when he took his seat in the House of Lords. At the election Sir
Charles Knightley was returned; he was noteworthy because he
kept the Nonconformists out of Preston Capes. One of his
tenants, a Baptist, held meetings in his house, and when Sir
Charles was unable to evict him he had the thatch taken off the
roof.

Although the Whigs lost the 1841 election, the Tories were compelled to carry on the good work of reform by the pressure of public opinion. The Corn Law, a relic of the war with France, was abolished in 1846. This had artificially kept up the price of bread, and now wheat from Canada began to arrive and the cost of a loaf slowly went down.

Much water had to flow under London Bridge before the working man had a fair deal, but the tide had turned, and from 1846 onwards living conditions slowly but surely improved. The rotten system of electing our MP had to be reformed, and bribery eliminated. It was years before the labourer had a say in the government of the country, but it came at last.

In 1884 the agricultural worker finally received the vote and, protected by secret ballot, could vote as he liked, whatever his landlord said. How things have changed! In 1881 only three in every hundred people here had a vote; in 1966, now that the women have come in, fifty-five in every hundred people had the opportunity to vote as to who should represent us in the House of Commons.

In that election of 1831, the Rev. Francis Clerke assisted in the canvassing, for one of the candidates was a relative of his. This was William Cartwright of Aynho, as Clerke's mother had also been a Cartwright of Aynho. The great stately mansion of Aynho, with its large rooms, lofty ceilings and all the comforts pertaining to gracious living, must have been very well known to Clerke. When he came to the rectory at Eydon in 1825 it must have seemed a come-down, for it was a rambling old house that had been altered many times during the centuries. Clerke followed George and Matthew Lamb, who had not been house-proud, but had farmed the glebe land themselves, and I believe had rolled up their sleeves and worked with the labourers.

Clerke was a well-to-do man and a bachelor. He was not interested in farming, nor did he care for the old rectory, so he decided to let both it and the glebe land and for himself he bought an old house on the Back.

He had part of this house demolished and a new west front of three storeys built. It stands on the high ground in the village and towers high above every other house. It is built of stone quarried here, finely cut, a splendid example of the stone-mason's craft. The old part of the house became the servants' quarters. From the new rooms an elaborate bell system was fitted so that they could be summoned to the master's presence, upstairs or down, just as they had at Aynho. The large back kitchen was fitted with a huge 'copper' for making beer, a smaller one for the washing of clothes, and a large oven for baking bread.

When Clerke died in Nice, the new rector, the Rev. Arthur J. Empson, arrived. He was described as a 'merchant in China' until, at the age of thirty, he had felt called to serve in the Church, and so had studied at Downing College, Cambridge, and taken his BA. To gain insight into a clergyman's work he spent a year with a Dr Hook at Leeds parish church. After he was ordained, at thirty-four years of age, he married Dr Hook's daughter, Anna Delicia, aged twenty, and they came to live at Eydon.

At first they lived in Clerke's old house, but soon they wished to build a new rectory of their own because Clerke's house, in the village, was quite lacking in privacy. Being such a compact village you could throw a ball into two, three or four neighbours' gardens from any other garden. There was no carriage drive to the vicarage front door, for the house was only a few feet away from the public road. So when an important visitor drove up in a carriage and pair there would soon be a mob of inquisitive youngsters standing round, all eyes and ears, watching the proceedings. Every passing vehicle on the road and folk talking in the street could be heard in all the best rooms, upstairs or down.

At night they would hear the men who had had a drop too much to drink at The Royal Oak talking loudly and shouting goodnight at the corner of Partridge Lane, where their ways parted. Behind the house is a small secluded garden, lawn and summer-house. No doubt they played croquet on the lawn and drank tea there on nice summer days, but only a few yards away was the carpenter's saw pit. Some days the screech of a cross-cut saw rent the air for hours as two men cut a tree into many boards. On the same side, a bit lower down, was Goodman's farmyard, complete with cows, fowls and heaps of muck that smelt both in winter and summer. Cows are quiet animals normally, but when one is parted from her calf she moos day and night, and so does the poor calf. We seldom hear a cock crow in these days, but then every farmer had a flock of fowls and many cottagers kept a few in the back garden. One joker used to start the dawn chorus; that woke all the others up, and for some time cocks would be crowing all over the village. Opposite the farmyard, between Empson's garden and the lane, stood several of the poorest cottages in the village. The folk who lived there were not what we should call 'nice people'. The large families meant squalling children, distraught mothers with raucous voices, rows at night when father came from the pub to be greeted by an angry wife.

The Empsons could not stand the noise, so the shepherd soon decided to get a bit further away from the sheep, for after all they are very smelly animals at close quarters. Plans were made for a new rectory on the glebe farm and the old rectory then became 'The Elms'. Twelve acres near the village were taken from the farm for the new house and grounds. In 1856 the house was built of stone quarried here; it was the last time any quantity of stone was dug out in the Bushes, although the face of the quarry was clearly visible as late as 1899. I have reason to remember the pit, for it was in the field my father rented for his cows. There was a small pool with newts in it at the foot of a miniature cliff, and solid stone underfoot.

To raise the money for the building a mortgage of £1,680 was arranged for thirty years – Chapman paid the final instalment in

1886. As Empson was a moneyed man it's likely the house cost considerably more than the mortgage. To quarry and cut the amount of stone required would cost many hundreds, even in 1856. The house, of three storeys, contains about fifteen rooms and is a gentleman's house of the period. A carriage drive to the front door, pleasure and kitchen garden, stables and stable yard make it a replica of Annesley's Hall on a lesser scale. No one has ever said in my hearing that it stands in a small park, but it does. Some of the trees were there when the house was built; others were planted by Empson. He planted an avenue of walnut trees – eleven, one for each child in the family. They were growing into handsome trees in the 1920s when that side of the park became the cricket field. The confounded cricketers moaned and groaned about the light, and the trees were blamed. They heard but said nowt. So to appease the cricket team the poor trees were grubbed up just when they were reaching the prime of life. One room in the house Sally Dancer called the 'Justice's Room'. Mr Empson was a justice of the peace, and for a few years he dealt with minor offenders there, though later all cases had to go to the Petty Sessions at Middleton Cheney.

I have never heard anything but good said of the Empson family. Mr Empson did his duty faithfully in church and village, and was friendly with the Nonconformists. There was no clash in his time. Mrs Empson and the girls were welcome visitors in many homes, and in the poorest they were most friendly without condescension. A sad loss to all the family is recorded in the school log-book as follows:

Feb. 17th 1868 The choir girls from the 1st and 2nd standards employed all day making new print dresses to be worn tomorrow at the burial of Miss A. D. Empson.
Feb. 18th The master and choir girls away attending the burial of the Rector's third daughter.
Feb. 19th A few of the girls away unwell from the excitement of yesterday.

Anna Delicia Empson was three years and ten months old. Calling her Miss was I presume a mark of respect on the part of the schoolmaster. In July that year, Cecil Annesley Empson was born, named after his godfather, Squire Annesley.

The school log-book gives a glimpse of a Sunday School treat in Empson's day, one I'm afraid which would not appeal to our twentieth-century youngsters:

May 1st 1867 The children brought flowers in the morning and assembled in the afternoon to proceed to the Rectory where they partook of tea and after finishing their various games, they marched to Church, where in lieu of a service, a beautiful Allegory specially adapted to children, was read by the Rector; the children being evidently impressed.
May 2nd School rather thinner, distributed the remains of cake and buns to the infants.

In March 1875, Mr Empson was stricken down with paralysis, and was called to higher service on June 28th the next year. The report in the *Banbury Guardian* says the church was crowded at the funeral service, the whole parish being present.

As a rector's house goes with the job, poor Mrs Empson had to find another home soon. She decided to settle at Rugby, and to simplify moving she sent the governess and some of the children to a south-coast resort. There Clement, a boy of fifteen, was accidentally drowned in September. They laid him by the side of his father in the churchyard and twelve years later Mrs Empson joined them on the east side of the church.

The irony of it was that the rectory, built to house a family of lively youngsters, has only once for two or three years heard the laughter of little children within its walls. Empson was followed by Chapman, who had neither chick nor child. We have had many rectors since his day, some childless, some with grown-up sons and daughters. Empson died there, and later Canon Rendell, but there hasn't been a child born in the house since John Basil Empson arrived in June 1871.

The size of the house and the extensive grounds have been a
bugbear to the church authorities for the last half-century. It was
built to house servants, now a well-nigh extinct race. The
difficulty of obtaining help and the cost have been a discourage-
ment to many of our rectors, so we have had many changes in
recent years. In 1955 we shared a rector with Culworth, so the
rectory was sold to Mr W. Oakey, an Aynho man who has
spent some years on the Gold Coast.

After Empson moved into the new rectory he'd built, Clerke's
old rectory, now known as 'The Elms', fell on evil days. With no
land attached it held no attraction to a farmer, and it was too big
to suit a tradesman. There were already three houses in the village
suitable for professional men, each with stable, coach-house and
room for a maid or two. So from 1856 to 1917 the house was
looked on in the village as a white elephant, and for most of the
time it stood empty. Towering above every other house in the
village, it stood gaunt, forlorn and forsaken. It was too well built
to become a ruin, so it stood like a proud old gentleman with
dignity and poise, yet clad in tattered garments. In 1900 all the
glass in the big windows was broken, so mischievous boys could
get inside the house. Boys will be boys; they love a bit of des-
truction, and whether it's an old house or a discarded motor-car
matters not to them. Door latches were broken, cupboard doors
hung precariously on one hinge, and wallpaper in tatters draped
the walls. When a strong wind blew doors slammed and the
whistling of the wind through empty rooms made strange and
weird noises. It was said the house was haunted. I am sorry to say
it was an old woman's tale, sorry because it would have been nice
in our history if we'd had a haunted house and a proper ghost.
I've done my best to find one but I came too late on the scene;
the folk who could have helped me write of the supernatural
all died many years ago. Thomas Kench held that some
of the queer noises heard in the house were caused by the
wind making the wires of the bell system vibrate. These

ran near the ceiling from the front rooms to the servants' quarters.

About sixty years ago a hunting man named Sturdy renovated the house and lived there for a few years. He built horse boxes and kept a string of hunters, so with grooms and hunters galore the premises became a hive of activity for a spell. Then once again the house was deserted. Between the wars two of our broken-down farmers lived there, John Henry Ivens and Tom Elkington; then for about ten years the house was again derelict.

During the last war these remote villages suddenly became very popular. Our long-lost city cousins remembered their country relatives; they came and brought friends. And so it came to pass that a Birmingham engineer, Mr B. Hassell, bought 'The Elms' as a refuge for his parents who had endured the rigours of bombing in London. Once again the house has been renovated and brought up to date, so again it is a house fit for a gentleman to live in.

Now I must make an apology, for I'm afraid this chapter will be very much like a game of snakes and ladders. We go back donkeys' years, then a few moves bring us up to the reign of George V, then back to 1865 and so forth. I've tried to piece them together so the joins don't show, but like the gaiters we used to put on motor tyres, you could feel the bumps as the wheels went round.

The Rev. A. J. Empson succeeded Clerke as rector; not only did he finish building the school and build a new rectory, he also made extensive alterations to the church in 1865. I'm sure no rector since his day would have been allowed to make such radical alterations, especially as it must have been a very costly undertaking. We like to think our church has stood just as it is for hundreds and hundreds of years; there isn't another like it in the country, it suits us, and you leave it alone or there will be trouble.

It is a delusion, I know, but why shouldn't we have a spot of delusion when it adds a spice to life and harms no one?

The old hands, Ivens, Malmsbury and Manning might admit the roof of the church needed repairing, but I doubt if they approved of the way the building was altered. For they would see the church in a different light from that vouchsafed to Empson. To them it was a truly holy place, made holy by associations and memories that few newcomers can appreciate. As they sat in their pews and should have listened to the sermon, their thoughts often wandered. They'd remember the funeral service when they took their mother and father there for the last rites, see the spot where the coffins rested during the service. They'd heard Mother talk about their infant behaviour when they were baptised in the font by Parson Lamb. Memories of boyhood days came to mind; they'd behaved badly in this very pew and Mother had smacked them when they got home. Though they were tough, hard men, they'd remember some service there in which they shed a few tears over a little child, or the loss of the best friend in the world. Often I see a patch of sunshine moving across the fields through a break in the clouds; so these passing thoughts in these men's minds made the church in a very real sense God's House to them. And so I'm sure they would have hated to see some of the alterations, but doubt if Empson met with very much opposition to his plans. He was a very wise man, so he did not propose altering the church as soon as he was settled in the rectory. It's probable he let seven years elapse before he even suggested the alterations. By that time he'd won their confidence and trust and, it may be, their affection.

To help him carry out the changes he wanted, Empson found a stalwart ally in Colonel Cartwright, MP, who now lived at the Hall. (Cartwright leased the Hall from Viscount Valentia, who had inherited it from his uncle, the Rev. C. F. Annesley, when he died in 1863. Viscount Valentia had several houses so did not wish to live at Eydon.)

The Colonel had no sentimental attachment to the building, for compared to his old church at Aynho it was a prehistoric building. At the time churches were being drastically altered and many enlarged all round us, and Eydon must not lag behind. 'We must keep up with the Joneses' is not a twentieth-century invention by any means. And so the church was enlarged just after the Wesleyans had built a new chapel to seat 145. The Quakers and Moravians had room for about 120, so the rest of the village folk would just about fill the church. Years ago old folk used to love to talk about the crowded churches and chapels of their youth. No doubt they were full on special occasions, but to infer that once upon a time every adult attended a place of worship on Sundays is, I'm sure, wrong. It was expedient for many poor folk here to go to church on Sunday; as Henry Peck often said, 'A man's a fool if he don't keep in with the folk with money.' But a Christian is bound to be an optimist, and Empson had the right ideas in his mind. He wanted to make the church lighter by the insertion of more large windows; comfortable, by warming it in the winter, and providing seats easy to sit in but not comfy enough to tempt his hearers to slumber during the sermon.

The architect they employed was R. C. Hussey, and the builder, Mr Watson of Napton. The musicians' gallery in the west end, put there only in 1828, was cleared away, and the nave reroofed. Two decayed pillars of red stone on the north side were replaced by pillars of Bath stone. A new east window over the altar replaced one of a different design. The north aisle was extended to make a vestry in the north-eastern corner of the church. The south wall of the nave was pulled down, and an aisle built with an arcade connecting it with the nave, much higher than the one opposite. The old box pews were removed and replaced by modern seating. The old pulpit went and an up-to-date one took its place. Mr and Mrs Empson gave the stained glass in the new chancel window; Miss Holbeach a new Bible, and old and present scholars of the school, the lectern. To warm the church a big square iron stove was placed near the south door. The iron smoke-pipe of this stove passing through the roof of the aisle caused a fire in the 1930s. They thought that by placing the stove in that position they would ensure that the air was warmed as it entered the church through the oft-opened door. That was what we were told when we complained of the position of the stove. All I know is it was nice and warm around the stove, but uncommonly cold if you sat very far away. Up to this time there had been no means of warming the church.

When the builder had done his work and the women had scrubbed the floor, and polished the woodwork and brass, I can hear them saying, 'Don't it look nice now?' But sure enough some of the old boys would say, 'Oi loiked it awlrite as it were.' The church was reopened on 1st June 1865. The clergymen met and robed in the school, then walked in procession to the church. The service was conducted by the rector, and the Dean of Chichester preached. Colonel Cartwright entertained the company to a most liberal luncheon in a marquee in the grounds of the Hall and later in the day the whole parish was entertained at tea.

The churchyard was enlarged by taking in a strip from the plantation on the west side, no doubt given by Viscount Valentia. Having persuaded folk here to dip hands deep in pockets for the church, Empson kept them at it while the going was good. 'Now we must have a pipe organ,' he said. So subscriptions were given and the organ installed in 1868. Before that time the singing had been led by a man named Amos, husband of Anna, who nursed the sick in the epidemic of fever in 1866. I have his photograph: a great big man seated holding an enormous wind instrument, nearly black in colour. I'm told it was a band instrument. I wonder if he could play any tune, or did they have to sing tunes that he could play?

Now before I leave the church I sit by the font to con over the

part this building has played in the life of the village through the centuries. For these venerable walls have seen so much of the joys and sorrows of mankind; they've seen the humble exalted and the proud brought low so many times, and the succession of men and women that have been joined here in holy matrimony, 'till death us do part'. Proud parents would bring a babe to be baptised, with hearts full of hope for the child's well-being in life. For the poorest couple in the village had the right to bring their baby here for baptism, just as John Browne had. Although John would hardly recognise the church today, I'm glad he heard one bell ring that still rings in tune with the others. Was that the bell that tolled the day they buried him in the church? I picture the church and churchyard crowded with the local aristocracy and village folk that day in 1691; the church full to the doors, the frail old rector, John Parkes, trembling as he read the prayers for he was on the brink of the grave himself, and died in the following year. And I think what a shame it is that they destroyed or hid the slab on the floor in memory of that good man, so deeply grieved when Thos. Smallbone became a Quaker. They could have set it up against the wall if they must have a new floor, so that when a stranger asked (for it was in Latin) 'What is this?', then we could have told how he and John Browne laid their heads together to do something about the Quakers here. It is the one thing I have against Empson, that he cleared away those slabs and those in memory of the little Caves. They were only names to him and I doubt if he knew anything about John Browne when he removed his sounding-board from above the pulpit. I think of the day they laid Empson to rest here – a crowded church and hardly a dry eye there. Dear old Sally comes to mind, and our beloved Canon Rendell, who ministered here the last ten years of his life. I think of humble folk, Aunt Ede and Lucy Edwards. Lucy sang in the choir all the days of her life and cleaned and dusted it for donkeys' years. How she loved the church with all her heart, mind and soul. She was one of countless numbers of men and women that have counted it a privilege to share in the church life: men and girls who loved to sing in the choir, hefty ploughmen who rang the bells, proud of their skill; sextons who kept the youngsters in order and told a new rector how to go on at Eydon.

Now I must get back home for the day is far spent. One last word: you may think these folks are all dead, but all I can say is, they won't be quite dead while I am alive.

Chapter 5

The two railways

My father was only twelve when Lady Palmerston cut the first sod of the East and West Junction Railway in 1864. It was nearly a mile from the village. I was six years of age when they started building the Great Central, only half a mile away. As they were almost parallel, when they were made they cut many good fields into bits and pieces which was awkward for the farmers. Now both railways are closed, and the fields cut in two could be joined again; but it would cost a dreadful lot of money to level the ground and make it as it was in 1864.

The building of the East and West Railway brought Eydon folk a very welcome alternative employment to agriculture, and it appears from this entry in the school log-book that the women and children set to work, not making hay while the sun shines, but bricks. The master, Tingley, records on 19th May 1865; '... Attendance on the whole fair, but many of the children are engaged with their parents in the brickyards making for the new railway.' Evidently local builders were given sub-contracts, for we know George Golby built the Preston road bridge. With a station at Moreton Pinkney and another at Byfield, two and a half miles away, this railway gave Eydon folk much easier access into the wider world. Another boon the railway brought was cheaper coal. This used to be brought from the canal or railway at Cropredy, or from the canal at Marston Doles in carts drawn by a pair of horses. The loading of the carts and the unloading, plus the seven-and-a-half-mile journey, would take a full day, for it would have to be a very good team of horses to do two journeys in a day. A boy used to be sent with a trace horse to meet the loaded cart and help them up the hills of the last two miles.

Although the East and West Junction Railway has been an asset to the villages along its route, to its promoters and especially to the unfortunate folk who provided the capital it was a sore disappointment. It was opened amid great rejoicing, ran for several years, then closed, to be reopened in 1884. This rural railway was for most of its life on the verge of bankruptcy, for as Sir Henry Dryden remarked, 'It never paid enough to grease the engine wheels.' The general managers' difficulties in making ends meet were eased in the 1920s when it became part of the London Midland and Scottish system. That was a very temporary respite, for it was the dawn of the motor age, and the beginning of the end of the little railway.

Probably the years when the Great Central was being built were the most profitable in the history of the East and West, for it carried vast quantities of materials used in its construction. I well remember the building of this railway and the upheaval during the four years of its construction. The light railway across the fields, the Moreton road crossing, a steam navvy at work near Lawn Hill and the raw earth and clay on the banks, I still see clearly after the passing of nearly eighty years. It began when Parliament passed a bill authorising the Manchester, Sheffield and Lincolnshire Railway to build a line from Annesley to Quainton. From Quainton to London trains would run over the Metropolitan Railway. The bill was not passed easily, for the railways serving the midlands and the north fought it tooth and nail in the Commons. They held that Sheffield, Nottingham and Leicester, the large towns on its route, were already served adequately by the main-line railways so that it would be a duplication of existing services. The verbal conflict ended, the bill was passed and received the royal assent in 1893.

The construction was delegated to six contractors, this section being built by Walter Scott and Co. of Newcastle-upon-Tyne. The supervisor of this section and representative of the promoters was Mr Duncan Fox, who set up an office at Brackley. Early in 1895 the work began and had got nicely going when a real hard winter set in. Hard frost and snow held up the work for weeks. The work here began in Woodford parish on the East and West Railway near the Black Bridge. The loop line was made that still connects the two railways. At Helmdon the Towcester to Banbury line crossed the route, so Helmdon and Woodford became important centres during the construction of the Great Central Railway.

This single-line, one-track railway brought to these sites the little tank engines and the steam navvies, as well as the coal they consumed. I use the name we used at the time for the steam-driven mechanical excavators. Steel girders for bridges, bricks and wood for buildings and workshop equipment came the same way. At Woodford and Helmdon long rows of huts were built as homes for the workmen. Stables for horses and workshops for blacksmiths and carpenters sprang up like mushrooms. As our local bricks were considered not good enough, first-class blue bricks were used for all the bridges. Local sand and gravel were used wherever available, and two pits were used at Woodford and one at Pebble Rump. When the Banbury branch was made two years later a pit was opened in the fields between Eydon and Culworth.

While the preliminary work was in progress, strangers were coming to the village in twos and threes, seeking accommodation. They were the contractors' regular men – engine drivers, foremen and skilled tradesmen. In those days most villages had empty cottages, but these were soon tenanted at what we thought exorbitant rents. A married man unable to find a cottage in one of the nearby villages became a lodger and kept an eye open for a cottage changing hands. Some of the poorer folk made a spare bedroom by squeezing the family together at bedtime, so that a lodger could be accommodated, glad of the extra shillings he brought into the house. The folk at the two Barnetts Hill cottages took in a surprising number of lodgers; they say the beds there never got cold when the steam navvy worked round the clock.

During the next four years these names appear in the school registers, all children of men working for Scotts: Jowett, Kerby, Woodhead, Lucas, Evans, Woods and Harris. Although they went away when the work was done, some names were remembered for years. A bathing place in the brook near Sidon Meadow was called 'Mark Edes' till the youngsters ceased to bathe there in the 1920s. Mark, one of the young navvies, regularly stripped and bathed in the brook during the summer months. The navvies, classed as unskilled men, followed the contractors up and down the country from one construction job to another. Here they were joined by many of the younger farm labourers out for the better wages the contractors paid. The average wage paid on the farms was in the region of 12s. a week. Scotts started a man at 3s. 4d. for a ten-hour day. They were employed on a daily basis, so if a man fell out with his ganger and got the sack he could walk to Charwelton and get taken on by Olivers, the contractors of the next length north. Most of them were big strong men with an amazing capacity for hard pick-and-shovel work. They wore bell-bottomed corduroy trousers with a leather strap below each knee. This was a help to a man using a shovel, for it saved the drag of trousers on his knee when it was bent. In shovelling, the knee is used to push the shovel into the material to be lifted, which saves the arms a good deal of exertion. They wore waistcoats with sleeves, a red kerchief loosely knotted round the neck, and a loose-fitting jacket of coarse, heavy cloth.

The navvies were a hard-working set of men; most of them consumed huge quantities of beer, and they swore like navvies. That phrase became a by-word with us at the time, and it's one we do not forget. During the summer many slept rough if they could not get lodgings, in a corner in one of the contractors' huts.

It is quite understandable that the building of the railway was not popular with the farmers in the district, for they lost many of their best men, and few returned to the farms when it was completed.

The first work in this parish was to cut gaps in the hedges and lay a light railway from Woodford. Very little levelling was done: it followed the lie of the land, and where it crossed the roads a level crossing was made. Early loads to be carried were bricks for bridges and mortar mills to mix the bricklayers' mortar. Every watercourse, large or small, needed a culvert. Every public right of way, whether it was a road or a footpath seldom used, had to be provided with a bridge.

Our parish council was very much on the alert during the construction; they kept a very watchful eye on Scotts' men, and lost nothing through not asking. They tried hard to get a halt at the Moreton road bridge, and when that failed they asked for a footpath down the bank from the Woodford bridge to the station. If this request had been granted, a foot-bridge would have been necessary over the permanent way, for the company could not allow pedestrians to walk over the rails at the entrance to a busy station. However, the proposed path has been used regularly by the railwaymen, and by many of us Eydon folk, in spite of the fact that we were trespassing.

We give the supervisors credit for having studied the ordnance maps thoroughly to enable them to provide for every public right of way, for they provided Eydon with a footpath crossing where no footpath existed. The 1833 ordnance map shows a footpath from Preston road corner down Long Leys to the buildings in the Barn Ground. As the path ended at the barn, it can have been useful only to the owner of the field. The result was the village folk had no use for it, so the right of way ceased to exist through disuse long before the railway came. Sixty-five years later the crossing was still there, but if I walked over it I was liable to be summonsed for trespassing. When a cow quietly grazing in the Barn Ground lifted her head to look at a passing train, she was bound to see the notice board solemnly warning her to 'beware of passing trains'.

While the bricklayers were busy on the bridges, a steam navvy travelled along the rails towards Culworth and set to work making a cutting through the higher ground. There another track was laid for the navvy to work alongside the first track. This enabled an empty truck to be placed by the side of the navvy. As soon as a truck was filled with soil a horse drew it away, and an empty one took its place. As a number were filled, a small tank engine drew them to the side of an embankment. The trucks were made to tip sideways – soon they were empty and on the way back for another load. At one time the work went on night and day, seven days a week, acetylene flares providing light in the hours of darkness.

During the construction the usual crop of snags and hindrances occurred, all except one that present-day contractors have to contend with – strikes. Mother used to talk of a bed of 'running sand' down the Preston road that added to the difficulty of making the banks stable. Later, when the Banbury branch was made, the new bank slipped away from the main-line bank several times. Making up had to be done, for it was some time before the two consolidated to form a stable union.

At the time of writing there lives at Brackley a Mr Law, eighty-six years old, who worked on the building of the viaduct there. This fine viaduct of twenty-three arches had to be built to carry the line over the valley of the River Ouse. He tells me that early in its construction it was considered necessary to give some of the piers extra support. This was done by joining piers together at the foundations by building a brickwork arch, an exact replica of the overhead arches.

Although the steam-navvy gang often worked on Sundays, for most of the men it was a day of rest. As it was the day after pay day, they had money in their pockets. Often during the summer when we were enjoying our Sunday dinner there would be a knock on the door. When we opened, a navvy would politely ask, 'Please would the Missus lend me a jug?' He would be a newcomer: the old hands knew it was no use asking for a jug at Tyrrell's; 'they didn't hold with such goings-on'. The man would find one of our neighbours more obliging, the jug would be filled at Gostick's, and with the jug in hand he would sit on one of the grassy banks by the roadside to enjoy his beer. On many Sunday afternoons ten or a dozen navvies were either sleeping or drinking at the top of the Moreton road when we went to the afternoon service.

Often there were quarrels that ended in a fight; some were soon over, others lasted many rounds. Rows were frequent at The Royal Oak, but Mrs Herbert, the landlady, was very strict. As soon as a man began to be quarrelsome she would order him outside, and outside he soon went. Usually, with her husband William's help, she could manage her customers, but one Saturday afternoon she sent for John Coy, the parish constable, to turn out an unruly customer. That was a busy afternoon for John, one he never forgot. He had two more calls for help, one to deal with a man threatening his wife, and the other from the neighbours of another couple because the husband was thrashing his wife. These carryings-on were discussed by the parish council and several times they asked for more police protection, but in vain. Then, as at the present time, our policeman lived at Culworth or Moreton Pinkney. He had the same troubles in his own village, and in the four or five villages that made up his beat. They were hectic times for all the local policemen, and the stories they told in after years of their adventures would have made a book.

I have mentioned that during the construction Scotts gave some of the work to sub-contractors. Parnells, the Rugby builders, built the station buildings, and the station-master's house at Woodford and at Brackley. The Brackley viaduct was built by J. Brooks of Kings Langley. The fencing along this length was done by two brothers who came from Market Harborough. That was quite a job, for every post hole had to be dug by hand.

As most of the money earned was spent in the district, all the local tradesmen shared in the prosperity of those years. At Culworth, Eydon and Helmdon shops can be seen that were built to cater for the increased trade of those boom years. By the end of 1896 the bridges were built and the cuttings and embankments completed; then the track was laid. On 29th July 1897 the first coal train came along the line on its way to London. The coal and goods trains that followed helped consolidate the track, for a lot of making up had to be done as the banks settled, more in some places than in others. The first passenger train left Marylebone, the London terminus, on 15th March 1899, drawn by a 4-4-0 engine, painted mid-green and decorated with flags. As the train steamed north it was a gala day in the towns through which the railway passed; bands were playing on the platforms with the mayor and aldermen present to confer a mayoral blessing on England's newest and most up-to-date railway. We could not rise to that height at Woodford, but the teachers and school-children were there to see the first train pass through the station. The vicar, the Rev. F. A. Smith, was there, and later he bought the first ticket at the booking office.

Now the main line was completed, the next stage was the building of the branch line to link up with the Great Western Railway at Banbury. The junction here is on the parish boundary, for it is over the brook that divides Eydon from the parish of Moreton Pinkney. This line winds between the hills in the parishes of Culworth and Thorpe Mandeville till it reaches the Cherwell valley at Chacombe. According to Fred Roberts, Scotts were responsible for the maintenance of the permanent way for twelve months, and then the company took over. We were not surprised that the cost of the railway considerably exceeded the estimates if the same type of claims were made all along its ninety-two miles that were made in this small section. After a lengthy correspondence our parish council were paid £30 for the reinstatement of the road at the Moreton road bridge. How much the actual work there cost I do not know, but I have a shrewd idea the work was done by the district road surveyor, Treadwell of Middleton Cheney, and was a charge on the district rate. For at the time the parish council was no longer responsible for the upkeep of the roads. Out of that £30 the council paid for the granite blocks that made a footpath from the Tudor House to Partridges Lane. Up to that time in the street there was nothing to indicate where the road ended and the footpath began. If the council spent anything down the Moreton road, then our first proper footpath was a remarkably cheap job.

The blocks are still in the street, as good as new, though some have been moved to the other side of the road.

In the early 1890s William Wright bought Farndon Mill, a water mill from Norman times, just outside our parish boundary, where he did a fair trade grinding corn for the farmers and pig-keepers in the district. When the railway was completed and the locomotive depot at Woodford in full going order, a large number of engines were stabled there in the sheds. To fill the boilers daily, water was taken from the brook that runs by Farndon Mill half a mile lower down. This reduced the water available for working Wright's water-wheel. He entered an action against the Railway Company for 'diversion of water, ancient water rights and so forth'. I believe it was settled out of court, by the company agreeing to pay the owner of the mill £40 per annum as long as it was used to grind corn. Wright installed an oil engine and carried on his business as usual, although the day of his mill was nearly over. These small mills were closing down on every brook and river in the country, for they could not compete with the big up-to-date mills at the grain-importing ports. A few years later Wright sold the mill to a Mr Goodwin, who ground a few sacks of corn for the farmers from time to time so that it qualified for the company's annual payment. When he sold the mill, the railway company bought it and let it to a signalman, Jack Jelly. That transaction brought the annual payment to an end after it had been paid for forty years.

When the bank had settled down it was sown with lucerne. For years the Eydon gang of plate-layers mowed it with scythes when it was ready for hay, and then it was sold as it lay in swathes. Henry Peck or Sam Spencer usually bought this length, for it made good hay in a fine summer. For about ten years it did well, then it began to deteriorate and rank weeds took possession of the banks. And so the bank, once an ugly streak in our valley view, has mellowed with the years and become a natural feature in our eastern landscape. It fits into the rural scene as naturally as the old Priory Church at Canons Ashby nestles among the tall elms where the sun rises. Every morning I would see it, and each night I looked to see if the signalman was in his box at the junction. A light in the signal-box told me one man in the parish was on duty while we slept, to see that the trains took the right road at the junction. On a dark night a brightly lit passenger train streaking across the valley was a cheerful sight to warm the hearts of boys of all ages.

The passing trains have not only been a never-failing source of interest, but men working in the fields found them useful to tell them the time, as few of them carried watches. The *Little Banbury*, a tank engine and two coaches, made five trips to Banbury from Woodford each day with clockwork regularity. *Sam Fay* (named after a general manager of the company) used to come down the bank in a desperate hurry at 4.35 each afternoon. For many years she ran non-stop from London to Sheffield, 160 miles in three hours. Another fast train, and one we often used after a day in London, left Marylebone at 6.20 each evening. We had to be careful to get into the last coach, for this was a slip coach for Woodford. Two guards were on the train, and half a mile from Woodford station one of them disconnected the coupling of the last coach. The train went through the station at sixty miles an hour, then a minute or so later the disconnected coach came slowly in and was brought to a standstill by the guard's brakes, punctually at 7.40 p.m. After the local passengers had alighted, the coach was taken on the East and West Railway to Stratford-on-Avon. On 21st December 1935 an accident occurred at Woodford station when the slip coach was derailed and thrown across the track. Several passengers received minor injuries and Dr Hays and the local ambulance were called on to help the injured passengers. Prompt action by Signalman Dale in stopping another train averted a much more serious crash. But as a result, the slipping of the coach was brought to an end.

Another train that made headlines when the GCR was very

young was the *Daily Mail* Special. A special train was chartered to take a load of this newspaper to the industrial north at express speed so that it could be on the reader's breakfast table long before any other London newspaper. The train, consisting of an engine and two coaches, came along the bank at 4.30 a.m., each coach displaying '*Daily Mail* Special' in bold lettering. One morning I went to Woodford station for our parcel of newspapers to find the platform stacked high with great bales of *Daily Mails*, said to be about twenty tons in weight. There had been some mishap to the train so that it had to be unloaded and the goods transferred to other coaches. The *Daily Mail* ran this train for several years, but then the company entered it on the timetables and it became an ordinary passenger train.

While on the subject of trains, we must not forget that between the two wars the longest-distance trains in the country came this way. Everybody knows that Aberdeen to Penzance is nearly as far as John O'Groats from Lands End. On the northern section the train was on the North British Railway to York, then the Great Central brought it to Banbury, and from there it was on the Great Western system to Cornwall.

For the first twenty years the third-class fare from Woodford to London was 5s. 9d. for a single ticket, 11s. 6d. return. When the company started excursions very few people paid the full fare, for on two days each week one could go to London for a day for 5s. 6d., or half a day for 3s. 3d. As half a day gave one about seven hours in London, this was a very cheap outing. Folk going there for a holiday went on the excursion train for 3s. 3d., and the return half of the ticket was thrown away. At Marylebone station lads were on the station premises cadging the return halves as passengers came from the platforms, so evidently there was a sale for them.

The new railway had brought us quick and easy travel to the north, south and west. Some cycled, others walked the two miles of road between the village and the station, and the busy folk and the infirm hired a horse and trap and rode there. Arthur Herbert of The Royal Oak kept a horse and trap for the job. One or two passengers rode seated high in the trap, while parties of up to seven travelled in style in a wagonette. This was a four-wheeler; passengers climbed steps at the back, and sat three each side facing each other.

Another boon the railway brought to Eydon was the national newspapers on the day of publication. As the railway was opened during the Boer War, we were all very keen to hear the latest news, for Eydon had three men in the fighting forces.

The railway brought an influx of new blood to the village; young men came to work for the contractors and remained in the company's employ. They found here a new freedom, for they had escaped from the feudal influences that were still strong in agriculture. They rejoiced that their employer, 'the Company', did not care two hoots whether they were Tory or Radical, church or chapel, or nothing at all. This attitude was fostered by my father, who soon tried to make friends with young men who had come to live in the village. He had an amazing gift of being able to find young men with an inclination towards the Radical fold. It gave him great satisfaction to have in the village a group of men who were Radicals and didn't care who knew it, a transformation from his early days in the political sphere. Among the new blood was a gang of five plate-layers. They came expecting to be here a year or two, but girls came into their lives, and that was the end of their travels. For the first few years they were paid 18s. per week, while the ganger received 20s. Then we always had a signalman living in the village; Bob Wilkinson came from Yorkshire to work at the junction-box, with no intention of staying in the village. 'I shaunt stop here when I finish, I shall goo back wheer I coome from,' he said many a time. But Bob started keeping half a dozen white leghorns at the signal-box. There was room for them to wander on the railway bank and a dry shelter under the signal-box, and Bob or his mate were always there to feed them and collect the eggs. His fowls increased in number, so he started keeping a flock on the allotments. And so when Bob pulled the last lever in the signal-box and drew his pension, what with his fowls and his garden, he was too involved here to make the break. When he left Eydon it was not for Yorkshire, but for that land from which there is no return.

When Gertrude Lines made a survey of the parish in 1928, twenty per cent of the men were employed by the Great Central Railway, the majority in the workshops and goods depot at Woodford. That is a fair average of the sixty-seven years since the railway was opened. Year in, year out, day and night, men have been walking, cycling, and now motoring there to keep the traffic moving on the last main line to be built in Great Britain.

One day in June 1965 I stood on Crockwell bridge to see the last train on the old East and West Railway. The engine and trucks were stationary, for a tractor with a fork-lift attachment was picking up the rails and sleepers and dropping them into the trucks. Then the train moved slowly on a few yards and the tractor got busy again. That was how they took away our first railway. I did not shed tears although I felt very like it. It was such a nice little railway, such a homely one. The Great Central was so big and grand with two tracks and no end of trains. The East and West was a single line, so each train had a length to itself, with no tearing past other trains on that line. It was a homely railway, as I said. The drivers used to wave to us youngsters, and the Moreton station-master, smart in his brass-buttoned uniform, was a personal friend. With only six trains a day calling he'd always time for a chat when my brother Percy or I called for a parcel of cloth.

Before this line finally closed, I recorded the following: 'The last *Little Banbury* ran on 13th June 1964. *Sam Fay* no longer thunders along the bank, leaving a billowing plume of smoke on her way to Sheffield, a reminder that it's nearly tea-time. There are no expresses now, no ordinary goods trains, just a few trains go along the bank containing maybe half a dozen people who look as if they'd got lost. Diesel locomotives add to the general despondency – no smoke, no fire, not even a decent whistle, more like a blooming ice-cream van. The friendly light in the signal-box has gone out, so there is now no one in the parish keeping watch while we are asleep.'

The running-down process was to have culminated in the closure of the section from Rugby to Aylesbury in April 1966. When the Labour Party was returned in November 1964 it was announced that there would be second thoughts before any main line was closed. . . . But on 23rd April 1966, the *Sun* reported:

... It was the end of the line yesterday for the old Great Central, the last main line railway to be built in Britain seventy years ago. The line which once carried from ten to twenty expresses each way a day between London and Yorkshire, and between South West England and North East, but never made a profit, will be closed. After years of controversy about its fate Mrs. Barbara Castle has agreed to the closure of the section between Aylesbury and Rugby and its link line to the Western Region between Banbury and Woodford Halse. It will save British Rail about £900,000 a year.

4th September 1966: ... It is all over, the last train passed along the bank this morning. How quiet it is here now. As long as I can remember, we could hear the passing trains, day and night, winter and summer. When atmospheric conditions were so-so, the railway seemed to come nearer to the village, for the roar of fast trains and the clatter and bumping of the trucks of goods trains were so loud one might have thought it only a few yards away instead of half a mile distant.

Yesterday evening I saw the last two trains, drawn by steam engines, pull out of Woodford station – the 6.40 to Rugby and Leicester and the 6.50 to London. They were packed by folk evidently anxious to make the last trip, and long-haired young men perched on bridges and messed about with cameras. Oh, it was quite a to-do. But the last train of all was a fast train from London, the one that started as the *Daily Mail* Special. At three o'clock this morning I stood at an open window looking across the valley at the light shining once more in the signal-box, listening. On the Banbury branch a diesel engine hooted as it came to a stop a few yards from the junction. That waited, and I waited and watched. Soon I saw a brightly lit train emerge from the trees, come along the bank at about 60 mph on its way north. I heard her pass through Woodford station, then as the sound faded away, a plane droned overhead. I knew where the train was going to, but the plane, goodness knows where she came from or where she was making for. In a few minutes the diesel came on to the main line, and stopped at the signal-box. The signalman put out the light, locked the door and boarded the diesel, and away they went towards Woodford.

That is the end, the line is now deserted.

6th September: Have been comparing notes with neighbours. We agree it's strange that we find ourselves quite unconsciously listening for trains. Today, busy grubbing up weeds in the garden, I pricked up my ears and said to myself, 'Why, that's a train on the branch, in the cutting.' It was only a combine harvester working in a field half a mile away.

It is fortunate this has come at a time of full employment. The railwaymen here have packed up one by one to work in factories in the nearby towns. Very few men regret the change of employment, and some wish they'd made the change years ago. Two men who refused to be other than railwaymen now work at Banbury on the old Great Western. As long as they live they'll mourn the passing of the Great Central, for things are done so differently in Banbury. Great Central men never did like the Great Western's goings-on!

Chapter 6

Neighbours and friends

When I sit by the fire thinking of Eydon I am reminded of so many friends who have left us, but the picture that abides in my mind is of life, not death. I remember all those people who have helped to make the village such a cheerful place, who have provided untold pleasure through the telling of stories about their goings-on. I see old Dr Jacobs coming to our house, I remember Jim and Harriet Treadwell who lived next door for fifty years. Then there was old Sally with her stories of the 1840s and John Henry Ivens whose farm was next door to the school.

Some of the people were well known to me personally. Others I have come to know well through legendary tales about them told to me again and again by Sally, Aunt Ede or Mother, such as the one about Thomas Pettifer, sheep dresser or Henry Peck, coachman. Anyone who gets around and asks questions as I do is bound to get answers of a sort, for some folk I know are never stumped. I'd known Ted Higham well but he would never tell about his early life, so I found out about it from others, from Father and Jim Treadwell.

i The doctor

One of my early jobs was to walk across the fields to Culworth for bottles of medicine from Dr Jacobs, sometimes for members of the family, but often for folk who could not do the journey. It was generally coloured, often very nasty, but it was good medicine and it did folks good. For everyone had such faith in Dr Jacobs. And I've more faith in a bottle of medicine than I have in the pills the doctors give folks in such quantities nowadays. He did not give his patients pills I'm sure, for they would have been light to carry, whereas four or five bottles of medicine were heavy for a boy to carry a couple of miles.

Adjacent to the old parlour of our house, a very small room was dedicated to Dr Jacobs, known to the family as 'the Doctor's place'. He kept a stock of medicine there, for some of his patients came to the house to meet him and he would fix them up with medicine and sometimes he would draw an aching tooth while you were saying Jack Robinson.

For over forty years H. R. Jacobs was looked on in this district as the model doctor, capable and clever at his work, kind and considerate to man, woman or child. I have never known a man so universally acclaimed by all sections of the community as a 'good man'. His name became almost a legend in the district and his standard of conduct and service became the standard by which other doctors in the district were weighed and measured.

In his day, like the good highwaymen of old, doctors used to charge the well-to-do folk plenty, so that they could doctor the poor folk for next to nothing, thus doing a bit of levelling in a kindly sort of way. At Culworth the doctor was the rector's right-hand man, serving from time to time as churchwarden and always very active in the Band of Hope. He was a keen and persuasive speaker on the value of total abstinence, and this soon brought him and Father together in the starting of the Rechabites Friendly Society at Culworth. The surgery brought him frequently to our house, thus giving Mother regular contacts with him; she used this to increase her knowledge of doctoring and first aid. I believe Mother had a more profound respect for Dr H. R. Jacobs than for any other man she had known and we were all taught to regard him as the epitome of wisdom and goodness. There was one thing Mother had known him to do occasionally that she thought was especially commendable. When he had done all that he could do for the comfort of a dying patient, if he felt it would be a help and comfort he would kneel by the bedside and in prayer commend the sufferer to God's mercy and love. He told Mother of his early life. He was a member of a rich Jewish family but he offended his father by marrying a Christian and being confirmed in the Church of England. His father struck him out of his will, so that all he had of the family wealth was the £1,000 his medical training cost. After he had taken his degrees he walked to work at St Mary's Hospital in London, before coming to Culworth in 1870.

In that year Dr Bishop died at Culworth Hall. He had supplemented his income by taking folk suffering from mental derangement into his home. Evidently it was a paying proposition for his widow carried on the home and brought the newly married Dr Jacobs to Culworth. It was agreed that he should give his services to her establishment free and have the rest of Dr Bishop's practice for his livelihood. This worked amicably for ten years, but then there was a hitch. On 3rd April 1880 Mrs Bishop was charged at the County Assizes with keeping an unlicensed lunatic asylum. There is a long account of the case in the *Northampton Mercury*, which ended satisfactorily for Mrs Bishop, so no harm was done at Culworth. On 8th May 1895 Dr and Mrs Jacobs celebrated their silver wedding, and this gave folk living round Culworth a chance to show their appreciation of the doctor. Canon Hill presided in a crowded schoolroom when Sir Henry Dryden presented them with a cabinet and a lamp, the gift of 281 subscribers.

The building of the railway caused a considerable increase in the population of the villages served by Dr Jacobs, which brought a corresponding increase in the number of his patients. To cope with the situation he took into partnership a Dr Glen Hays, who came to live at Eydon and work the area round Woodford.

The two doctors did a job in our house that I have never forgotten and one that is not likely to be done at Eydon again. In the early years of the century one of our tenants was Bill Garner, with his wife and youngest son Walter. Poor old Bill was crippled with bad legs, and for years had worked only for short periods. One leg got so bad they said it would soon kill him, so Dr Jacobs decided to amputate it above the knee. The two doctors came with a nurse, they had Mrs Garner scrub the kitchen table, they operated and it was quite a success. After a long interval Bill got about again; he used to get round the house with the help of a chair about a year after the amputation. Dr Hays obtained an artificial leg for Bill from the Medical Aid Association. Mrs Garner called me in to see it, carefully wrapped in a long cardboard box. It was a beautiful leg and no mistake; the joints worked and it had a most lifelike foot. Bill wore it only two or three times, for he never broke it in, saying it was too fast for him. So he carried on scrabbling about with the help of a kitchen chair, and the leg went back to its bed of tissue paper in the cardboard box. Several years after this event, I asked Walter what the doctors did with his father's real leg, and he said they had him dig a deep hole in the garden and Dr Hays brought it wrapped in a sheet and they buried it. If at some future time human remains are found in front of the house, no one need be alarmed.

Mary Kench tells me that when she was a child she had a cyst on her eye. Dr Jacobs did all he could for some time, but it got worse rather than better. The doctor said to Mr and Mrs Kench, 'I could remove it if you will say the word.' They agreed he should operate. Mary remembers sitting on her father's knee and the doctor giving her a whiff of chloroform. He removed the cyst and made a good job of it so that no scar remained once it had healed.

Mother held that he saved many a life by tackling, often single-handed, operations that are now done only in hospitals. We believe he liked to try his hand at some of the tricky jobs doctors have to do. He often talked to Mother about the extra-ordinary cases he had, for he knew how interested she was in medical work and nursing. There were cases of illness here in poverty-stricken homes that he knew were caused by malnutrition. Some of these he discussed with Mother, then put half-a-crown in her hand and said, 'Spend this on them, will you, you'll know what to send.' Kate remembers taking rice puddings to the Garner family as a gift from Dr Jacobs, who knew perfectly well he'd never be paid for his services. All the folk round us knew Mother was a very capable nurse, so that in illness and accidents she was often called on for help. A neighbour sent for the doctor to see a sick baby; when he called he asked, 'Has Mrs Tyrrell seen the child?' and when the mother said no, he replied 'Why didn't you ask her? She is as good as a doctor any day.' He felt that with experience of children she had a practical advantage over the doctor with his theoretical training only.

ii Jim and Harriet Treadwell

From 1900 to 1950 the tenants of the cottage next to the farm-house were Jim and Harriet Treadwell. In that tiny three-roomed cottage they brought up a family of six children out of ten born. I say tiny, but to be more exact, the rooms were all seven foot six inches across. When they became tenants the rent was 2s. 6d. weekly; then for some years it stood at 3s. and the last few years they paid 3s. 6d. which included rates. During the latter years Harriet always paid the rent before nine o'clock on a Saturday morning, but for the first twenty years they were always heavily in arrears. They were not unduly pressed because we knew where the money went and Jim often did a job of work for Father in his spare time to pay a bit off the rent owing. Harriet was the most stupid and ignorant woman I have ever known, which was one of the reasons why she lost four children in infancy. She spoke in the broadest dialect, more pronounced than anyone else in the village. There was one fact in relation to her accent worthy of record. When speaking of Eydon she always said 'Ayden' to rhyme with maiden, whereas everyone else makes it rhyme with Weedon.

Although Jim was classed as an unskilled labourer he was a good and capable worker and was one of the last men to make bricks at Eydon. I remember going with Mother one Sunday evening for a walk to see him at the Woodford road brickyard. He was tending the fires round a kiln burning bricks, a night-and-day job till they were properly baked. If his wages had been carefully spent they would still have been poor folk, but with Jim drinking and Harriet a poor manager it was a very poverty-stricken home. Normally Jim was a peace-loving individual and would do anything to avoid trouble or a row, yet when he had had drink he became as brave as a lion. After turning-out time at The Oak he'd get as far as the bottom of Partridges Lane; there he would look up the street and down the street as he shouted loudly for his enemies to come and see what he'd do for them. It might be Jim Dancer or Ike Blencowe he'd invite to come and be slain. We at home couldn't help hearing the rumpus and after a time we'd hear Harriet speaking very softly in a wheedling tone, 'Come on Jim, come on home, do come Jim', and eventually she would guide his unsteady feet homewards. I believe the drink was a lure to him because it gave him courage he naturally lacked; it made him feel a proper he-man.

In addition to the four children they lost in infancy, a girl died at the age of ten from diphtheria and Edith died in her early twenties in the 'flu epidemic of 1918. During the frequent cases of illness in the family Mother used to supervise the nursing by frequent visits, usually taking something tasty for the sufferer, for to use Mother's own words, 'Harriet hadn't a bit of gumption'. On one of these occasions she was alarmed to find that a bottle of medicine containing enough for three days was nearly empty after only twenty-four hours in the house. 'What on earth have you done with that medicine?' she asked anxiously. 'Did you give her a spoonful at a time as I told you?' Harriet's answer was, 'She drunk it out of the bottle,' which made Mother really angry, 'You fool, woman, it's a wonder you haven't killed her.' 'Oh but she didn't have it all, the others had some,' Harriet assured her. This answer did not pacify Mother's anger. The idea of the others taking sups out of medicine the doctor had provided (well knowing he would never be paid) made her furious with Harriet. When Alice lay ill with diphtheria Mother kept away, for Jane Higham helped with the nursing. It was the only time Jane helped anyone outside her own home. She did it because Ted, her husband, and Jim worked together and were very friendly and she would do anything to please Ted.

There was great rejoicing in the cottage when the last child was a boy. Jim went to The Oak that night to celebrate with Harriet's full approval and came home drunk as expected on such a special occasion. Harriet made a terrific fuss of the boy for a year or two, then began to change her tune. 'I do'ant want no more boys,' she said. 'They be more trubble than all the gels put together.' Poor Harry was weak and ailing most of his short life and tuberculosis brought it to an end when he was thirty.

Not long after the son was born Jim went to bed one night full of drink. During the night he was doubled up with severe pain. 'I thought I should have died,' he told us afterwards. It frightened him so much that he left the drink severely alone; we were highly amused, for the fright did what Father and the Band of Hope had failed to do – it made Jim a teetotaller.

Although his hands were rough and calloused with hard work Jim could take a clock down, clean and reassemble it, working by the light of a small paraffin lamp. These were jobs for the long winter nights. He did several for us and made a good job of them, but as he grew old his eyes failed him for fine work. One day Harriet had a word with Mother, 'I hope you wunt give our Jim any more clocks to mend, for he can't see the little bits and he drops 'em and has to go on his hands and knees to find 'em and it makes him swear so, and that makes me swear.' Jim tried spectacles but they were either Woolworth's sixpenny ones or Father's cast-offs, so they were not much help. We suggested he went to Banbury and had an optician test his sight, but he would not hear of such an expensive procedure. The last few years of their lives the pension made them very comfortable; in fact Harriet saved money week by week out of their pensions. They lived in the cottage till the end came when they were nearly eighty years of age.

iii The village carriers

An important person in any fair-sized village was the carrier to the nearest market town. For centuries Banbury has been our town for trading purposes. It is six miles nearer than Northampton, and that is a long way in a carrier's cart. Very small villages unable to support a man were served by carriers passing through from a larger village. 'Picking up on the way' it was called.

Village shops could stock only goods in constant demand, so hand tools and implements, boots and clothing, as well as the stock in the shops, had to come from town in the carrier's cart.

Old George was not a first-rate carrier. He became a bit deaf and often misunderstood directions, which made him seem more stupid than he actually was. He and his father were poor folk. I doubt if they were any better off than the farm labourers. I don't think he ever grumbled, for it was his way of life. They spent their lives going to and coming from Banbury fifty-two weeks a year – no holidays for a country carrier.

In John Browne's correspondence the carrier is mentioned as bringing the letters from Banbury. This was very soon after a postal system had been instituted by private enterprise; in a few years it was taken over and made a government monopoly by Oliver Cromwell. Whenever possible the mails were carried by stage coaches running to a regular timetable; if no coach was available they were carried by men on horseback from town to town. As not many people wrote letters in those days and the Post Office had to make a profit each year, letters for Eydon came only on the days our carrier journeyed to Banbury. For well over three hundred years a man set out for Banbury probably twice a week, driving a horse and cart and carrying an assortment of goods and a few letters to post. Not many, for letters were costly till the penny post came in 1840; then in a very short time the number of letters trebled. About that time we were transferred from Banbury to the Daventry postal area, and we could buy a stamp and post a letter in the village.

William Potts records 208 carriers visiting Banbury in 1838; in 1899, 166 made 397 journeys there. Our man went each Monday and Thursday. For well over a century three generations of Hunts made these regular trips to Banbury up to the First World War; this important service was maintained summer and winter, irrespective of the weather, and with no holidays. The carrier rode in a cart, with a light semi-circular roof covered with tarpaulin to keep his goods dry. The village carrier was always a trustworthy man. He had to be straight and above-board in all his dealings or he would never have made a living. The carriers took passengers on the understanding they walked up the hills, to ease the horse. You might have to sit on an empty vinegar barrel or a hamper of butter, as there was no room for padded seats. If you rode to Banbury with our man, it was no use your being in a hurry, for you were three hours on the way. He went the field road by Trafford House and Edgcote Park, the shortest and easiest road to Banbury, picking up goods and receiving orders at the houses on the way. There were eight gates to open this side of Trafford Bridge and seven through the park, and carriers' horses were never renowned for speed. They had to be well-mannered, so no carrier bought a mare till she was well past her giddy youth. The horse very soon learnt the way to Banbury; she knew just where to stop at the gates, according to which way the gate opened, and every house to call at for an order or a parcel. The road this side of the bridge goes through the middle of the Ewe Ground, an eighty- or ninety-acre field. On a dark night in winter, with a fall of snow that obliterated the track and the feeble light of a candle lamp to guide your footsteps, only a good horse could have kept in the right track that led to the gate on the far side. There were mishaps: Mother used to tell of George Hunt's grandmother breaking a leg on the way home from Banbury.

George was a kindly old boy, who did his best, but he wasn't in the same street as the super carriers from other villages that wended their way with clockwork regularity to Banbury. Every tradesman and every shop in town named William Cherry of Boddington as one of the best. A keen business man and very methodical, he did a roaring trade all his long life. Farmers gave him cheques on Thursdays to cash at the banks for wages to be paid on Saturdays. On one occasion he handed the money over, but the next time he called the lady of the house met him and said, 'Mr Cherry, you left a sovereign too much on Thursday.' 'Did I?' he replied, 'Well then, it must have been the bank.' So William goes to the bank, lays the sovereign on the counter and says, 'You gave me a sovereign too much on Thursday.' The clerks hold a confab, then one says, 'No, Mr Cherry, our accounts were correct, so we couldn't have made a mistake.' So very reluctantly William pocketed the sovereign, but he wasn't at all pleased, for he prided himself that he made no mistakes.

No one here would have trusted George Hunt to change a cheque. He was honest all right, but he had his limitations and Eydon folk knew them. William Cherry was busy on Wednesday afternoon getting orders, so that he could start in good time on Thursday morning. George left everything till the morning, so he was always late in starting to Banbury. One morning he called on Mrs Coy between ten and eleven o'clock. 'Shan't you soon be off, George?' she asked him. 'Oh no,' he replied, 'Oi shan't be off yet, for oi've still got to call on the three Ps.' To Mrs Coy's further enquiry, he replied, 'Pick, Peck and Pettifer.' So George used to arrive in Banbury in the middle of the afternoon, when William Cherry was starting to pack up and get on the way home. George put up at The Wagon and Horses, one of the smaller inns that catered for many country carriers. The two hotels, the Red and White Lions, catered for the gentry, farmers and dealers, that thronged the High Street on market days. Many a farmer found the markets a good excuse to have a day off. He could always tell the missus he was looking for a horse or a cow, and on his return say they were too dear. The landlords of the Red and White Lions not only thought of the customers that thronged their bars, but also had to bear in mind the horses that brought them to town. It would never do to have their stables and yards cluttered up with country carriers so that there was no room for more profitable customers. At The Wagon and Horses George parked his cart in a row of carriers' carts under an open shed, and stabled his horse, giving him water and a feed of chaff and oats. Next he went round the shops with written orders, nails and iron for the blacksmith, cloth for the tailor, leather and springs for the shoemaker. Later in the day, the goods ordered were dumped by the side of George's cart, which meant that in bad weather they were under cover. When Raymond Gostick wanted a quantity of goods for his shop he went to fetch them; but always there was some commission for George, if it was only for a case of matches or a keg of lard. He brought ready-made clothing for men and boys, and materials for the home-dress-makers, cough mixtures and pills from the chemists and an armful of newspapers from the *Advertiser* and *Guardian* offices. These are only a sample of the miscellaneous collection of goods that filled the carriers' carts at Banbury, up to the First World War.

As George was late starting in the morning he was usually the last carrier to leave Banbury, so in the winter he had darkness to contend with all the way home. Getting in and out of the cart to open gates in daylight is bad enough, but at night it is ten times worse. There were stops at Edgcote and Trafford to deliver parcels and newspapers, all done with the help of a candle lantern. George was about five hours on the road from town during the winter, and longer if snow was on the ground. For years he tried the patience of Eydon folk sorely. Some folk wanted to see the *Banbury Guardian* before they went to bed, others needed a parcel he was bringing; all they could do was sit and listen for the rumble of his cart in the street.

He was continually being teased and compared to the cow's tail, but he would parry complaints with some light-hearted remark; he was never in a hurry himself and he couldn't understand why other folk were; there was plenty of time.

George lived with his sister Binah in a cottage that I think was built especially for a carrier's home. I'm told there was a similar carrier's house at Steeple Aston; apart from these, I do not remember seeing another like it in the district. There was a recess in the wall, open to the street, about ten foot long by five foot wide. Above was the floor of a bedroom. To the left was the cottage door, to the right the stable door; facing you, a door into a store for hay and corn. This enabled the carrier to leave his fireside to give his horse a feed, and yet still stay under cover. The carrier's horse was all-important; he must be cared for well to keep him up to the work on which his master's living depended.

Just before the armistice George made his last journey to Banbury; a month later everyone in the village knew he was near the last journey of all. I recount this incident as Aunt Ede told it me recently. She was Mrs Teddy Amos; Teddy was the village roadman and one of the village barbers:

We had just finished breakfast one Sunday morning when Jumbo came with the message, 'Would Teddy go and cut George Hunt's hair?' 'Yes, I'll be along later,' Teddy replied. Well, he washed, shaved, cleaned his boots and did the usual Sunday morning jobs, when another message came to the same effect. 'I be coming,' Teddy replied impatiently. 'What's the hurry?' Taking his tools Teddy went along to Hunt's cottage, walked upstairs and opened the door of George's bedroom. The old man looked up from the bed and said to Teddy, 'I be glad you be come Teddy, I should like to go nice and clane.' Teddy pulled him up in bed, put a cloth over his shoulders, then cut his hair and beard. After he'd made George comfortable, Teddy bid him good day and went home to his dinner. I'd just finished washing up, when Sarah went by and said old George had gone.

Evidently as soon as the old man was 'nice and clane' he lay down and died.

George was not the only carrier around these parts. There was one called Frank from Moreton Pinkney who was always a bit wild even at the best of times. He's an old man now but still hale and hearty, I'm glad to say. Years ago no one thought he'd even live to be old, for he was a speed merchant long before the motor came into general use. A carrier to Banbury and Northampton, he did quite a bit of dealing in pigs, fowls or anything he could make a bit out of. He travelled the villages round here in a spring cart drawn by a fast cob. When Frank climbed into the cart and got hold of the reins his horse was off and going in top gear before you could say Jack Robinson. If a horse couldn't trot fast enough for Frank he had to canter; they very soon learnt what was expected of them and no horse of Frank's ever let the grass grow under his feet.

Now that was at nine o'clock in the morning; but later in the day when Frank had wetted his whistle at two or three pubs the pace can only be described as fast and furious. There were times when his horse was in such a hurry to get round a corner that he took it too short, ran the wheel up a bank, tipped the cart over, and Frank came a cropper. Of course, it may have been Frank's driving that was at fault, and not the horse, I can't say who was to blame; I can only tell you what happened and why we are surprised Master Frank ever drew the old-age pension.

At the time of this incident there lived close to Frank a Mr Fletcher, a musician: a tall, thin, aristocratic-looking man, quite a gentleman. The schoolmaster in the village was Mr Jones, a short stocky man with closely trimmed whiskers. For rather a small man he had a terriffic big voice, deep bass. I well remember the first time I heard him sing: it was at the school here at Eydon when I was quite a youngster. He sang 'With my bundle on my shoulder, I'm off to Philadelphia in the morning'. He sang that song with such power and gusto, I quite thought it was true, and he was off to America the next day. But he never went.

No, he came to Eydon again years later and sang that same song on a night that he didn't forget in a hurry. It came about this way.

Henry Peck got up a smoking concert at The Royal Oak club-room in the winter. An invitation was sent to Mr Fletcher to come and play the piano and to Mr Jones to sing.

Frank tells them he's coming too; he likes a smoker at Eydon, and they may as well travel with him. Now they know Master Frank; they know he's apt to get a bit aerated (or merry as other people might say) on these occasions and they're a bit dubious. After all they are middle-aged men. But it's three miles to Eydon, and it's wintertime. They had no desire to walk, nor horse to bring them, so when the concert came off they rode with Frank in his spring cart. Well, the concert went off very nicely, I'm glad to say, and our local talent rose nobly to the occasion. Billy Brum sang first. He was always ready with a song; he'd sing any time or anywhere. He earned many a pint with a song. They said his voice never broke; at any rate he sang in a high-pitched falsetto voice, more like a woman's than a man's. He could whistle, too, like a lark; he'd go walking down the street whistling 'Onward Christian Soldiers' and when he came back it would be the latest music-hall ditty; we always knew when Billy was about.

George Tompkins, the wheelwright, sang too. He was a proper John Bull of a man; his bass almost took the roof off when he really got going. How he loved to sing 'Black and stormy is the night' and he sang it with great style, I can tell you.

Then I remember the chairman looking down the room and calling out, 'We haven't heard from you yet, Dan Leno.' So old Teddy Wills, wagoner on the Hall farm, shuffled up to the piano —he was a tenor. It was comical to see Teddy sing; before he made a start he screwed his face up in the funniest way imaginable and shut his eyes; and he didn't open them till his song was finished.

All I remember of his first song was the refrain 'Waiter, waiter, 'ot pertater, How about your veal and 'am'.

His second song, the favourite here at Eydon, ran to many verses. These four give the gist of it. If Teddy was here to check my copy, I'm sure it would be improved, but there it is, it's the best I can do.

1. I'm a jolly young swell, well known round here,
   And I come from Warwickshire,
   With a jolly life and Nance for my wife,
   I live from year to year.
   And every night by the firelight bright,
   When the children round us play,
   It makes me think of the days gone by,
   And about our wedding day.

Chorus
   The bull did dance, and the cows did prance,
   The pigs all grunted in the sty,
   The dogs did bark and the pretty little lark
   Sang merrily in the sky.
   The cock did crow to let folks know,
   The hens all cackled on the perch,
   The ducks and the drake, what a row they make,
   When I took our Nance to church.

2. When I first met our Nance,
   It was on the village green,
   She was dancing round the maypole,
   She was called the village queen.
   She gave consent to see her home,
   So she took me by the arm,
   I was making love to her all the way,
   Until we reached the farm.

3. I shan't forget one moonlight night,
   As I stood by the old farm gate,
   I kissed our Nance's rosy cheeks,
   I said I'd know my fate,
   I met the old farmer toddling home,
   I told him what I meant,
   Young Squire, said he, with all my heart,
   Your marriage I'll consent.

4. The pretty little birds did gaily sing,
   T'was on a summer morn,
   The wedding bells did gaily ring,
   As we walked across the farm,
   The lads and lassies round the church,
   Soon then did they arrive,
   Wishing long life and happiness,
   To me and Nance my bride.

As the evening got on some of the young 'uns who wouldn't sing earlier got braver and had a go. We admired their pluck if we didn't enjoy some of their songs. Mr Fletcher was at the piano. Few of the singers had any music, but he could play well enough, for a song he didn't know as well as for one he knew well.

So the evening passed harmoniously: the songs were sung, the pipes were smoked, the glasses were filled and emptied time and time again. You could hardly see across the room for smoke—rank smoke from aged pipes filled with shag tobacco.

Fletcher and Jones had kept an eye on Master Frank, and they were pleased to see that he had been moderate with the drink, so towards the close they gave one another the wink as much as to say, 'We'll be all right, Frank's quite all right tonight.' Just before 'God save the King' Frank whispers to Jones, 'I'll go and put the horse in so we can get off quick.' So Frank puts on his topcoat and goes outside. But instead of going to the stable for the horse, he slips across the yard into the bar and treats himself quickly to two or three tots of gin, no doubt to keep out the cold on the drive home.

When Fletcher and Jones have said goodnight to everybody and got outside, Frank is busy putting the horse into the cart; the two candle lamps are lit and very soon they are on the way home. It was an uneventful drive over the three miles; they were nearly in the village and Fletcher and Jones were thinking what a pleasant evening they'd had and a comfortable ride home. But as luck would have it, an orchard gate stood open by the side of the road.

Frank had a brainwave. In a moment he turned the horse through the gate. 'Now I'll show you what old Frank can do,' he hollered, giving the horse a clout with his whip. For a few minutes he made the horse tear round among the trees, turning, twisting in and out among them like a mad thing. Fletcher and Jones crouched down in the cart, holding on tight and expecting every moment to hit a tree and be capsized. But the worst didn't happen, I'm glad to say. When Frank was quite satisfied he'd demonstrated his skill as a driver he turned the horse back into the road and took them quietly the rest of the way home. If Fletcher could play the piano and Jones could sing, Frank could drive a horse, and he knew it.

iv Sally

Monday was washing day at our house; while we sat having breakfast the clatter of buckets and washing trays from the wash-house below would warn us that Sally had arrived. Soon the place would be full of steam as Mother and Sally tackled a big heap of dirty clothes. Mother worked, talked to Sally and kept an ear open for the shop bell; sometimes she let Sally talk while she listened. About ten o'clock Sally took off her wet sacking apron, rolled her sleeves down, buttoned them at the wrists and came up to the kitchen for her lunch.

Sally Dancer was of medium height and spare figure, with a face all wrinkles round her grey twinkling eyes that missed nothing. Sally was proud of the fact that she hadn't a tooth in her mouth, but could eat anything, for she seemed to look on teeth as quite unnecessary for a woman of her age. Her lunch was always a cup of cocoa and a slice of the family cake. Mother explained that when Sally was a girl tea was so expensive that very little was used in her home and in after years she had never acquired the taste. At dinner time Sally sat at Mother's left hand at the table. Sometimes one of the youngsters would refuse one of the vegetables or the pudding; not often, for Mother did not hold with picking and choosing. Whenever that occurred it was sure to set old Sally off. 'Turning yer nose up at good vittles,' she'd say, very sarcastically. 'If you'd bin at our house when I were young you'd be only too thankful to eat such good vittles.' We heard many of Sally's reminiscences at these times. One that made a mark in my mind was her story of breakfast time in her home. She was one of a large family; the mother died young and the eldest girl had to take the responsibility of the family. Bread was strictly rationed in the home: the boys had a slice and a half of bread for breakfast and the girls one slice.

I believe Mother thought it was good for us to hear Sally's reminiscences for she always listened very attentively and we were expected to do the same. Having known Sally, I can quite understand the men of her generation smashing the newly invented machines coming into agriculture. How she hated the mowing machines: from her talk it appeared that they were little better than inventions of the devil to rob poor men of their livelihood. 'They don't cut the grass,' she declared, 'they mangle it.' According to her account, 'No lattermath grew behind the mowing machines like it did the scythes, and what's more it killed the mushrooms, so they never grew where the machines had been.' When Sally made this very emphatic declaration it was more than I could stand. 'Right oh, Sally,' I said, 'I'll bring you a nice fry of mushrooms out of the lattermath this autumn.' Later in the day Mother gave me a blowing up for my impudence: it didn't matter if Sally was right or wrong, it wasn't my place to put her right, and I'd better learn to keep a still tongue in my head. Years after this episode I read Hardy's Wessex novels, where I met many folk strangely like old Sally, the same blind obstinacy, the same clinging to the old ways when the better ways had dawned. Sally was fifteen years old in 1840 and she lived through the worst years of the period we now know as the 'Hungry Forties'.

The wages of an Eydon farm labourer at the time ranged from

7s. to 9s. weekly, according to the skill of the worker. A 4 lb. loaf cost 1s., brown sugar was 6d. per lb. and tea was 4d. per oz. One can see why little children had to go into the fields winter and summer to earn a few coppers and why they were ragged, shoeless and generally hungry.

No wonder Sally hated to see a scrap of bread wasted. 'Throwing away good vittles,' she'd say if she saw a scrap thrown to the fowls.

It was a sad blow for Sally when her husband Joseph died in 1879. Their only son, Bill, was working in Birmingham at the time; he came home at once, presumably to help keep the home together. But Bill was a broken reed, and Sally would have been better off without him. He was a frail type, too fond of strong drink; most winters he was laid up for weeks with bronchitis. Sally often talked to Mother about Bill and her anxiety as to what would happen to him if she should be taken first. Sally, however, was very much alive at the time, keen, shrewd and with a sharp tongue for anyone that crossed her or tried to take advantage of her. This was well known to the village wits and wags.

One day as she was on her way up the street she met Bill Hemmings, and passed the time of day with him as they met. A minute later Bill turned round and called Sally; both retraced their steps till they met again. 'How fur should you ha' got if I 'adn't called yer back?' Bill asked. 'Twice the length of a fool and you lay down and measure it,' Sally replied short and sharp.

Mother must have got the following tale from Sally. She and another girl, both in their teens, were swede-cleaning at Trafford. It was the hunting season and the hunt came and put in the nearby wood. The girls downed tools and set off to see the hunting. Later in the day, when hounds had gone far away, they were making their way back to work when a gentleman in a red coat came up. They held a gate open for him to ride through. He looked at them and noticed Sally was wearing a new pleated smock. 'That's a nice smock you're wearing,' he remarked to Sally. 'Yes, sir, it is,' she replied. 'What will you take for it?' he asked. Sally soon told him it wasn't for sale. 'Come on, come on,' he said, 'I'll pay you a good price,' and he rattled the money in his pocket. As he persisted, refusing to take no for an answer, Sally stated her price, 'I want two fools' heads and you've only got one'; and that ended the encounter.

This is Sally's version of the cracked gravestone that stood by the wall of the north side of the churchyard, near to the graves of the Ivens family. It is a story, with minor variations, known to all the old people in the village. The stone was cracked right across but two irons stays had been inserted to hold it together. It has now fallen and is covered with debris. At the time Maude and I wrote these verses at Sally's dictation; we went to the churchyard and checked them by the stone, for the lettering was quite clear. We found the inscription and verses quite correct as told us by Sally:

> Elizabeth, daughter of James and Elizabeth Ward,
> Died September 11th 1783, aged 32 years.

> I had a husband who should have been,
> The greatest comfort unto me;
> But quite the reverse to me he proved,
> He was to me the greatest foe.

> When God saw fit to ease His child,
> And take her from this wretch so vile;
> My parents dear and friends don't mourn,
> To think how soon she's dead and gone.

> I only came just for to see,
> The world and its great vanity,
> Weep not for me, it is in vain,
> I hope to die to live again.

> I think I shall at that great day,
> Arise, and to my husband say,
> Thou vilest wretch to me on earth,
> I hope God blessed you after death,
> May Christ his mercy on you show,
> For God knows where your soul must go.

The story is that Elizabeth, a Quaker, married against her parents' wishes and the marriage turned out very unhappily. At last she left her husband and went back to her parents. During the illness that ended with her death she composed these verses and requested that they should be engraved on her tombstone. This was done and the public reproach so enraged her husband that he hired two men to go by night and smash the stone. They went and had struck the first blows when a terrific clap of thunder startled them and a flash of lightning lit up the church and churchyard with the brilliance of daylight. This was the prelude to a storm which so frightened them that they slunk away convinced that the wrath of heaven would be upon them unless they ceased their evil work.

Mrs Prestidge, John Coy's eldest daughter, remembers some of Sally's walking exploits. It seems that for some years she walked the ten miles to Banbury each week to do a day's work at The Leathern Bottle. During the winter she came home out of town with a lantern in her hand as the lamplighter was lighting the street lamps. The last part of the road home through Edgcote Park, under the great elm trees and through the fields from Trafford, was an eerie walk in the darkness. Memories of the old ghosts and bewitchings were then still strong in many people's minds and still half believed. Father used to laugh at a fright he had in the park one dark night when a donkey the other side of a hedge let out a blast—hee-haw—startling him till he realised the source of the commotion. There was no need for Sally to walk that twenty miles to earn a shilling, for she could have earned that at Eydon; we think she must have had some extras in the way of a basket of food as well as her pay.

In the early 1880s an Eydon man lay ill in Northampton Hospital. His wife, a friend of Sally's, wanted to visit him but could not afford the fare. 'I'll walk with you,' said Sally, so the two women set off. After visiting him they went into an eating house, sat down to a cup of cocoa and a penny bun, all they could afford;

then they set off on the eighteen miles home. Weary and footsore they trudged down the street as the church clock struck midnight.

v Thomas Pettifer – 'The Original Firm'

A century ago the Eydon man best known over a wide area was undoubtedly Thomas Pettifer, sheep dresser and veterinary surgeon (uncertified). The fact that it is seventy-five years since he passed on and yet he is by no means forgotten shows that he made a mark which time has only partly erased. Evidently he was well endowed with vim and vigour, loved a joke and the company to be found in public houses.

While I cannot vouch for the truth of this incident, the fact that it is remembered and linked with his name gives us an idea of the type of man he was. He is reputed to have said to some of his cronies, 'When I be gone you can put on me gravestone,

> Who lies here?
> Who do you think?
> Old Tom Pettifer,
> Give him a drink.'

Many men whose business took them from one village to another, calling on farmers, completed the call with a drink. The drink was expected by the traveller – and it was not a cup of tea. There would be occasions when the difficult calving of a cow, or attending a sick horse, would keep Thomas busy for hours at a farm. Then a meal would be laid for him on the kitchen table: a joint of meat, bread and a jug of beer was the usual fare. A drink here, and a drink there, and the result at the end of the day was that he was bubbling over with high spirits. Sometimes he got into trouble, as this report in the *Banbury Guardian* shows:

Middleton Cheney Petty Sessions June 27th 1864: Thomas Pettifer, sheep dresser of Eydon, charged with being drunk and disorderly at Farthinghoe on June 4th. Defendant said there could be no doubt that he was guilty. He had been to Bicester and had lost his mare. He had been looking for her all night, and had got so thirsty that he had been obliged to have recourse to sundry drops of brandy and water.

Thomas was fined £1 and 12s. 6d. costs. He did his rounds on horseback and it was no uncommon thing for his mare to come home without him. Sometimes he was away for two or three days, but no one at home worried; they knew he would turn up sooner or later.

By a strange coincidence, when Thomas faded out Sam Spencer, a man carrying on the same type of business, had the same failing: he often came home at the end of the day as drunk as a lord. I've often seen Sam's horse walk down the street drawing the sheep dipper, with Sam lying prone on the floor, apparently sound asleep. The horse is a very intelligent animal, and these men's horses knew the roads as well as their masters did; the most stupid of horses is sharp enough to know the way home to its own stable.

Mother used to say Thomas was often in court, charged with drunkenness; the authorities got tired of fining him, so one day at Daventry the magistrates gave him a shock. That morning when his name was called he walked into court as bold as brass, chinking the money in his pocket. Looking at the magistrates he addressed them 'Good morning, gentlemen; how much do you want this morning?' The chairman looked at him, 'Don't be in a hurry Mr Pettifer; we don't want your money; you will go to gaol for seven days.' They say Thomas was very careful afterwards; the week in Northampton Prison had a very sobering effect on him.

The *Guardian* describes him as a sheep dresser; we should have called him a sheep dipper; during the spring and summer he went from farm to farm, over a wide area, driving a horse drawing a box-like wagon lined with sheet zinc. A large bath he carried was filled with water impregnated with chemicals. The sheep were thrown into this and washed to clean the wool and check infestation by maggots during the hot weather. This side of his business worked in with his main work as a horse and cattle doctor. In his day qualified veterinary surgeons were few and far between; most of their work was done by the blacksmiths or men like Pettifer. My wife remembers her father, the Boddington blacksmith, making horse pills the size of golf balls to be taken by an ailing horse; this was in about 1900. By all accounts Thomas was a very good man at his job; probably he had a natural gift which he developed by observation and experience. He mixed his own medicines, using his own closely guarded secret recipes. He grew and used medicinal herbs and it was probably the low cost of these that led him to boast that he made 11½*d.* profit on every shilling. Someone repeated this to old Dr Page; he soon went one better: 'I make 11¾*d.* on every shilling,' he asserted.

Thomas had one daughter, Judith, and one son, Stephen. Judith and Stephen helped mix the medicines at home, and Stephen went about with his father, helping to dip sheep and doctor sick animals. One day the old man loaded a cart with his wares and started Stephen off with instructions to sell them in the Chipping Norton area. Journeying down the Cotswolds, selling on the way, Stephen kept on and on till he reached Malmesbury with an empty cart and a pocketful of money. There in the sheep country he could see good prospects, so he took a house and started in business, making the same medicines he had learned to make at home. Judith married Ernest William Stanton, a Heyford farmer, in 1875. They were bad years for farmers, so before long Ernest came to the conclusion that there was more money in his father-in-law's medicines than in farming. He was a shrewd and far-seeing man in that he had a deed of partnership executed in 1877 whereby he became a partner with Thomas in the business, trading as Thomas Pettifer and Co. Four years later he shook the Heyford dust off his feet and brought Judith and their two small daughters to Eydon. He rented Cherry House, then owned by Sir William Clerke.

Ernest left the veterinary side of the business to Thomas, and the dipping of sheep to an employee, while he concentrated on selling their wares in the local cattle markets. Soon he was a well-known figure at Banbury, Northampton and Stratford markets, with his stall of liniments, herbal mixtures and sundry pills and potions. He not only sold his wares but was ready with free advice for every potential customer on the cure of animals' ailments. Gradually he increased the area covered, from the local agricultural shows to the Smithfield Fat Stock, the Birmingham and the Royal. All were brought within his sphere of action. The promoters of these shows were left in no doubt that Thomas Pettifer and Co. had arrived and needed a space for their stall, in or very near the front row. Attending these shows (some for one day, some for several days) involved travel and nights away from home for Ernest and the two men who accompanied him. They erected the stands and hung out the large red bunting banners to let everyone know that Pettifers of Eydon had arrived. Potential customers were encouraged with a ham sandwich and a glass of beer, and sometimes mistakes were made as to the amount of an order. Often a farmer would order half a dozen bottles of 'green oils' and a dozen would be despatched. This was one way of increasing sales, and often the trick worked. Whether it paid in the long run is another matter, for often the customer would only be had once – afterwards he would keep well away from Pettifer's stall. Ernest was a very able salesman; he could tell a tale and enjoy a joke in any company for he was shrewd and knew that a laugh helps to put men at their ease, which is good for business. He also knew the value of a good appearance, for he always turned out well dressed in black morning coat, striped trousers and a squat top hat; he looked the prosperous business man he meant to be. While Ernest was here, there and everywhere his wife Judith kept a keen eye on all that went on at home. She knew far more about the medicines than he did, for she had mixed them for her father for years. So at home she supervised the mixing and packing, and saw to it that the men got on with the work while 'the Master' was away. She was a very busy woman, for soon after they came to live here she had three girls and a boy to care for.

While this expansion was taking place, Stephen Pettifer, trading as Thomas Pettifer and Son, was doing a similar trade with the farming fraternity down in Malmesbury. As both firms sold the same type of goods at the same markets and agricultural shows, customers were often puzzled and muddles occurred through letters going to the wrong Pettifer. Ernest found the situation intolerable, and he was not the man to sit down under a handicap. His solicitors at Northampton, Becke and Green, entered an action in the High Court in London to restrain Stephen from using his father's name in his business transactions. The case was heard by Mr Justice Matthews in the Queen's Bench Division of 28th and 29th June 1883. Stephen's main defence was that the deed of partnership between his father and Ernest Stanton was a forgery. He held that a witness to the document (now deceased) could not write, and so could not have signed the deed. That brought my father into the case; he was summoned to give evidence at the court. He stated that he had seen the witness write his name, and that he knew the man who had taught him to write long after the witness had reached manhood. During the hearing old Pettifer did not come out any too well, for it appeared that although he had entered into partnership with Ernest, his son-in-law, he had given more help to Stephen, his son. The Eydon branch of the family won the case, for Stephen was ordered to trade under his own name. While the case was on Father stayed with my Uncle Edward in the Burdett Road. He quite enjoyed the experience of attending the court and listening to the arguments of the learned counsel, and – very important to him at the time – all his expenses were paid by the plaintiff.

From that time on all the firm's stationery and advertisements were headed 'Thomas Pettifer & Co. – The Original Firm', and a trade mark was registered, which consisted of a bold red cross.

Stephen was not pleased with the verdict, so he retaliated by sending one of his salesmen, William Brain, to live almost on Ernest's doorstep, at the Pound Cottage, and to sell his wares in the district. A stock of his products was kept at The Leathern Bottle in Banbury. Ernest countered this move very neatly, for before long Brain left Stephen's employ to be one of Ernest's salesmen, and he served him well for the rest of his working life.

The winning of the lawsuit and Ernest's rise in the social scale through the money he made were often the subject of conversation round our table in my early years. 'Why, they were as poor as church mice and down at heel when they came to Eydon,' Mother often said. We were amused too that they paid the school pence at the farmers' rate, while we considered them tradesmen, who paid a penny a week less than the farmers. One could hardly call selling cattle medicines farming.

Soon after the lawsuit Ernest changed his surname by deed poll to Pettifer. That was easily done at the cost of a few pounds, but to get Eydon folk to address him as 'Mr Pettifer' was up another street. 'You know, he isn't really a Pettifer,' I've heard folks say many a time. Quite twenty years after his name was altered George Ward of Woodford sent his boy Tom to Eydon to pay a bill he owed. Ernest looked at the envelope Tom gave to him, and saw it was addressed to Mr Stanton. That did it; he gave it back to Tom and said, 'Take it back to your father and tell him my name is Pettifer.' Poor Tom had to walk back home to get the name on the envelope altered.

During the next twenty years the business continued to expand. Salesmen and agents were appointed, so that most of the country was being worked by one or another of his men. Here at home bay windows were put in Cherry House, and a two-storey block of offices erected to house the clerks who were kept busy booking and filing the sales. Mrs Pettifer set up a maid: a girl straight from school soon became a smart damsel arrayed in a black dress, fancy lace cap and white apron. For years ten to fifteen people, men, women and boys, were employed here at Eydon. The business was built when labour was cheap, so labour-saving ideas did not enter into the programme. Although he was a keen business man, Ernest did some things we thought anything but business-like. He rented Cherry House, improved it, built offices, and then in the 1920s had to buy it and no doubt pay for the improvements he had made. In a field named Manitoba he grew two acres of herbs on land owned by the parson. Then in 1905 he built the Spice House for the processing of herbs; half a mile from the village in another direction, he erected two buildings in another field called New Zealand, then owned by Viscount Valentia. We used to say that Pettifer's men spent half their time walking slowly from one building to another for this, that and the other; it caused endless leg-pulling and jokes galore.

Moreton Pinkney was the station Ernest used for the despatch of parcels and the receipt of such heavy goods as barrels of linseed oil, turpentine and cases of bottles. He was such a good customer of the East and West Junction Railway that he received the same preferential treatment as was meted out to Sir Henry Dryden. These two gentlemen never missed a train at Moreton, for the very good reason that the train would wait for them. The station-master's life would not have been worth living if on market days he had let the morning train to Northampton go without Ernest William. He never let the railwaymen forget what a good customer he was; it helped to keep them on their toes, for he expected to be waited on in double-quick time. This was encouraged in the lower grades on the railways by a tip from time to time; on his constant travels it helped to get him the quick service he felt his due. Six days a week he was busy here, there and everywhere from morning till night, absolutely immersed in his business, but on Sundays he and his family went to church. The business was closed down each Good Friday, so that the family could attend the morning service; the men were paid for the day if they attended the service, but absentees were not paid. We often smiled at one of his foibles: returning from church on a Sunday morning, if he met John Coy in the street, he'd stop him for a message of this sort, 'We don't want to talk business today, do we, John, but I wish you'd send a man up in the morning to put a new lock on the surgery door.' Ernest was a staunch supporter of Church and State; he often served the Church as churchwarden, and the State with an annual subscription to the Conservative Party. He was very patriotic, for whenever we had a coronation or a jubilee he always found time to come to the parish meeting and help get a programme made for the day by promising a substantial subscription.

Early in the 1900s an Act of Parliament became law by which all manufacturers of medicine were compelled to make them under the supervision of a qualified chemist. The first chemist Thomas Pettifer and Co. employed was E. D. Coleman, a married man with a family, who lived at Stoneleigh for some years. Up to this time the business had been run on cheap labour, for Ernest paid his men a little more than the agricultural rate, but not much; a man and a strong lad cost him about £1 a week up to the outbreak of the First World War.

Ernest was an old man and beginning to fail when the following incident took place. He came pottering along the street one day to the Red House, to have a few words with Father. For some time they sat in the sitting-room enjoying themselves, talking of the old days when both were young, before Ernest came to the reason for his visit: 'I've been telling my son, Mr Tyrrell, what a great help you were to us in the lawsuit, and what a good thing it was for us that we won the case. So I should like to make you a little present.' He handed father a cheque for £5 5s. and they shook hands and parted, both men pleased with the transaction.

When Ernest died in 1923 his son Tom took control, but soon it became a limited company, and the variety of goods sold increased considerably. A break with Eydon came in 1955, for that year the offices were transferred to Northampton, and the making of medicines to a London firm of manufacturing chemists who use the same prescriptions for some goods that old Tom Pettifer used a century ago. He used to set out from Eydon to sell his wares astride a horse; now his great-grandson Ronald sets out on the same errand driving a Cortina for the 'Original Firm'.

vi Edward Higham – manslaughterer

The year 1883 is memorable for a court case that made a sensation at the time and that, unlike the Pettifer lawsuit, was one our parents very seldom mentioned. In a cottage at the back of the Wesleyan chapel (long ago demolished), there lived at the time a widower named William Higham with his two younger sons. When the mother died I do not know, but I am sure that her death had a lot to do with subsequent events, for Edward was the youngest and probably the wildest of the family. I believe she died when he was an infant and that the eldest girl had to mother the younger children. One of Ted's brothers went out to India and became a warder in an Indian prison on the Andaman Islands.

This is an extract from the school log-book dated 29th June 1864: 'Admitted John and Edward Higham. Neither had been to school before; the Rector had great difficulty in persuading them to come now. They are the wild Arabs of Eydon but bribery will ensure their coming.'

The master was right in his prediction, for on 3rd October he records, 'The three Highams paid for by Mrs. Empson have earned their pinafores promised for a month's regular attendance.' Two years later he writes, 'The Higham family still as untidy but attend school regularly.'

In 1883 Ted was twenty-three years of age, a strong, hard-working, hard-drinking fellow, quarrelsome in drink and frequently embroiled in fights. After one drinking bout they told him at closing time that he had drunk twenty-two pints that day – he himself had quite lost count.

He went home after closing time at The Oak one night in May 1883 to find his brother in bed and his father sitting by the dying fire. Ted sat down by the fireside and began unlacing his boots as his father made for the stairs. 'Ain't there a bit of supper for me?' asked Ted, looking at the empty table. 'You be as well able to get it as I be,' his father answered.

According to Ted's account he threw a boot at his father, who stepped quickly back and fell, cutting his head on the door sill. The neighbours heard a row and William scream, then Ted call out, 'That's done you now, you old b——.' They were so alarmed that they knocked on the door and when Ted opened it they offered their help, but he told them to mind their own business and shut the door. The next morning William asked one of them to bind up his forehead; this she did but strongly advised calling in the doctor. 'No,' William replied, 'it 'ud only get Ted into trouble.' He kept about for a few days, then at the end of a week Dr Jacobs was called in as poor William lay dying. A post-mortem was held, and at the inquest at The Royal Oak Dr Jacobs gave evidence of the lacerated forehead and three broken ribs; these injuries had brought on pneumonia, the cause of death. Ted was arrested, taken to Brackley and charged with manslaughter. From there he was sent to Northampton Gaol to answer the charge at the assizes.

Baron Huddleston was the judge at the trial which took place on 9th July 1883. Higham's neighbours, Ann Cubbins and Sarah Blencowe, gave evidence of hearing the row and William scream and of their offer to help which Ted rebuffed. Ted's brother, who was in bed at the time, took the same line as his father and tried to shield Ted in his evidence. The police and Dr

Jacobs gave their evidence and soon the trial was over and the jury's verdict was 'manslaughter, with a recommendation to mercy'.

Ted was sentenced to twelve months' imprisonment with hard labour. This he served in the old gaol on the Mounts which stood where the fire station is now.

The women witnesses came home and said if they had told all they knew, Ted would have been hanged. They believed Ted knocked his father down and repeatedly kicked him, breaking his ribs – I've no doubt they were right – but as they could not see through stone walls or a closed door, their thoughts would not have been considered evidence.

At the end of the year Ted came home to Eydon but there was no work for him. It soon became evident that the farmers had laid their heads together to boycott him and drive him away from the village. He was a hard worker. He could cut a hedge, plough a field or build a rick in first-class style, for he was always reckoned one of the best men in the parish; no one would dispute those good qualities or that he had done a wicked action. But Father felt Ted had been punished enough and so he stood by him. He and John Tomlin gave him some casual work and encouraged him to stick it. That summer he found work in the hayfields at Byfield and Woodford and by autumn the boycott had faded, so there was work for him at home.

In the autumn of 1885 Ted had a half-day off to attend the Byfield flower show. There he met Jane Batchelor, his future wife. Jane was a Byfield girl but for some time she had been living at Bradford and working in a cloth factory; now she was on holiday.

They were married the next year and, to secure a home, Ted took a job at Chacombe with a cottage. Their home was simply furnished with the money Jane had saved during the time she worked in Yorkshire. Years after Ted told me of many incidents during the three years they lived at Chacombe but he did not tell of his furious drinking there and how he ill-treated Jane. A relative of Jane's tells me that it was a great disappointment to Ted that there was no child of the marriage and this was the reason why he would turn on his best friend when he was drinking.

After they had been at Chacombe two years, a change took place at Eydon destined to alter the pattern of their lives completely. Our neighbour, John Tomlin, had prospered in farming Goodman's land and now he needed more land for his stock. Father suggested to John that he apply for the tenancy of Lawn Hill Farm which had become vacant. It was largely his faith in John's ability which overcame his fear of the financial risk involved at a time when prices of produce were steadily going down. When John was accepted as tenant he needed help to work the larger farm. Ted Higham was glad to come back and work at Lawn Hill and to live in a cottage John had secured for him in the village.

John had been wild in his early years through drink and had been a very skilful poacher. Ted was still wild and was a very artful poacher, as everyone knew, including the local policeman. As master and man had much in common they became very friendly and John, much the wiser of the two, soon had Master Ted weighed up. One summer day they were scything a crop of clover together and, as they ate their lunch standing in the shade of a hedge, the conversation got round to money. John mocked Ted on the grounds that although he was always at work and earned good money, he was always short because too much was spent on drink. Ted said he would chuck it up, to which John replied, 'What's the use of you talking like that, Ted? You know very well you can't.' ' 'Course I can if I make up me mind,' Ted answered. 'Well, if you'll keep off the drink for twelve months, I'll give you a sovereign.' 'Right oh, master.' Ted had accepted the challenge because to tell him he couldn't do a thing was to put his back up straight away.

He came home that evening very quiet and thoughtful. Jane

said afterwards she wondered what was up. As they sat at the evening meal, Ted told her of the challenge and his determination to show John Tomlin how wrong he was in his judgement of Ted Higham. Jane fully agreed with him that John had made a mistake and so the two decided that John should pay for his error. That was how Ted became a teetotaller for a year. Everyone in the village knew it but not the reason why, for Ted and Jane were very close and Tomlin said nothing further on the matter, not even to Ted.

When the anniversary of the day came round, Ted reminded John of the challenge and at the end of the day he called at the house and John put a golden sovereign in his hand. That evening as Ted and Jane sat eating their bacon and beans, the golden sovereign lay on the table between them, a feast for their eyes. Jane told Ted how, when she was in Bradford, she had paid money into the Post Office bank and how sixpence was added to each pound yearly. Ted's schooling had been so intermittent that he could neither read nor write; this bank business was a new idea to him. They agreed on a plan: Jane paid the money into the Post Office at Byfield bringing home a new bank book. This transaction had to be kept secret from Eydon people as the folk at the Post Office here could not be trusted.

Before long Jane scraped together another sovereign to go on the book and that was how they started saving. Ted did not remain a strict teetotaller for long, just occasionally he would get drunk, but the drink had lost its lure for him and often he'd go weeks without a drink. The years he worked at Lawn Hill, from 1888 until John died in 1896, were very happy years for Ted, for the two men had so much in common.

Years after, whenever Ted spoke of John, it was always in tones of profound respect for a good man and a very good farmer. He wouldn't work for a bad farmer if he could help it. He hated to see land badly farmed and horses and cattle neglected. I believe it really hurt him.

Father was frequently at the farm with them, giving a helping hand haymaking or getting in the corn at harvest. During the winter there was nothing he liked better than a day's rabbiting with John and Ted, and when the three were there not many rabbits got away.

When John died, work on the new railway was in full swing so, when Mrs Tomlin left the farm, Ted went on the railway. His basic wage was 20s. weekly, overtime extra, and this extra money helped the bank account to grow faster so that when that railway work came to an end, Jane held a bank book with a balance of over £100.

For the next seven years Ted worked for William Wright, the Farndon miller. His job was to drive a horse and cart around the villages, delivering flour, barley meal, toppings and bran, and picking up corn to be ground. Many of the customers paid Ted, and Wright was amazed that he made no mistakes, for he had a wonderfully good memory. Jane walked by Byfield every few weeks and put a few shillings in the savings bank.

While on this job, Ted heard that a Maidford man was prepared to sell a cottage at Eydon – it is in Partridges Lane, quite close to the chapel. Ted came and consulted Father; he advised him to buy as the price was reasonable, and so in 1907 he bought a sound detached cottage and garden for £140. The tenant was Jim Dancer, a labourer of about the same age as Ted. They had been to school together and had often worked together in the fields. News of the house purchase soon went around the village and when Jim heard, he went off the deep end. If a tradesmen or farmer had bought his home, well, that would be quite in order, but for Ted Higham to buy it, a farm labourer and a middling character who could not read or write, was beyond endurance. Jim felt something must be done. He must let off steam somehow, so he went into the garden and cut down two apple trees and one plum tree, well-established trees, ten to fifteen years old. They could be seen from the road, so the news soon went around the village. We were very amused and waited for the next move now that Jim had declared war. When Ted heard, he came for Father to go with him to see Jim and to act as his friend and adviser. They went, and after the preliminaries were over Ted asked Jim, 'What did you do that for? You'll have to pay for them, Master Jim.' After a good deal of bluster, Jim intimated that he had had an accident with a saw – it was more the fault of the saw than his. The upshot was that he paid for the trees and soon vacated the cottage; Ted was not a man to be easily done.

This property deal made Father very proud of Ted. I have heard him tell lots of people that Ted Higham was the only agricultural labourer he had ever known to own his own house. He was a good gardener and very soon young fruit trees were growing, the garden was in first-rate order and there was a little pig in the sty. Ted dug the ground and planted it. Jane did the rest and also fed the pig with scrupulous care. Several times a day she would walk down the garden path, her keen eyes surveying the ground for weeds; as soon as a tiny one appeared, out it came in a hurry. The sparrows had no place in her garden for she kept vigilant watch and as soon as one settled she would rush down the path and shoo him off before any damage was done.

During the first ten years that Ted and Jane lived in their own cottage I became a frequent visitor in the winter evenings. For Ted's benefit I read aloud several books, including *Oliver Twist*, sitting close to the table to get the light from a small paraffin lamp. I'd read for about an hour, then close the book and we would talk. A bookmark was not necessary, for Ted and Jane always remembered just where we had left off the previous reading. Frequently Ted would say in devout tones, 'I wish I were as good a scholar as you be.'

He never mentioned his early life or his parents or the tragic affair which landed him in gaol. Much of the talk centred around his strength and skill; how he wheeled a barrow loaded with bricks – I am not sure if it was six or eight hundredweight, but it was far more than the other men could manage – the day they had a contest at the brickyard. Ted could cut and lay a hedge in first-class style but it seemed to me a pity he should speak slightingly of the other hedgecutters in the village. He has assured me in most impressive tones that Michael Pratt killed every hedge he cut and he was a regular hedge-cutter, whereas with Ted it was an occasional job.

I learnt a lot during those evenings but my tale would be very incomplete if I hadn't listened to Jim Treadwell talk of old Ted with a twinkle in his eye. For Ted, the senior by a few years, always treated Jim as if he were a boy; this suited Jim, as he was quite content to play second fiddle. While Ted was very proud and boastful, Jim put on a very humble demeanour, under cover of which he very cleverly led Ted into some sticky situations. I believe Jim was the only friend Ted ever made during his life, for both he and Jane were very suspicious of nearly everyone and most unsociable towards the village folk. He had respect for and some trust in Father – Master Tyrrell, he called him – but Jim was really a friend. They went poaching together on dark nights, not always very successfully. One night they fell over some wire and made such a rattle, every rabbit in the vicinity made for cover in a hurry. Jim ended up the tale with, 'Oh, how old Ted did swear.'

During the years from 1908 to 1914 both Ted and Jim worked at Crockwell for Newbury, who also had two young men living at Tile Barn working for him. All four were first-class men. No one, not even Newbury, would have liked to say which of the four was the best man. But Ted knew and he wittered and badgered Newbury, until for the sake of peace he gave Ted an extra shilling a week. He could not rest until the boss thus acknowledged his superior skill. His mates made no complaint for it was better for all concerned to have Ted contented than suffering a grievance.

Eydon, from the south with the Hall in the foreground.

1907, the Wesleyan Chapel is on the right, the bakehouse
and baker's cart opposite.

Opposite above: Grandfather Joe and Grandma Flora.

Opposite below: Silver wedding group, 1901.

The Tyrrel family hay-making, 1916.

Opposite above: Frank and Percy Tyrrel, 1917.

Opposite below: Syd at Gibraltar, 1917.

Grandma Flora and Dorothy Jean outside the
Red House, 1926.

Opposite above: Garner's Cottage, Partridge Lane.
This is now garages.

Opposite below: The stocks at Eydon. The lodge at the entrance
to the Hall is on the left.

Syd with his grandchildren, 1972.

One of Jim's tales was of how they competed in the flower show allotment competition. Both had plots in 'the Pits' and both were very good gardeners. During the month before the plots were judged both were working long hours harvesting and were unable to devote any time to their plots, for Sunday work was quite out of the question. Ted's plot was kept in apple-pie order by Jane so no weeds flourished there, but Jim's became sprinkled with tiny weeds by the time the plots were judged. In spite of this, Jim was awarded the first prize. Each morning they would walk to Crockwell together but the morning after the judging, Ted started early, before Jim made a start. When Jim got to Crockwell, he was soon told how amused they all were at his victory. 'Old Ted, he was wild Jim had beaten him. He's like a bear with a sore head.' Later in the day Ted and Jim were working together and for some time Ted preserved stony silence. After a time, he stood up very straight and looking hard at Jim, he demanded, 'What did they give you the prize for, mullock?' I remember asking Jim the reason why he came first and the answer was, 'Old Ted plants his things too close together; why his brussels grow up like spinney trees.'

Jane was a great help to Ted in his gardening operations for she would do any job to help him or please him, and this was at a time when women in general were very careful and choosy in doing what they called men's work. The women of the village were scandalised that Jane would wheel a barrow of manure up to 'the Pits' and would regularly clean out the pigsty. They said, 'She ought to have been a man.'

Another of Jim's tales was of how he and Ted cut a crop of peas in a hurry. Newbury had grown several acres and, at harvest, he asked Ted if he would hack them as piecework. Ted said he would if he could have Jim to help him, and as Jim was agreeable, this was arranged. When Ted asked Jim if he had done much pea-hacking, Jim intimated that he had had very little experience but Ted assured him that he would soon get into it.

They started the job. With a bent stick held in the left hand they lifted the peas from the ground, then cut them with a hook, a tool shaped like a sickle. Ted started first, cutting a wide swarth, and when he had done a few yards Jim started. He said, 'I was very careful to take as wide a swarth as old Ted, so he couldn't say mine were narrower.' In a few minutes Ted looked back and Jim was just behind him, so he got down to it and worked just a bit harder to leave Jim behind. Jim said, 'I kept just arter him.' And the next time Ted straightened his back, he took out a handkerchief and wiped his brow, then set to furiously to get away from Jim. But Jim wasn't going to be left behind; he was enjoying the situation. He had got Ted where he wanted him so he kept just behind his victim. Both worked furiously for two hours, Jim keeping close behind Ted, who worked like a madman. At last he straightened his back, wiped his brow and, looking wildly at Jim, said, 'I don't know what you think, but I think us be going on the way to knock ourselves up.' And so a truce was called.

Jim's stories were always matter of fact, strongly spiced with humour. Ted had little humour and his tales were coloured by superstition. He was the only person I have known who believed in ghosts and witchcraft. Many folk talked of the occult with tongue in cheek and some old people I have asked for information have alluded to it as 'Tommy rot'. Ted was always careful each spring to plant his seeds the right time to suit the moon. He felt that was the reason why his vegetables thrived so much better than his neighbours'. Many of his tales were of churchyard incidents and ringing the bells at midnight with strange noises and shadowy figures hovering in the background, of how the other bellringers were scared to death, all except Ted.

I learnt from him that there used to be a witch at Woodford, a widow named Harris, and how she put a spell on a farmer living near her cottage so that he never did any good afterwards. All because some of the branches of her apple tree hung over his garden and his children pinched some of the apples. The yarns always seemed to me to be very vague and indefinite; this, Ted implied, was because the spirits and their world were so different from ours.

He told me of the Warden Hill ghost that caused so much trouble there about 1870. The farmer there was a harsh, over-bearing man, disliked by his employees for his unjust and spiteful ways. One evening at harvest time the farmer and a man were loading sheaves of corn on a wagon – he was on the load. He fell to the ground and broke his back. They reckoned the accident occurred through the carelessness of the man on the ground. The farmer died that night in great agony. They said he came back; at any rate, there were such goings-on, no girl or man would stay in the house more than a few days and they left scared to death. The cows would be tied up ready for milking, contentedly munching hay, when all of a sudden a draught of wind would blow all the doors open, the ties would drop off the cows' necks and they would tear off back to the field with their tails in the air as if the old man himself was after them.

Ted said things got so bad that they got Parson Empson and some of the old men to go and lay the ghost. They said they laid him in a whisky bottle in the pool in Blankey Piece; at any rate that pool hasn't been cleaned out from that day to this, for they reckon if the bottle got broken, he would come back. I managed to keep a straight face, for that was essential, and to ask very simply, 'How did they do that, Ted?' The answer was, 'Ha, you know, Syd, they wouldn't let us young 'uns know that.'

One evening we were talking of an accident which had occurred in a spinney at Chipping Warden, where a man using an axe had slipped and badly gashed his foot. He lost so much blood before he was found that it nearly proved fatal. 'But you know, Syd,' Ted asserted, 'he needn't have bled like that if he'd said the right text.' 'What do you mean Ted? What text is it?' I asked. 'I can only tell you part,' he replied, 'you must find it in

the Bible for yourself. It's "Passed by and saw thee polluted".'
At home that night, with the help of a concordance, I soon
found the passage in Ezekiel 16:6.

I believe that years ago religious belief was very widespread
in the countryside. Ted, at any rate, implicitly believed that
repeating that passage of scripture would staunch the flow of
blood from a wound.

According to his account, there used to be very strange
happenings when he lived with his father and brother. He would
go home late at night and, sitting at the table having a bit of
supper, the table would move across the room to the fireplace,
then go back to its normal position. Doors would suddenly
become unfastened and slam of their own accord. No one took
much notice or became unduly alarmed. Ted held that the spirit
was mischievous rather than angry.

One of his tales I found highly amusing, for it showed how
Ted, at a time when he appeared to have no religious scruples
whatever, knew where to draw the line. It was as if in the background of his mind there was a fragment of Christian ethics, so
that his conscience warned him, 'So far and no farther.' Soon
after he went to Chacombe there was a very showery spell during
the corn harvest. Corn was cut and stood stooked in the fields for
weeks, too wet to put into ricks. Farmers were in despair; it
looked as if the corn would be a total loss. Then for a few days,
the latter end of a week, the rain ceased and the corn dried. A
neighbouring farmer decided to start carrying on the Sunday
and, knowing Ted was free, asked him to lend a hand. 'No, I'll
be damned if I will,' Ted replied. 'Not if it's never got in, will I
work of a Sunday.' Well, the farmer carried his corn and 'ours
was out in the field another three weeks afore us got it in'. 'But
you know, Syd,' he went on, 'when that corn was thrashed it
came out fusty, but when my boss's was thrashed out it was first
rate. It were so good, he sold it at Banbury for Yeoman wheat
and it weren't Yeoman arter all.' Ted's condemnation of Sunday

work together with his apparent approval of selling wheat under a fake label I thought took the biscuit.

Ted and Jane spent eleven very happy years in their own cottage, years that compensated Jane for the unhappy years of their early life when she suffered through his drinking and brutality. She was never known to utter one word of complaint; her devotion to Ted was beyond praise, for she waited on him hand and foot. Nothing was too much trouble if it pleased Ted.

I think at some time in his life he must have joined the Salvation Army at Byfield. For he told me one night that when he was gone, he wanted the brass letters 'SA' in the drawer upstairs buried with him. In latter years he came to the chapel services. When we stood up to sing a hymn Ted stood up but held no hymn-book in his hand. Often a preacher noticed this and took Ted a book but Ted shook his head. Books were no good to him as he could not read.

Jane faded away and died in the autumn of 1918. Ted never slept in his cottage again; very soon he sold it and rented one on the estate. I've a notion that he was afraid to sleep there alone. It was very near the cottage in which his father had died through his brutality, and he really and truly believed in ghosts and evil spirits. Maybe he was afraid his father might do as the Warden Hill farmer did, come back and cause trouble. He joined Jane in 1929; they lie side by side in the old churchyard. Occasionally I've tidied up the graves for old times' sake.

vii Henry Peck – coachman

Now I must tell you about Henry Peck, a personal friend of my father. Even now it seems strange to me, for in religion, politics, disposition and outlook they were exact opposites. For years Mrs Peck used to come to our house about eight o'clock on a Saturday night to talk with Mother. She had been a domestic servant in mansions of the aristocracy. About nine o'clock Henry **would** come straight from The Royal Oak, puffing a cigar, to **escort her** home after he'd had a chat. I am glad now I sat and listened, for in my life I've met a few snobs, but never two such horrible snobs as Henry and Mrs Peck.

Colonel Cartwright, a member of one of our old county families and an old soldier, was as autocratic as Mrs Cartwright and Eydon folk would allow him to be. Henry Peck, his coachman, reigned over the stables, the eight to ten horses housed therein, the groom and the stable boy with an iron hand, for Henry was far more autocratic than his master. He loved to tell the tale of how he bested the Colonel over his old horse, Crockwell. This is how it was done.

Another carriage horse was needed in the stables and Peck was told to be on the lookout for a suitable horse. He soon found a horse on John Ivens's farm, Crockwell, a strong five-year-old bay of about seventeen hands. He had the horse on trial and put him in the stables but said nothing in the house. That evening, as luck would have it, the Colonel decided to have a walk round the stables after dinner. When he got to the box and saw this horse, rough and unkempt, straight off the farm, he was aghast.

'What's this?' he cried, and the groom tried to explain he was on trial for carriage work. 'Send him back, I won't have him on the premises,' he cried, and went back to the house in high dudgeon.

The next morning this was reported to Peck but, instead of carrying out the order, he rolled up his sleeves and set to work on the horse. He was curry-combed and groomed, his hair was trimmed and his hooves polished so that his appearance was entirely altered. A day or two later Mrs Cartwright ordered the carriage to take her to Edgcote. Peck drove her there and back in the carriage, drawn by the new horse. He took the carriage at a spanking pace along the level, and up the hills quite easily in his stride.

On the way home Peck asked Mrs Cartwright what she thought of the new horse. She knew nothing of the Colonel's order and, of course, Peck said nothing of the incident. So the good lady replied that she thought he was quite a good horse and would suit them admirably.

The result was that the Colonel paid Ivens for the horse and Peck called him Crockwell. He served the family well for ten years and when the Colonel died Crockwell was given to Peck. It was a comedown for him, from the spit and polish of the Hall stables to drawing a muck-cart on the farm which Peck eventually rented. On market days Peck harnessed him in the spring cart and drove to market, usually with a litter of small pigs, kept aboard by a strong rope net. I knew Crockwell well the latter part of his life. One of my early jobs was to lead him as he drew the cart being loaded in the hayfield. He lived to be twenty-eight and when he was so infirm that he could hardly walk they led him down to the old gravel pit and there he was shot and buried. Peck was not a sentimental man by any means but he grieved when he lost his old horse, a link with the happy years he spent in the Colonel's service.

Henry Peck cannot justly be counted a leading light in the

village, for they would not have made him a churchwarden at any price in Chapman's day. Still, he shone in the village with some of the reflected glory of Colonel Cartwright – a true bulwark of Church and State.

When I read of the men on horseback who escorted the Colonel the last mile the day after the election he'd won in 1865, I at once ascribed it to Henry Peck, for he loved mounted processions. As long as he could possibly get together ten or twelve men on horses it would be a feature of gala occasions here. Needless to say, Henry would lead the procession and, come to think of it, he was remarkably like the Duke of Wellington. But I find that the election procession happened before he came on the scene, for he could not have been the Colonel's coachman in 1865. He came in about 1880 from London. There he had been Lord Grenville's coachman, which explains his terrific swank. He was a Lincoln-shire man and I believe his father had some land, but mainly depended on dealing. There he learnt one thing about Quakers, the one and only thing he ever did learn about them.

When he was a boy he went with his father to have a deal with a Quaker farmer. When they had done the farmer turned to Henry and said, 'Would you like a bit of pie, me buoy?' Henry said, 'No thanks.' The farmer then asked his father and he said, 'Yes please.' They went into the kitchen and a nice pork pie was placed on the table, which Henry senior was soon enjoying. Henry stood by his side and very soon altered his mind; he wanted some too. But the Quaker said, 'You said Nay, and Nay it must be,' so poor Henry had no pie and learnt very early in life that Quakers are different from most people.

He was a tall, well-set-up man, with a face of the Roman type, tanned and weather-beaten, adorned with side-whiskers. There is no doubt he was a smart man at his job; when he drove the carriage and pair to the Hall door to take the Colonel for a drive there were no flies on the outfit. The nickel plating on the horses' harness glittered, their coats shone, their feet would be black and the carriage spotlessly clean, inside and out. Henry and the footman, both in livery and top hats, sat bolt upright on the driving-seat as proud as Lucifer.

When the butler opened the front door and the Colonel descended the steps this was the precise moment for the footman to alight and open the carriage door for the Colonel to take his seat. The door closed, the footman climbed into his seat, Peck made a clicking noise – a signal to the horses – and away they went. Those horses were trained to start like soldiers on the right foot when the signal was given, all as smart and efficient as a parade of the Royal Horse Guards. It was not Henry who cleaned the harness and made the nickel shine like silver, for he had a groom and stable boy under him and they did most of the routine work of the stables. Henry's job was to see they did their work properly and he was very efficient indeed. 'You sweep the corners out well,' he'd tell the stable boy who was sweeping up the yard. 'The middle is sure to be all right.'

He expected a high standard of work and cleanliness from his helpers and if they did not reach his requirements they would have to go. Two lads he trained from the village became in later life a feather in his cap of which he was very proud. Two of Bill Hemmings's boys, Charles and Peter, started in the stables with Henry, then went away for promotion. Later Charles became coachman to the Duke of Devonshire at Chatsworth and Peter served the Duke of Portland in a similar capacity at Welbeck Abbey. As they came to Eydon each year for a holiday, Henry kept in touch with them and when Charles drove King Edward VII on his visits to Chatsworth and the King presented Charles with a gold tiepin Henry Peck was a very proud man indeed.

When the King or Queen wants a tip-top royal procession and a lot of carriages and horses, he or she borrows trustworthy coachmen of the nobility to help the staff at Buckingham Palace; and so the two dukes lent Charles and Peter to drive coaches at the 1897 Jubilee and at the Coronation of Edward VII. How Henry used to blow out his chest on those occasions – it showed how clever he had been when he taught those boys how to be first-class coachmen.

For several years Edward VII visited Chatsworth in January for a week's shooting with the Duke. To cope with the extra work this visit involved, Charles Hemmings had to employ more hands in the stables. For several years Henry went to assist his old pupil. It was a nice change for him and he came in for a share of the £20 the King gave Charles to be divided among his staff. I ought to be able to tell you how many folks accompanied the King and what their baggage weighed, but I'm sorry, I have forgotten.

Returning from one of these visits, Henry brought home a couple of pheasants and gave my father one. We had it for dinner on a cold day when Father and I were at the muck cart, an annual job getting away the pig manure. The fresh air and exercise gave me a rare appetite, and it was a treat, I can tell you, to eat a pheasant that had perhaps been shot by the King at Chatsworth.

There is no doubt that Henry served the Colonel well and they got on well together, but occasionally a clash came. When the Rev. W. H. Chapman started his 'workingmen's club' at the old Black Moor's Head, he appealed to Henry to join and help make it a success, but was given an emphatic refusal. The Colonel was chairman of the club committee; Chapman was artful and had a strong influence over the Colonel, so he told him that his coachman, of all people, would not support the club they had started for the benefit of the Eydon men. That warmed the Colonel up; he was very indignant, sent for Henry and let out at him hot and strong that it was his bounden duty to join the club and help make it a good thing in the village. Henry listened very respectfully to all the Colonel had to say and replied that he wasn't going to 'sit there at night with a lot of unshaven clodhoppers for anybody'. Now Colonel Cartwright knew as much about social distinctions in the village as anyone and he soon began to realise that it was asking a lot of Henry – his head coachman – to expect him to consort with farm labourers; the matter dropped and Henry did not become a member of the 'workingmen's club' after all.

There was plenty of grass land between the park and the brook, but as there was no arable land, the clover, straw and oats used in the stables were bought off the local farmers. Woe betide the farmer selling these to Colonel Cartwright if he omitted to get on the right side of Henry. Sure enought the clover would be musty or the oats light and the Colonel would very soon hear of the poor quality of the said goods and that farmer would sell no more to Eydon Hall.

These were perquisites pertaining to his office on which Henry looked as his lawful gain; but he was never very comfortable, always feeling that the butler, cook and gardener fared better in these extras than he did and they were all very jealous of one another. The cook sold the dripping to the village folk at 4*d*. per lb., and Henry said she'd put two or three pounds of butter costing 1*s*. per lb. in with the very substantial joints of meat to make more dripping to sell. We used to smile at some of his tales and remember that it was the pot calling the kettle black.

One yarn I remember was of his London days when he was coachman to Lord Grenville.

His Lordship was visiting a country house in Sussex and Henry was with him and the carriage and pair. When the visit was over, Lord Grenville returned to London by train, after instructing Henry to drive to Grinstead and put the horses and carriage on rail for London. 'When I got to Grinstead station,' Henry said, 'I found I should have to wait nearly three hours for a train that would take the horses and carriage. I enquired of the booking clerk just what it would cost and then drove out of the station yard on to the London road. I let the horses take it very gently and when we got to Dorking I made for a hotel yard which I knew. Here I had the horses out, stabled them, rubbed them down and made them comfortable. While they ate their food and had a rest, I got some dinner. I gave them a couple of hours' rest, then we got on the road again and reached the West End of London about five o'clock; the horses were tired but were none the worse the next day for the forty-five mile journey.'

When Henry sent in his next account to His Lordship it contained the item 'Railway charge for carriage, two horses and self, Grinstead to Waterloo, £3 14s. 10d.'. This was duly paid to Henry!

With a regular wage and some very useful extras Henry was getting money together, so he began looking for paying investments. He took the keep of some grass fields, and bought a bunch of store cattle to graze them. A regular daily job at the stables was the exercising of the horses, so he would exercise a horse by riding to his fields to have a look at his cattle – 'shepherding' he called it.

About the time that Colonel Cartwright died George Whitton left Eydon and so a house and small grass farm became vacant. Henry became the tenant and started farming. The house was next door to ours so he was our neighbour for about thirty years. Not that he settled down to six days a week regular work – that would have been going backward for Henry, as he was now a farmer and dealer. He attended all the local markets on the lookout for profitable deals. Riding high in a spring cart with Crockwell in the shafts, he became well known for miles around.

Henry would buy anything if he thought it would make a profit, and dealing in pigs became his speciality – 'higgling' he called it. A litter could be comfortably carried in the spring cart, kept in by means of a net.

He prospered, bought a few fields at Moreton Pinkney and a

plot at Eydon, on which he had built the Jubilee Cottages in 1897. His initials can be seen on the south end, cut in Eydon stone.

For many years he was an active member of the 'Ancient Order of Foresters', holding various offices, and as a trustee he rendered valuable service in the investment of the court funds. He kept a keen eye on the finances of the court, saw that all members paid their dues, and was specially vigilant when a member drew sick pay. If, in the winter, a farm labourer fell sick, he would be suspected by Henry of malingering. 'He's getting as much from the club as he'd get at work,' he'd say; that he was not popular in all quarters will be readily understood.

Yet Henry was a wonderful man. Six days a week he was busy, here, there and everywhere, and on Sunday he went to church. He played a good game of cricket and kept on playing until well past middle age, when his 'gammy leg let him down'. This was his excuse when he had to drop out of the team. He loved to dance and was in his element at the flower show dances on the Hall lawn. Dancing there certainly went with a swing when the Blakesley Silver Prize Band made the music. It was a lovely setting for a dance on a summer evening – a good lawn among the high trees with the Hall in the background.

Henry loved a joke, he'd an apt word for anyone, rich or poor, and to the ladies he could be very gallant indeed. In politics he was a staunch Conservative; not that he gave the political divisions any serious thought, but he never pretended to. To him it was a matter of common sense and expediency to be on the side of those with position and money.

Now let us leave Henry for a moment and consider the graceful art of riding a horse successfully. By that I mean retaining one's position in the saddle and looking quite comfortable in that elevated position. I can say from experience that it is not as easy as it looks and to fall off is to find the ground a very hard landing-place. Now a well-set-up man, dressed in a smart riding outfit and mounted on a good horse, makes a good picture any day and I've a notion that people who ride horses know it. We that walk have to look up to them and they look down on us.

Henry Peck did a lot of riding in his life and I'm afraid he got into the habit of looking down from his elevated position on us of the common herd.

They say, 'He got too big for his boots.' He enjoyed a good dinner followed by a cigar. He liked a glass of whisky and, above all, company, and these he found each Thursday at Banbury Market. I've recorded some of his tales but this incident did not come from Henry. After dinner at the Red Lion one market day he and a farmer friend were talking billiards. Henry said he could do 'so-and-so' with the balls, which his friend doubted. Henry offered to bet £5 that he could, and the bet was accepted. They went to the billiard table, he tried the shots, failed, and was £5 the poorer all in two or three minutes. Once we were talking of someone that had done a very foolish action and Henry remarked, 'We are all a bit loony at times.' Maybe this incident was at the back of his mind when he spoke.

Of course he knew a lot about horses, even those he had never seen, for he always knew which horse would win the St Leger and the Derby. Occasionally it came off and we would hear how right he had been when he said so-and-so would win, but there were long periods when he said nothing.

Then we heard that he had sold the fields at Moreton Pinkney, and later Charles Hemmings, who by this time had left Chatsworth and was living at Northampton, bought the Jubilee Cottages from him.

His decline took place very quietly and over a period of time. The years took their toll. He was growing older and losing much of his vim and vigour. The upward trend in land values after the First World War presented Captain Cartwright with a good opportunity to sell his Eydon property, and as a result Henry's house and land were put up for sale. He gave up, bought the corner cottage in School Lane for £50 and began drawing the old-age pension.

In his old age he became a churchwarden at a time when we had no rector here. He kept the church accounts in a far more healthy state than he had nursed his own finances. Strange to relate, he served on the last committee of the workingmen's club, a committee formed to wind up the club affairs and dispose of its property. Years before he had refused to help the squire and parson make the club a boon in the village, but he came into the club funeral willingly. All Henry had when he died was the £50 cottage and an extensive wardrobe of old clothes of which he had been very proud; but to his credit, it must be said, he built two cottages that remain to remind us of Henry Peck, and that is a good way to be remembered in any village.

viii John Henry Ivens

Sixty years ago the school was surrounded by farm buildings, the centre of John Henry Ivens's farming operations. The house he lived in and the adjoining buildings constitute one side of School Lane and on the north side of the playground was the farmyard and rickyard known as 'Mokel', a corruption, I believe, of Malt Kiln.

John Henry's orchard at the lower corner of Bufton was a temptation to boys each autumn when the apple season came round, and each autumn some were pinched. Each autumn he came to school to complain to the master, a short stocky man with a red face and side-whiskers, very much like the cartoonists' 'John Bull'. We were duly warned of the consequences likely to ensue, but the culprits were seldom caught, for there were so many gaps in the hedges that escape was easy in any direction. Once I remember him waylaying some boys in the orchard; he threw his walking-stick at them and hit a tree. Looking back to those days, I find John Henry and the school so linked together in my memory that this section is a blend of the man and the institution. For we worked at school (when we did work) with the sounds and smells of his farming operations coming from all directions, so that we knew just what was going on on his premises. In the winter three or four horses and carts would be busy for days carting vast quantities of manure from Mokel yard. The moving of the manure and the throwing of it into carts liberated the rich old fruity smell that permeated into every room in the school and hung in the air for days. 'It's a healthy smell,' they used to assure us.

Another winter task was threshing; that brought a pall of dust and we worked at school for days with the steady drone of the threshing-machine in the background. Some of the boys were sure to know when this exciting job would be done; it was exciting because John Henry's ricks always contained more rats and mice than the other farmers' ricks; they said he always kept his corn until it was half eaten by the vermin. On those days, as soon as we were let out of school his rickyard was invaded by a noisy mob of ten to twenty boys, armed with sticks and out for blood. When the men threw the thatch off a rick and began to throw the sheaves on the threshing box a mouse would jump off the rick now and again. But as the rick was lowered, the game became fast and furious; rats and mice dashed out in a frantic endeavour to escape; men's hobnailed boots, terrier dogs and boys' sticks took heavy toll of the little animals; but these were so many and there were so many holes and corners to give them refuge that many escaped the slaughter.

During the scripture period in the spring the bleating of sheep and lambs would be explained by a whisper going round the class – 'They be cutting the lambs' tails'; or it might be, 'John Henry's shearing.' In either case, as soon as school was over half of the boys would be there to watch the men at work. I used to like to watch the shearing, but the operation on the lambs held no attraction for me; I felt it was cruel and that a lamb ought to have a tail to wag the same as a dog. As the severed tails were thrown on the heap, there was much laughing and joking about the 'lambs'-tail pies' so-and-so would have for dinner. I have been assured that they are extra good to eat, but I am inclined to put them in the same category as the 'sparrow pies' which were a figment of the imagination in 1900.

The rats and mice in John Henry's corn were only a section of his enemies; they were joined by moths, worms and weevils of all descriptions in ceaselessly eating away his produce. Mother remembered him keeping a barn half full of wool because the price offered was so low and it remained there for years until it was worthless. That would have been in the 1870s. He farmed in hard years for farmers, for the market prices of their produce was declining year by year while wages, tools and implements were on the upgrade. In his early years it may have paid sometimes to hold produce back, but not in the 1870s. No doubt he was a very stupid man, or maybe he felt he was fighting a losing battle and whatever he did the final result would be failure. He had no one dependent on him and no near relatives in the district; I think he was a very lonely man, farming because he'd always been a farmer, but with very little heart in the business.

John Henry never married. He had a housekeeper, a grim old lady named Adkins; she was almost a recluse – never went any-where. Whenever I had to go to the house I'd knock on the door and she would open it about three inches and peek through the opening. Her face always reminded me of a witch: it was just what I expect to see if ever I should see a real witch; for as Mrs Treadwell used to say – 'You never know.'

The Ivenses were, for over a century and a half, a well-to-do and influential family in the village. There is no reference to them in the Enclosure Act, but the name appears in the registers from 1763, the year after the Act became law. The name Thomas Ivens, churchwarden, appears on the No. 1 bell, the only one cast by our local bell-founder, Bagley of Chacombe, in 1790.

M. Bryden gives a glimpse of the household when John Henry was a boy:

> At Christmas time we children sometimes journeyed in a tilted cart to Eydon to see Grandfather Stockley. It was quite an adventure to us children, crossing the Grange ford and over Warden Hill. We enjoyed and were made much of at old Ivens', such mince pies and good fare in those days. An old servant Bet was so good to us and told us ballads and yarns over her lace making. Her mother and sisters were such nice people and all made lace.

Of John's family, four died in infancy; William entered the Church, became a canon and spent most of his life in Birmingham; Arthur became a doctor and all I know of Fletcher is that he died at sea in 1877. John Henry was the youngest of the family. He was so called to distinguish him from his father and another John Ivens at Crockwell. Mother described them as big strong fellows who could pick up a sack of corn and throw it over the side of a wagon. A sack weighed about two and a half hundredweight and the wagon would be about five feet from the ground. She never forgot how cruel some of the men of the family were to John when he was an old man; it was said he often turned aside into the farm buildings and shed a few tears in private after they had had words. When he was old and becoming infirm they expected him to do his share of the work just as he had done in his prime. They showed no mercy on him whatever.

Now I am not sure whether Mother's description applied to John's four sons or to John and his brother, Martin, when they were young men. I do not doubt its accuracy, but I hope it was not the doctor and clergyman who were so hard on an aged father.

Although John Henry never recovered from the slump in agricultural prices of the nineties he remained by far the biggest farmer here in terms of acreage. He owned Welshman's Farm and rented the glebe land, and Ashby's Farm from Sir William Clerke. All the fields were his from the Moreton Road, across the Preston Road to the Woodford Road and the Windmill Ground; and from the village to the railway with the exception of Farmer Lines's fields.

He employed six or seven men regularly. Jesse Avery, the wagoner, was a skilled and trustworthy man. Sometimes he had a good shepherd but the majority of his men were what Father used to call 'poor tools'. They did not reach to Henry Peck's saying, 'strong of the arm, weak of the head', for they were anything but strong. Sally Dancer's son, Bill, was a fair specimen; nearly every winter he was on the sick list for weeks, with bronchitis. Being a 'Forester' kept the wolf from the door during those times and when we met him out wearing a heavy overcoat we knew Bill was on the Club. On the farm they could not be trusted to do work which needed skill and judgement but did heavy manual work under supervision.

Fortunately for old England, they, like their master, never married; so we have no group of that type in the village now, and the machines do the work they did so laboriously. John Henry was a benefactor here in one respect, for he would always find a job for the duffers, at a low rate of wage, of course. His shaky financial position forced him in 1910 to leave the Rectory Farm and the house which had been his home since he was seven years old. He went to live at 'The Elms', which, if you remember, had been the Rev. Francis Clerke's old rectory.

That house had been vacant for years, and in fact up to 1940 it was looked on as a white elephant, for as I have already mentioned during the ninety years since Empson enlarged it no one had lived there for long and it had been empty for years between tenancies. A few days before the move took place, John Henry met Harriet Wills in the street; she was the charwoman at his house. This is her account of the conversation: 'John Henry says to me,

Harriet, he says, we be going to move next Friday, he says, so
get repaired.'

There was a sale at his house of farming stock, implements and
junk of all descriptions from the house and barns; much of it
belonged to his father's and grandfather's days. I well remember
seeing in the back kitchen a high wooden box with a lid, half full
of a brown substance like meal with a pungent smell; they said it
was malt dust. Half buried in it was a ham, very dark brown and
almost mummified. Henry Peck said it was cured the year John
Henry was born, 1846, and that in the house was a bottle of beer
brewed the same year.

Recently I have been told that in many of the old farming
families it was customary to keep a ham and a bottle of beer of
the year a boy was born, to be consumed at his twenty-first
birthday celebrations. It is said that a well-cured ham will keep
for twenty-one years in malt dust and be quite edible; but I am
sure that ham was dried to a cinder; it sounded like wood if
tapped with one's knuckles. Bearing in mind Mother's account
of strife in the family, I think it very likely that when John
Henry's twenty-first birthday arrived, no one in the house felt in
the mood for a celebration, so the ham was never eaten nor the
beer drunk; and what was done with them after the sale I do not
know. I am sure the box and the ham went for a song, and I wish
now that I'd bought them.

John Henry spent much time pottering about in the garden; it
had become a wilderness but with Raymond Needle's help they
soon had it spick and span. Henry Peck helped him with the buying and selling and, after his death in 1917, settled up the estate.
The rise in prices caused by the war, combined with Henry's
vigilance, so turned the scales that when all his debts were paid
he left £500 to his brother's children.

His housekeeper, Miss Adkins, first came to Eydon as house-
maid to his mother, and when his mother died in 1889 stayed
with him as housekeeper. Although I remember her as a very

formidable sort of person, she was very kind to many folk and she nursed John Henry with wonderful devotion, some folk said for his mother's sake.

He died on a sofa in the sitting-room and when John Coy and Jesse Avery carried the coffin into the room and John saw the corpulent body on the sofa, he exclaimed, 'Oh dear, Jesse, this is very awkward, I don't know how we shall get him in.' The ever resourceful Jesse replied, 'Put the coffin on the floor and roll him in.'

That was the end of a proud old family of yeomen farmers and the end of a hundred and fifty years which the Ivens family had spent cultivating the good brown soil on Eydon Hill.

Part Three

The Tyrrells

Chapter 7

My family

The village had seven shops in the 1840s: two butchers, two combined baker and grocers, one baker only, a draper's and a general shop. There were also many craftsmen, a shoemaker, harnessmaker, clockmaker, stone-mason, woodworker and Thomas Kench who did plumbing and decorating. John Addison was tailor here until 1841 when my great-grandfather Edward Smith took over the business. Edward and Patience Smith had three sons, Lorenza, John and Edward, and three daughters, Ellen, Bessie and Mary Ann, who was my grandmother. There were two other girls but they died early on in life.

Lorenza, the eldest son, learned the trade and settled at Priors Marston, where he worked up a good tailoring business and was one of the stalwarts of the Wesleyan Chapel for a long lifetime.

John also learned the trade, but he soon forsook the tailor's bench. He had many jobs, but probably the one he did best was as manager of the Temperance Hotel at Banbury. Then, as a part-time occupation, he became a Registrar of Births and Deaths in the Banbury district. He was a local preacher, one of the long-winded sort, and thought nothing of preaching for an hour, so that his services were never less than an hour and a half long. He had houses built and speculated in property. According to his account he lost a lot of money during his lifetime, but Flora always explained to us that it was money he never had, but should have had if his deals had worked out as he anticipated and other people had done what they should have done.

Edward became a customs officer at the London docks, a local preacher and active worker in the East End Mission. He served for years on the local borough council and it was said he was asked to stand for Parliament by the Poplar Liberals. He worked wholeheartedly with the Rev. Peter Thompson, the founder of the Wesleyan East End Mission. Edward's home was in Burdett Road, and Mother and the elder members of our family occasionally visited there. The story is told that soon after Thompson started work he arrived at the chapel in tears. The drunkenness and fighting in the streets, the ragged women and children had so shocked him that he cried. A steward trying to comfort him said, 'Never mind, Mr Thompson, you will get used to it.' Thank God Peter did not get used to it, for by his work and that of his helpers he helped clean up that part of the city.

Three of Edward's daughters had settled at Northampton. Ellen became Mrs John Margetts; she and her husband lived over their grocery shop in Gold Street and were very prosperous for years, till the multiple firms invaded the town with cut prices and John's business faded away.

Bessie married Harry Adams, manager of a clothing shop in Bridge Street. Their home above and below the shop was a most alluring and romantic dwelling to us youngsters. It was a house of four storeys, a dark old kitchen and cellars under the ground and above the bedrooms a large attic with a window in the roof. On our visits there with Flora we'd wait patiently till the adults were busy talking in the sitting-room, then quietly slip off upstairs to the attic where a handy set of steps enabled us to climb through the window on to the roof. It was thrilling to peer over the parapet to the street below, and watch the traffic from the dizzy height of a four-storey building rooftop.

Mary Ann became the wife of William Carey, believed to be a relative of Carey, one of the pioneer missionaries to India; if so, in later life he bore remarkably little resemblance to his famous relative in life and character. The Careys had a family of four, Flora Lizzie Ellen Jane, Sidney, Louie and Edward. I give Flora's name in full for she was my mother and now takes a prominent place in this record. She was never allowed to forget her formidable name; 'twas the subject of many a jest. Flora was the eldest grandchild and a frequent visitor to Eydon; at one time she attended school here. It's quite likely she was a favourite with the old folks, for they were very proud of their family, and their children's children.

When Flora was about eleven she would have sat down at table in her grandfather's house with their apprentice, young Joseph Tyrrell. He would have been about fourteen then. Just when they fell in love we do not know, but by the time Joe was in the final year of his apprenticeship they had decided to make a match.

I used to think my grandmother Tyrrell (Joe's mother) was very queer, for if I'd asked her, 'Do you know where Sally East is?' she'd reply, 'Her be gone up the street, her wunt be long.' We did not talk like that round here; that's the Warwickshire dialect. She came only from Tysoe, fourteen miles away as the crow flies; and I'm pretty sure it was the longest journey she ever made in her life. She never rode in a railway train; carriers' carts took her to and from Tysoe and Sulgrave. Although she lived at Sulgrave for about sixty years she never became reconciled to the fact, for it was in her estimation a poor sort of village compared to Yysoe. Everything at Tysoe was grand, everything at Sulgrave poor and mean. This intense loyalty to her birthplace seemed very strange to me, for her people were poor people there in the 'hungry forties'. Hers was a hard life, for her husband died in his forties; still, she was spared the cruel poverty many endured, for she and her family never went hungry and were always decently clad. She came to Sulgrave in about 1840, as maid in a farmer's household. In a little trunk containing her clothes she brought a New Testament, inscribed on the flyleaf 'Hannah Raisin, Tysoe Wesleyan Sunday School 1833'. As there was no Wesleyan chapel at Sulgrave, Hannah went to the Baptist chapel, the next best thing on a Sunday. She went under protest, as she never approved of the Baptists or their ways; still it was a shade better than going to church. There she met and later married James Turrell, a young farm labourer. They set up housekeeping at Plympton, but a year or two later returned to live in a two-room cottage near the now famous Washington Manor House. Later Hannah brought Wesleyan preachers to Sulgrave, so instead of Hannah becoming a Baptist, James became a Wesleyan. There's no doubt about it, she was a strong-minded woman and James wanted a bit of peace and quiet in life. I knew very little about him; the following shows he had some initiative for I've never heard of anyone else doing the same thing round here. Father said in the winter when work on the land was short he'd get permission from farmers, and go round the hedgerows digging out briars. He tied them in bundles of a hundred, and sent them to nurserymen for rose budding.

James and Hannah Turrell had only two children, Joseph and William. This helped them financially, for boys soon brought money into the house, whereas girls going out into service were a dead loss as far as the family budget was concerned.

Joseph, my father, went to school and learnt to read and write, and when he was nine started work on a farm as wagoner's boy. These little lads were put in charge of the big shire horses and heavily laden carts, and on rough roads when one wheel dropped into a rut, the horse would lunge, for the boy was not big enough to have any real control over the horse. They say it's a wonder he was not killed one day when the horse ran away down a hill. It was a hard life, for often the wagoner was a brute to the boy put in his charge.

Hannah managed by hook or by crook to bring a bit of extra money into the house; one of the Malsburys would call on her for help on all special occasions. If it was a birth or death, a wedding or a pig killing, Hannah would be there, the family's right-hand woman. There was a lot of work to be done when they killed a pig weighing between three and four hundred pounds, which would not be a record by any means. Salting the bacon and hams, making pork pies, sausages and pig's puddings kept Hannah busy for days; she looked on herself as an expert at the job, and no doubt she impressed others with her ability. And so by hard work and frugal living James and Hannah spared their boys the hunger and degradation found in so many homes around there. They then set about getting Joe an apprenticeship.

By the time Joseph was fourteen, Hannah was well known to the Wesleyans in the villages around Sulgrave, and at Eydon a Wesleyan tailor named Edward Smith was willing to take an apprentice to his trade. Hannah was ambitious for her boys to have a better chance in life than farm work offered, so it was arranged by the trustees of Robert Gardiner's bequest at Sulgrave for Joseph to come to work for Smith for a trial period.

What a blessing it has been in days gone by that good men and women thought of poor folk when they made their wills. To administer these charities is a headache to many of the trustees in these days; and what they do with the money now matters little. For many long years after the donors died their money helped many a poor dog over a stile, and brought comfort and cheer to many a poor home. That was exactly what the kind-hearted folk wanted their money to do. It is good that we know the name of Robert Gardiner, though I wish we knew more about him. According to Whellan he left at Sulgrave in 1763: £7 16s. in bread to the poor, £5 to the schoolmaster for teaching six poor boys, £5 for an entertainment to the trustees annually. He also left £500, the interest to be disposed of on St Valentine's Day as follows: 21s. to the minister for preaching a sermon on that day,

21s. to the county hospital, 15s. to entertain the trustees, £3 for clothing six poor boys, £9 3s. to be distributed to the poor in beef and £10 for apprenticing a poor boy.

Good old Robert, he thought of the poor, he remembered the parson, and knowing that the administration of the legacy would involve the trustees' time and thought he left enough for them to have a jolly good dinner each year.

On Joseph's fourteenth birthday, 29th April 1866, Hannah tied his new clothes together in a bundle, said, 'God bless you my boy', and Joseph walked by the old windmill to Culworth, then across the fields to Eydon. The trial period being satisfactory to both parties, he became an apprentice to Edward Smith.

The following is the indenture that bound Joseph hand and foot, as he described it in later life:

This Indenture Witnesseth, that Joseph Tyrrell, A Minor of the age of fourteen years or thereabouts, son of James Tyrrell of Sulgrave in the County of Northampton, labourer, with the consent of his said father testified by executing these presents
doth put himself Apprentice to Edward Smith of Eydon in the County of Northampton, Tailor to learn his Art, and with him (after the manner of an Apprentice), to serve from the 29th day of April 1866 until the full End and Term of seven Years from thence next following, to be fully complete and ended.
During which Term, the said Apprentice his Master faithfully shall serve; his Secrets keep; his lawful commands everywhere gladly do. He shall do no damage to his said Master, nor see it to be done of others, but that he to his power shall let of forthwith give Warning to his said Master, of the same. He shall not waste the goods of his said Master, nor lend them unlawfully to any. He shall not commit Fornication nor contract Matrimony within the said term. He shall not play at Cards, Dice, Tables, or any other unlawful Games, whereby his said Master may have any Loss. With his own Goods or Others', during the said Term with License of his said Master, He shall neither buy or sell. He shall not haunt Taverns or Playhouses, nor absent himself from his said Master's Service, Day or Night unlawfully. But in all things as a

faithful Apprentice, he shall behave himself towards his Master, and all his, during the said Term. He shall give a true and just account of his Master's Goods, Chattels and Money committed to his charge, or which shall come to his hands, whenever required so to do by his said Master. And the said Edward Smith, in consideration of the premises and of the sum of ten pounds of lawful money of Great Britain to him in hard cash paid at or before the execution of these presents by the Ministers, Churchwardens, overseers of the poor of the Parish of Sulgrave aforesaid as Trustees of Charity Funds left by Robert Gardiner for apprenticing poor boys of the Parish and for other purposes and of the further sum of ten pounds to be paid to him by the said Trustees in case the apprentice shall be in his service on the 29th October 1870. His said Apprentice in the Art of a Tailor best means that he can, shall teach and instruct, or cause to be taught and instructed; and find unto his said Apprentice good and sufficient Meat, drink, Clothing, Washing, Lodging, and all other necessities during the said Term. And for the true performance of all and every said Covenants and Agreements, either of the said Parties bindeth himself unto the other by these present. In Witness whereof, the parties above named to these Indentures have set their hands and Seals the Ninth day of November in the thirtieth year of the Reign of our Sovereign Lady, Queen Victoria, by the Grace of God of the United Kingdom of Great Britain and Ireland, Queen, Defender of the Faith, and in the year of our Lord One Thousand Eight Hundred and Sixty Six.

Signed, Sealed and Delivered in the presence of
Joseph Turrell
Charles Watts Overseer
James Tyrrell   his cross
Edward Smith

Joseph signed Turrell, as he had learnt at school. The Sulgrave rector, the Rev. Harding, said it should be spelt Tyrrell, and so James, who could not write, had his name written according to the rector's ruling, and it has been so spelt ever since that day. I'm glad they altered the spelling, because we might be descendants of Sir Walter, who shot William Rufus in the New Forest many years ago.

In the indenture there is no mention of hours of work or wages for the boy, but very definitely of £20 for Edward. One of Joseph's first jobs was to help Edward alter a carpet at the Hall for Mrs Cartwright. Later on he was often there, sometimes for a week, sewing carpets that were cut where worn and made to fit a smaller room. As their pressing irons were heated in the kitchen he soon knew his way about the house. And he learned to keep on the right side of the servants, which was almost as important as pleasing Mrs Cartwright.

The tailors' workshop was a small building in what is now a garden; the one window looked over the fields, for the back was on the street. Years before it had been a room in the house with a window on the street. This did not suit one of the Annesleys, for when he walked up the street, the tailors used to look up from their work to see the squire pass by. So he had a new workroom built. This had one advantage for Edward: no one in the street could look in the window and see if he'd any visitors. During the winter evenings they had many callers, some to have a gaff in the warm, some on business. When the new groom at the Hall came to be measured for a suit of stable tweeds, after the business was done Edward would enquire where he'd come from. Most men like the opportunity to talk about themselves, and the tailors might hear of a ducal mansion or a faraway town. The schoolmaster came to talk to Edward, and Joe heard of the difficulties he had in getting the youngsters to school regularly. Moravians and Wesleyans came and Joe for the first time in his life heard discussions on religious beliefs and practices. Edward had a son in London and daughters in Northampton, so he knew all about the political discontent in those two hotbeds of revolutionary ideas a century ago. When the conversation was about what Gladstone and Disraeli were saying at Westminster, voices were hushed to a whisper, lest they be overheard. Joe kept his ears open, for he was getting glimpses into the wider world through these conversations and contacts with people, so different from those he'd met in

Sulgrave. He learnt a lot besides tailoring during those seven years of his apprenticeship.

Edward was not likely to see the London newspapers that came to the village, but it's probable his son in London posted him one occasionally. He certainly posted to Joe in 1899 an evening paper announcing the death of Gladstone, knowing how interested he was in the Grand Old Man.

On Sundays Joe would visit his parents at Sulgrave for the day, or go with Patience to the new Methodist chapel. Edward, being a lay preacher, was generally away preaching in one of the villages grouped in the Banbury circuit. A ten-mile walk to an appointment was a fairly easy day for him. The big day of the year was in the summer when he went to Tysoe to preach. No doubt he used the footpaths across the fields for part of the way but that day he must have walked well over thirty miles, reaching home in the early hours of Monday morning.

In the tailors' workroom Edward and Joe started work at six in the summer and seven in the winter and normally worked for twelve hours, but, during the busy periods or when black clothes were needed at short notice for funerals, long hours were worked in the dim light of paraffin lamps.

Not long after Joe started learning the trade Edward brought the first sewing-machine to Eydon, a 'Howe', and Joe learnt to use it. It made quite a sensation, and all sorts of folk came to see this new-fangled contraption at work; heads wagged and most folk expressed doubts as to whether the sewing would last like the good old-fashioned handwork.

Joe described how Edward was addicted to sleep-walking and on one occasion he rose in the night, mixed a bucket of food for the family pig, carried it down the garden path and as he lifted it over the wall to empty it in the trough accidentally spilt some on his bare feet; the shock woke him up.

His wife, Patience, was according to all accounts a very frugal housewife; she made rules for her household and rigidly enforced them. One spoonful of sugar was her allowance for each person at the table and Joe maintained that the sugar spoon had been beaten nearly flat so that it held only a minute quantity.

Another rule was that she never served anyone with a second helping after she had eaten her portion; so if Joe wanted a bit more pudding he had to gobble his up with an eye on her plate, or be too late to get one. 'Quick at eating, quick at work' was one of her maxims.

During the latter part of his apprenticeship Joe became very friendly with Thomas Kench. They were both Wesleyans and had joined after a mission held at the chapel. Thomas was a voracious reader, and very fond of Dickens's novels – *Pickwick Papers* was being published in instalments at that time. During the winter evenings when Joe was alone in the workshop sitting cross-legged on the bench and busily plying his needle Thomas read aloud the instalments and together they enjoyed the adventures and exploits of Pickwick and Sam Weller.

Between instalments of *Pickwick* they studied theology, for both were preparing to become local preachers and, before they could be accredited, an examination had to be passed. This was an exam before the local preachers' meeting, and every statement made by the candidate had to be proved by the quotation of a passage from the Bible; this needed both a good memory and thorough knowledge of the Bible. During the long summer evenings they went for walks in the fields and, as they strolled, discussed the pros and cons of the textbooks they were reading, and the questions they anticipated being asked.

At the time the East and West Junction Railway was being built. This work was of great interest to them and many evenings they went to see the progress being made, in what was then to Eydon folk a sensational, modern development.

The exam took place at Marlborough Road Church, Banbury,

and both passed, and very proud they were to go to the village chapels around and preach, simply for the love of the work. Often they walked five or six miles to their appointments, such as Upper and Lower Boddington, and Sulgrave and Greatworth. These were counted short journeys, hardly worth the trouble of getting out Thomas's horse and trap, so they went on 'Shanks' pony', as walking was often called.

This friendship was a lifelong one and although, as they grew older, the differences in their outlook and characters developed and they had little in common on political affairs, nothing ever marred the friendship established in those early years.

It is not surprising that when Joe entered the seventh year of his apprenticeship the terms became very galling to him – no wages or even a bit of pocket money when he was twenty years old. He had hoped to earn more money by learning a trade, but he felt worse off than the farm labourers, for they had some money in their pockets each week and he had none. He wasn't one to suffer injustice without protest, so he grumbled and complained with the result that after long delay Edward relented and paid him a few shillings in the final months of his seven-year term.

For a time after his apprenticeship he worked for Edward for wages; after Patience had deducted his board and lodging I should say it would be 6s. to 8s. a week.

Edward and Patience were old. Their girls were settled at Northampton, and before long they decided to retire and let Joe take over the business. There was quite a stock of cloth, linings and so on, and all the odds and ends that go into the making of men's clothes. These were valued by the two sons, Lorenza and John, at £120. Joe had had no business experience and no one interested in him to advise on the transaction. Before long he realised he had been had by allowing men financially interested in the transaction to carry out the valuation. For some was old stock that had depreciated in value and it was booked to him at the original price. This may have been done quite unwittingly, for they may not have known that a qualified valuer would have allowed for depreciation. Joe agreed to pay by instalments – the old folk departed to Northampton and he was left to carry on.

Now Joe had a house, but he never was much good at housework or cooking, and Flora's parents had moved to Redhill, Surrey, where her father was a very popular ticket inspector at the station, so soon it was arranged for Flora to come to his assistance.

The wedding took place at Redhill Wesleyan Chapel, on 18th October 1876. They came home that evening by the Great Western Railway to Cropredy, where George Whitton met them with a horse and trap, and drove them home.

Joe and Flora moved into the house at the lower end of Blacksmith's Lane. Joe employed a tailor to help him; he lived with them and received wages each week, so from the first Flora had an extra one to cook for, extra washing and housework. When a rush order came and the men were working sixteen or eighteen hours a day Flora took some of the plain sewing to help get the work completed on time. Later on Joe suggested to her that it would be helpful if she learnt to work button-holes in the tailor's style. Flora thought a moment. 'I think I know enough,' she replied, and that was final.

Their best customer was Colonel Cartwright. Each year he provided suits for the butler, the footman and the men employed in the stables, and at intervals livery – long coats with tails, and many bright buttons, made of expensive cloths, and involving much hand sewing. Other customers were in neighbouring villages, especially Chipping Warden, Aston-le-Walls, and the Boddingtons. These Joe visited on foot on a Saturday afternoon and evening to measure, deliver the goods and collect the cash. It was not a ready-money trade by any means, and many garments were paid for by instalments. Joe became a well-known figure in that district, stout walking-stick over his shoulder supporting a parcel of clothes. He knew all the footpaths over the fields, and on the darkest night tramped the roads and fields, without a glimmer of light of any sort, reaching home between nine and ten o'clock. As he never smoked he never carried a box of matches in his pocket.

One dark night Flora sat by the fire waiting for his return, ten o'clock struck, then half past and no Joe appeared. Flora began to get anxious. What made him so late? Had he had an accident? Her mind conjured up all sorts of dire possibilities. By eleven o'clock she could sit no longer, so went outside the gate to listen. Before long whistling was heard, and Joe comes down the lane cheerfully whistling a tune. How that vexed Flora! Joe received a telling off for being late and whistling when she was so worried, for Flora had a sharp tongue at times.

When the children came, Joe's mother Hannah came over from Sulgrave to officiate as midwife and housekeeper; she rather tried Flora with her old-fashioned ways and ideas, and her cooking was very different, but there was no option: Hannah came and took charge at these times. She was all for boiling food in one pot, potatoes, beans and turnips in net bags along with the meat. We all thought it very queer, but no doubt it was a relic of the days when few cottagers had ovens.

Agnes was born in 1877, Percy in 1878, Kate in 1881. With three little ones to feed and clothe and no higher income, life became a struggle to keep out of debt and preserve a decent standard of living and dress the children respectably. I think they must have got behind in the payments for the stock, for the uncles who carried out the valuation obtained a bill of sale on their furniture, so that if the worst came to the worst their household goods would have been sold to pay the debt.

That was a bitter pill for Flora, one that she never forgot. For they had trusted the Smiths when they took over the business. Now they found they had been had. However, the bill of sale never had to operate, for by dint of hard work and frugal living the payments were maintained till the last instalment was paid.

That was a great day for Joe and Flora. A great load was lifted from their minds, and I am pretty sure they sang together that day, 'Praise God from whom all blessings flow'.

Joe and Flora had not been brought up in at all the same way, nor were they used to life in a village such as Eydon. Eydon was a Tory village, as the squire, rector and estate steward were of one mind. The few folk who were independent were like Brer Rabbit: they laid low. Henry Peck bluntly said what many folk thought, 'One was a fool not to keep in with the folk with money.'

Flora's early life had been spent in very different surroundings. Her mother in early life had learnt the hat trade at Luton, and in the 1860s she had a house and a hat shop on Abington Square, Northampton. Her father was a railwayman and worked at Castle station. The family were keen Methodists, active loyal workers at their chapel.

Northampton at the time was a hotbed of revolutionary ideas. Among the cobblers were double-dyed radicals, atheists, agnostics, free-thinkers and republicans; societies for the spread of their ideas flourished. The working men of the town were of the right mood to welcome those two outstanding Radicals, Bradlaugh and Labouchere, and to send them to the House of Commons in 1880.

Flora did hold with a lot of the goings-on in Northampton, but she was a staunch Radical, and a loyal Methodist.

Joe's early life was spent in a quieter world. His father never voted in his life, and his mother's thoughts never soared above the chapel and the daily round and common task. They were peasants, and I must confess I can find no tangible grounds for the notion that we Tyrrells have come down in the world. If we come of Norman stock, if our forbears came over with William in 1066, we have been hewers of wood and drawers of water for so long that any signs of our aristocratic heritage vanished years ago. Having said that, I am left wondering if Joe's pugnacious instincts were derived from the warrior strain. Although he was never a soldier, or even a boxer, he gloried in a fight; and both the Radical Party and the Wesleyan Methodist Church provided an arena where young men could win their spurs.

He had not forgotten the whispered conversations about political issues in Edward Smith's workshop, and now under Flora's strong influence he soon saw the way he should take. They were united in condemning the verse often sung at chapel:

> The rich man in his castle
> The poor man at his gate
> God made them high and lowly
> And ordered their estate.

It was wrong, they believed, to charge the Almighty with making the chasm between the rich and the poor which was the result of man's greed. They thought it could be bridged. They dared not come out openly at this time, for ejection orders were easily obtained and Thompson would have turned them out without compunction. Everyone believed he would, so was very careful not to give him the opportunity. Joe and Flora began to realise they would have no real liberty while renting a house on the estate.

One of the leaders of the chapel was John Foster, a dealer. I have been told that in the 1850s he bought pigs till he had a drove, then had them driven by road to the London markets, about a week's journey. Evidently he was in financial straits in 1883, for part of his property was for sale by order of the mortgagee. This is rather surprising, for John, being a well-known Wesleyan, would have had the financial backing of Arthur Fairfax, a Banbury solicitor, also a Wesleyan.

Any prominent worker in the church could go to Fairfax for a mortgage and unless it was a hopeless proposition business would be done. He and his successor, Harold Barfield, propped up for many years Wesleyan tradesmen and farmers who would have been bankrupt but for their support.

I think on this occasion Foster was so deep in debt that Fairfax persuaded him to divide his property, sell one block and move into his house next door. That sale consisted of three cottages and a garden; one cottage was very poor, little better than a hovel. The roof of the best cottage was in a very dilapidated condition, there were great holes in the thatch, and some of the timbers were rotting. This cottage stood empty, and as it was a cheap block of property Joe bought it in 1883 for £100. As he lacked the wherewithal to pay for it he went to see Sam Allen at Chipping Warden; he readily lent Joe all the money he needed. Sam was the proprietor of the Red Hill brickyard, a shrewd, hard-working, hard-dealing man.

The roof was put in order, with new rafters where necessary, and thatched, and a room was altered to make a tailor's workroom before the family moved up the street to the new home. The whole family felt they had moved into another land, a land of freedom, for now, as long as the interest was paid regularly to Sam, they were safe. He cared nothing for politics, so there was no fear of offending him and causing trouble.

Many and many a time in after years Joe and Flora thanked God that they had taken this step in their early married life. Joe was a young man at the time, and he had not been bred and born at Eydon, so this transaction did not enhance his popularity among the Wesleyans, and we fear the Fosters never forgave him for buying their old home.

Colonel Cartwright was Viscount Valentia's tenant of the Hall, and he did not have quite the same standing in the village that ownership conferred. The Cartwrights were highly respected in the village, and undoubtedly were a very fine family, long remembered for their kindness and consideration. The real bulwark of the Church and State in the village during these years was Charles Thompson, Viscount Valentia's steward. As he farmed the home farm he employed several men, and was in charge of George Harding, the estate carpenter. He was responsible for letting and collecting the rents of twenty-eight houses and cottages in the village, which gave him a standing he made the most of. Churchwarden, first representative of the village on the Brackley Rural District Council, first chairman of the parish council, and captain of the fire brigade, Charles was a man of authority in the village for many years. Except in the hottest days of summer he wore a bowler hat and always carried a stick, so it was always handy to give a horse a clout, or lay it round the backside of a cheeky boy.

The Rev. W. H. Chapman, the parson, was another autocrat. He was a terrifically hard worker, organising clubs and societies galore in the village, and he loved compiling statistics: I could tell you how many sixpences and pennies were collected at church in 1888. He was a very outspoken man. He did not love our chapel folk, and one would not think he loved his own folk overmuch, by the dressings down he gave them at church sometimes. What he'd said in the sermon was often the talk of the village the following week. Old John Henry Ivens used to call the pulpit 'coward's castle' while Chapman was here.

In 1884 Gladstone extended the franchise by giving all householders the vote, and two years later he was defeated in the House of Commons on the Irish Home Rule Bill and a general election ensued. Joe bought a picture of Gladstone and hung it in the sitting-room over the mantelpiece. Everyone in the village by this time knew Joe was a Radical, for he was never one to hide his light under a bushel. He set to work for Carmichael, the

Radical candidate, trying to influence the working men who were voting for the first time in their lives.

There was widespread suspicion as to the secrecy of the vote; many expressed a belief that 'they would know'. Joe did his best to reassure the timid ones that no one would know which way they had voted. It had to be done very quietly; at this election he did not openly canvass for votes as he did at later elections. There were Radicals among the tradesmen who lay low and said nothing for business reasons.

On the great day Charles Thompson in his trap decorated with the Tory colours, and a trap from the Hall, were busy all day long taking voters to Byfield to record their vote. Several working men chose to be independent and refused to be identified with either the Reds or the Blues by walking to Byfield. That day only one man in the village dared to be seen talking to Joe in the street. He never told us the man's name, but I believe it was his great friend John Tomlin.

The Tory candidate was Sir Rainald Knightley; he had been the Member for years, and it was said he had spoken only once in the House of Commons, and that was to tell an usher to 'shut that door'. He won the election by 316 votes. Without a doubt Colonel Cartwright and Chapman were very uneasy; they did not know how the men had voted and it was the first time there had been open opposition to their rule in the village. No doubt they felt that Joe was a dangerous character, and a threat to the peace and harmony of the community.

When Chapman came to Eydon he found Nonconformity a powerful influence in the village; he hated the 'sects', as he called them. He also hated Radicals and feared the spread of their ideas amongst his flock. If he could not get at a man direct, he often could through Colonel Cartwright, and that is how he tried to silence Joe. Everyone in the village knew that Chapman could twist the Colonel round his little finger.

Joe was working on the annual order for clothes for the Hall servants when a message came from the Colonel countermanding the order. This came as a shock to both Joe and Flora; it was a struggle to make ends meet already, and if the best customer failed the outlook was very grim. Joe was always optimistic, but Flora's courage ebbed away; she had a few sleepless nights and visions of the home being sold up to pay debts haunted her mind. Something had to be done, so Joe asked for an interview with the Colonel and eventually a message came for him to be at the Hall at nine o'clock in the morning.

The butler ushered him into the Colonel's room and then joined the family and the household staff in the front hall for family prayers. The Colonel went to his room to see Joe, and Mrs Cartwright led the prayers that morning.

Afterwards the butler told how he listened, trying to hear what the Colonel was saying to Joe in a loud voice, instead of following the Bible reading and prayers of the lady of the house.

After passing the time of day, Joe asked the Colonel if his work hadn't been satisfactory; was that the reason the order was cancelled? 'That's quite all right,' the Colonel replied, and then launched into a long tirade. 'I'll tell you what, Tyrrell, there's you and old Foster and John Ivens, you are nothing but a lot of psalm-singing humbugs.' And so he let out hot and strong; the gravamen of the charge was that he did not like their chapel-going ways, and said they did not support activities run for the good of the village. Probably he had in mind the meagre support given by the chapel folk to Chapman's workingmen's club. When he had given utterance to all his complaints he cooled down; then Joe spoke up and had his say. The Colonel listened and peace was restored. Finally, Joe asked about the work on order. 'You can get on with it,' the Colonel answered. Joe went home with a light heart and reported the interview to Flora. There's no doubt that she slept well that night; Joe used to boast he could sleep any time, anywhere, even on a thorn faggot.

The year 1885 was the Colonel's last election here; when the next came in 1892 he had passed on, and T. W. Holland was at the Hall. The candidates this time were T. L. M. Cartwright, Tory, and D. C. Guthrie, the Radical. On the morning of the election day Guthrie left his East Haddon home, driving a coach drawn by four horses, complete with footman blowing a post horn at intervals. He drove around the constituency, and I believe this is the only time a coach and four horses has been seen at Eydon.

The next day Percy was sent to Byfield to wait for the result to be posted up at the Post Office. Guthrie won by the narrow majority of forty-eight. Percy says he got back as quickly as he could, running, then walking, then running again, for he was so pleased to bear the good news, which was received at home with jubilation. They say the blackbirds that year sang 'forty-eight, forty-eight', in this part of the country, and nearly drove some of the old Tories dotty.

During this election Father first came into contact with a very keen Radical worker at Boddington – Frederick Kitely, shoemaker – and a lifelong friendship ensued. He was the younger brother of Thomas Kitely, the Woodford shoemaker, as keen a Tory as Fred was a Radical; both were big hefty men as strong as a horse. They worked independently, but bought supplies of material together; this necessitated meeting occasionally at Byfield, half-way between the two villages. After they had settled the business transactions, sure enough, if an election was pending, the conversation would drift into the political arena, and before long the temperature would rise and blows would be exchanged. Sometimes the dispute developed into a ding-dong fight; Father used to say they fought like long dogs. When Thomas got really excited at Woodford he could shout 'Tory up' so loudly that it was clearly heard at Eydon two miles away.

I believe it was on the night before this election that Father said to Mother, 'I'm going to have a day for Queen and Country tomorrow.' He had come to believe every man ought to serve his country by taking some part in politics, or in village affairs; that no man should spend all his time working for himself. So when Charles Thompson left the village in 1918 Father took his place on the Brackley Rural District Council and the Board of Guardians. In 1905 he had become a school manager, to Chapman's great disgust, and in 1924 he was made a justice of the peace. It was a bitter pill for Chapman having the rebel sitting as bold as brass at the meetings of the school managers, for there was no love lost between them.

Many times Joe expressed his relief that through coming to Eydon he had escaped the life his father lived, that of a farm labourer. I believe it is true that at that time farm labourers did the hardest work for the lowest wages of any manual workers in the land. The only way a man could escape once he became a farm labourer was to leave the village and seek work in one of the towns, or join the army or police force. That door was closed to a married man.

Thanks to the Sulgrave charity, Joe became a tailor. Yet he always kept one foot on the land. It was always one of his great interests in life. I believe his heart was always in agriculture rather than the craft he followed in the workshop. Most weeks, after spending long hours plying the needle, on Saturday afternoon he would put on a pair of stout boots and set out to walk a round of ten to twelve miles. He walked the paths across the fields from one village to another and on the darkest nights he never went astray, or used a lantern.

These walks brought him a welcome relief and refreshment of spirit after the close confinement of the workroom. The smell of the damp grass, the animals and birds and those sights and sounds we associate with Mother Nature were to him the very breath of life. The weather seldom bothered him; in fact Flora thought he liked rough weather for she said above once, 'If it was a wetter and more windy day than usual, he was sure to have some business to take him to Adstone or Maidford.'

When in later life he rode behind the pony, there was ample time as she trotted along the road for his eyes to take in the fields and their contents on both sides of the road. He would count the cows in a herd of milkers or the massive Shorthorn bullocks grazing in Edgcote Park. He would praise a well-built and thatched rick of hay or corn and I believe the sight of them gave him real pleasure. It grieved him to see land badly farmed and one field near Middleton was a bugbear for years, both to him and to Thomas Kench. Thomas was not really interested in farming but as they drove by this particular field he remarked to Joe, 'I'm ashamed that man Wheeler is a Wesleyan, and such a bad farmer.' 'Ha,' Joe would reply, 'he's like the cow's tail, always behind.'

His keen interest in local agriculture was fostered in the 1880s by the political propaganda of the Liberals during Gladstone's term as Prime Minister from 1880 to 1886. One of his team, Jesse Collins, toured the country advocating, 'three acres and a cow' for the countryman. This fell on fertile ground and brought a ray of hope to labourers – still the bottom dog, still badly paid and miserably housed. Country folk have long memories, and many labourers of the 1880s remembered through their grandsires how they had been 'done' when the common fields were enclosed a century before. Many believed that this was the root cause of their poverty and utter dependence upon the farmers for a livelihood.

Another factor in making the farm labourers restive was the work of a local man, Joseph Arch of Barford, near Stratford-on-Avon. He was no ordinary farm labourer, being a champion hedge-cutter, a Wesleyan local preacher and a fluent speaker. He started the first trade union to cater for the farm labourers, 'The Agricultural Labourers Union', and he did it mainly by speaking on village greens. He spoke by the Cross Tree at Byfield and, although his voice was never heard at Eydon, his message came through crystal clear calling the workers to unite and adding to the fermentation going on in people's minds.

Joe made it his business to let the labourers here know of the three-acres-and-a-cow proposals and also the work Joseph Arch was doing to try and improve the labourers' lot in life. No union branch was started here, for Cartwright, Thompson and the parson still ruled the village with what Joe called 'a tight rein'.

The extraordinary thing was that, at that time, I believe quite half of the labourers in the village believed if they could get one foot on the ladder, they would soon be farmers on the way to prosperity. Some labourers did become farmers, and poor men around them said to themselves, 'If he can do it, so can I.' A very dangerous delusion to start with. If a man could save up and buy a heifer calf and persuade his wife to graze her on the roadside grass while he went to work and earned money, he had got a start. In the course of time, the heifer would present him with a calf and milk for butter. Soon he would have two cows, then he would rent a small field for his cows and he was well up the ladder of success.

Chapman was no fool – he knew very well what the men were quietly discussing and he knew Joe was talking about Jesse Collins and Joseph Arch and what they wanted done in the country for the labourers. Long before he came, one field of glebe land, 'the Pits', had been let as allotments. Eleven acres divided into sixty-nine plots meant they were all small, hardly big enough to grow potatoes and greens for a family. Chapman was a man of action, so when the three-acres-and-a-cow stunt blew up he moved speedily. Somehow or other he got possession of the Bushes and Manitoba, about twenty-six and a half acres. He divided Manitoba into twelve holdings and the Bushes' grass and bushes into three fields, one of which he let to Joe. He also rented two acres in Manitoba. Whether this was an attempt to get on the right side of the agitator, I do not know. I do know every few years they had a row about something or other.

Subsequent events showed that twenty-six acres were sufficient to meet the real needs of the men for land, but at the time the men wanted more. The year after they had taken over Manitoba, on 12th December 1887 a meeting was held in the schoolroom to which all interested in the provision of more allotments were invited to attend.

There were twenty-seven at the meeting, including Chapman, the parson, Malsbury and Thompson, farmers, the Maubey brothers, brickmakers, Bob Franklin, the cooper, and Sam Spencer, sheep dipper; the rest were labourers. The parson was elected chairman and my father, Joe, secretary. All were agreed on the need for more allotments and the men asked, some for an acre, others for halves.

It was decided to write to all the owners of land in the parish and ask for their help by making land available for allotments. As every bit of land in the parish was tenanted and farmed, some landlords could not help, and some who might have helped were not in that frame of mind. Negotiations proceeded and meetings were held during that winter, so that by the end of March Viscount Valentia had agreed to let them have 'Whit me Ley' at a rent of 25s. an acre. I have never heard the field referred to by that name; we have always known it as New Zealand.

The field was divided into thirty-one plots and the men drew lots as in the pre-enclosure days. They took possession on March 1st and as part of the field was planted wheat, it was agreed to pay Ambrose Inge, the tenant, £1 per land for the growing corn, with thanks for his kindness in giving the men early possession. The grass growing on the road through the field was sold to Richard Hunt for 9s. 6d.

Only nine genuine farm labourers drew plots in New Zealand. Sam Spencer came in for four; the rest went to the Hunts, the carriers, carpenters, Joe and such-like.

In the spring of 1888 the men set to work in earnest. The weather during the next few years did not help them, as dull showery summers brought poor crops, with the result that several men lost heart and gave up. New Zealand soon proved to be a white elephant. The soil is heavy, almost the consistency of clay, and it needed power to plough it. One tenant, Sam Spencer, owned a horse but to plough there a team of three horses was needed. The farmers had the horses and a good and trusted wagoner might borrow his master's team to plough his acre; but on no account would they be lent to some of the men. If a man paid the ordinary rate for ploughing his plot there was drilling and cultivation to be done, all expensive work. So New Zealand was not ploughed many times.

Joe had drawn an acre by the Rough Ground hedge, and when his neighbour packed up, he took it over; then, a year or two later, the next acre. At the other side of the field Sam Spencer was doing the same, for there was no waiting-list of tenants at New Zealand. Joe put up a post and wire fence on the open side of his three acres and laid it down to permanent grass. In ten years the field had reverted to pasture, in four separate plots. The owner had no objection to the change as he continued to receive the same rent. As the field was no longer let in plots, the allotment society ceased to function after a life of ten years.

The men working in Manitoba fared rather better, for there the soil is light and easily worked, though as it is near the iron-stone they say it is very 'hungry'. In Manitoba Joe grew corn and potatoes, varieties that were popular in those days being White Elephant, Magnum Bonum and one with a very nice name, Beauty of Hebron. The potatoes were sent to Stratford-on-Avon market. He had to pay cartage to Byfield station, the railway carriage and the salesman's charge, and as prices were low there was not a lot left for much hard work.

Joe soon came to this conclusion and here he spoke for several of the men who were keen to try their hand at cultivating land: 'To have to pay for land to be ploughed and drilled and the corn cut at harvest time, on top of the rent, takes the gilt off the gingerbread.' The allotments could have been a success only if the full co-operation of the farmers had been secured at the start, for they had the horses and machines absolutely necessary for the work.

This was not done, so the men worked under a heavy handicap. Some paid for their acres to be ploughed, then did the rest of the work by hand; the seed was sown by hand and in the autumn the corn was cut with sickles and bound into sheaves in the old-fashioned way. As machines could do these operations quite as well in a fraction of the time, all this hard work went very much against the grain. The ricks of corn were placed close together, then a threshing-machine was hired to thresh the entire harvest.

Several of the men who clung to the old ways grew wheat and, when it was threshed, sent it to the mill to be ground into flour for bread-making at home. That could be done only if the housewife liked to bake her own bread, and was in accord with her husband in scorning 'baker's bread'. As Gostick's bread was only 4½d. for a 4 lb. loaf, few wanted to go to all the trouble of making bread at home. 'What with the yeast and the firing, there's nothing in it,' they said. A crop of barley, ground and used to fatten a pig, was far more likely to win the housewives' approval.

While all this was taking place, Father was tenant of part of the Bushes, so that he could keep some cows. I remember hearing Mother tell folk what bad luck they'd had, how they lost four cows in two years. Percy said the first cow turned out to be a screw and had to be sold for next to nothing; the second one was a topper, she made 8 lbs. of butter a week. Alas, she went and died with her second calf. I remember seeing one lying covered with bags in a hovel in the Bushes; I presume she was dying. And I remember the muck they made in the yard, and what a job it was to swill the bricks clean enough to suit Mother. I hated the job. So of all the things I've wanted in this life, I have never wanted to own a cow – they're such dirty beasts. Why this venture turned out such a failure I do not know. I think Father packed up and bought a pony soon after we moved into the new house.

My memories of Manitoba go back to about ten years after it had first been let for allotments. By that time the early starters had dropped out and the acres were getting into the hands of tradesmen. Pettifer's had an acre growing herbs for their business and Henry Peck had one or two acres. Looking at the field today, one could write off the allotment society of 1887 as a failure. The men that hoped to make money by cultivating an acre were disappointed, though others made good by being able to feed a pig and keep a few fowls on their surplus produce. Men worked incredibly long hours during the growing season to raise their standard of living, but at the same time it helped satisfy the land hunger in their hearts. For the peasant of pre-enclosure is not quite dead in us yet. I find when I walk in the fields or along the brookside that, quite unconsciously, I am looking for something to take home – perhaps a few blackberries or a bit of wood that has fallen out of a tree. I hate coming home empty handed. You see, my forbears had always had to be on the lookout for something to eat, so sticks had to be carried home to boil the pot. I think I'm a bit of a throwback, for most men of my generation have outgrown such foibles. Yet in the eventide of my life I feel the call of the land very strongly, much more compellingly than in my early life.

Chapter 8

Our childhood

We three younger members of the family were born in the Fosters' old house that Father bought in 1883. When a birth was imminent Father would walk across the fields to Culworth to call Dr Jacobs, then go on to Sulgrave to warn his mother that she was needed while Mother was laid up. Mother always remembered the weather on these occasions. She never forgot that Kate was born on the eve of the bitterest winter in living memory, 1881, the year Harry Bull was laid up for three weeks with frostbite and several deaths occurred in the district through exposure.

They said that when I arrived eight years after Kate, in 1889, Grandmother Tyrrell remarked, 'Poor thing, he ain't come for long.' The old lady was only too familiar with the high mortality rate of babies, which was about thirty per cent in the first year. But I didn't die, and nor did Maude who came in 1892. I reckon when Frank was born in 1895, Mother said, 'This will have to be the last, Joe.' 'Yes,' he said, 'this is the dillin,'* for he knew Mother had ideas in her head. Scott's had just started work on the new railway and men were coming to the village looking for vacant cottages. Any landlord with one empty could have two or three

* The dillin, or, as some say, the runt, is the last and often the smallest of a family, whether animal or human.

times the normal rent while the contractors were here. Village shops flourished as never before, for the men on the job earned big money, and they spent it. The two shops in the village were grocer's; no one sold any drapery or odds and ends. Henry Bayliss, a Woodford man, used to come round with a basket containing pins, needles, reels of cotton and tapes. Mother could see there was an opening for a drapery shop in the village. Father and she had two cottages to let, but one was a very primitive poor sort of house. I can just remember it. I should think it was sixteenth-century and probably it was the poorest cottage in the street. If they could build a new house in its place, our house could be divided, and that would make three cottages to let at good rents. But they had no ready money, so they consulted Harold Barfield, their solicitor. He soon found that Father had an insurance policy for a term of years, taken out soon after they were married. 'It's quite easy,' he told Father, 'You can borrow £50 on this, and I can fix you up for the rest of the money.'

Of course it soon became known in the village what was afoot, and very soon Chapman came to see Father. 'I hear you are likely to build a house of bricks,' he said. 'I wish you'd build it of stone, you can open the stone pit and have all you need without any charge whatever.' Father thanked him and promised to look into the comparative cost. He very soon found it would be far more expensive to build with stone, so brick it had to be. And so it's we Wesleyans who have spoilt the street with brick buildings. First the chapel in 1860, a great big factory-like building towering high above the road. Then later Thomas Inge replaced the stone front of Midway with a brick front some years before Father built the Red House. The Moravians, not quite so brash as the Wesleyans, built a brick chapel, but they put it in somebody's garden, out of sight. Aunt Mary and Winnie thought the Red House pretty awful, but when Winnie looked at it in 1967 she said, 'It's not as bad as it used to be, it's toned down quite a bit.' But how opinions do vary; one old Eydon man said to me recently, 'You know, I like it.' The style was popular at the time, and the brickwork is relieved by a bit of fancy work around the front door and over the windows. The plans were drawn by Tom Kinch, a man who had been in the building trade in London, and his father was the bricklayer who built it. He was one of our local preachers, a whiskered old boy with a fierce glint in his eye when he preached. He always reminded me of Elijah on Mount Carmel defying the prophets of Baal. In the pulpit he laid down the law in a loud voice till the end, then very quietly he'd say, 'I'll finish with a few verses of poetry.' He called it poetry, we called it tripe, for we could make nowt of it. He was a better bricklayer than preacher; he'd worked in the fast building trade in London, and very soon he was by no means popular around here among the men in his trade. He worked too fast for them. Most bricklayers were served by one labourer, but Kinch needed two to keep him going on a piece of straightforward work. Then he'd get his line set, and when all was ready he'd tap his trowel on a brick and call out, 'Boys, we are all ready to begin.' He could lay a row of bricks while you were saying Jack Robinson, and his two labourers had to run to keep him supplied with bricks and mortar.

The contractor for the building was George Johnson of Hinton, another Wesleyan. He agreed to build the house – seven rooms, shop and workroom upstairs – for £235. Before it was half built he began to moan and groan that he was losing money on the job, so he tried to charge extras that my folk reckoned were in the contract. They complained that best Leamington bricks had been specified, and inferior local bricks were being used. It was a painful situation. It would not have been so bad if Johnson had been an unbeliever, but all the parties concerned were Wesleyans. There is no doubt he lost money on the job; he undercut other builders so often he soon got into Queer Street. For years Harold Barfield, the solicitor, propped him up financially, but Johnson was never able to stand on his own legs.

When the house was ready and we moved in, the old house was altered to its original size, before the panelling was put in the parlour, so that the old stable was now two cottages. How proud Mother was of her new house, nice level floors in all rooms and no steps. You see she'd lived in old houses where the living-room floors were big stone slabs. They wore with the continual walking, so that just inside the door was a depression. Another part worn down was round the fireside, the result being that in some parts of the room a chair stood on only three legs. The table had to be in just the right place, or it would rock. If you nailed a bit of wood on one leg to keep it steady, and it should be moved an inch or two, it rocked worse than ever. Mother had had such a packet she thanked the Lord for nice level floors that could be covered with linoleum to walk on. Another great boon to her was a sink in the kitchen and a tap; she'd always had to fetch water from outside the house, and go outside to empty dirty water down a drain. The new kitchen range was the very latest, it had an enclosed boiler by the side of the fire. You put cold water in at the top, and drew hot water out through a tap low down on the front. The fire had such a fierce draught that the oven got hot in less than no time; never had Mother cooked our food so easily. How she revelled in all these comforts. I should have forgotten them years ago if Mother hadn't talked so much about them. The preachers who came to tea with us on Sunday heard all about them, travellers who came for orders had to hear the story before they could do any business; and friends and relations who visited us were shown all the latest conveniences in our new house.

To stock the shop Mother went to Banbury shopkeepers, many of whom sold goods at wholesale prices to village shopkeepers. She went in for drapery, stationery, children's toys and all sorts of odds and ends. But never sweets: she held that we youngsters would eat all the profits, and no doubt she was right. If she was busy in the kitchen and the shop door bell rang one of us had to get behind the counter to serve the customer. And so I am able to inform you that up to 1914 a reel of cotton or Sylko cost a penny; that would also buy a tin of boot polish or a yard of elastic. A boy could have a fishing line for a penny, complete with hook and float. Sixpence would buy a jointed fishing rod; I believe they had three lengths. Boys used to go fishing regularly in the summer in the ponds and the brook, so we did a good trade in fishing tackle. We catered for all their games; each had a season and when that was over another took its place. At one time half a dozen groups of boys could be seen playing marbles in the street. Ordinary coloured clays were ten or twelve a penny; glasses were more expensive, two or three a penny. Then there was the spinning-top season. Tops were a penny each. You wound the lash of a whip around the top, put the top on the ground and started the top spinning by smartly pulling the whip lash. Then by lashing the spinning top it could be kept going for a long time, the longer you could keep it spinning the greater expert you were at the game. These were in my line, so I'm sorry I can't tell you much about Mother's drapery.

When we moved into the new house, Frank was a toddler and Maude and I were at school; while Kate in her teens had so many boy-friends that Mother kept a sharp eye on her. Percy was working with Father as a tailor's apprentice, and when he wasn't working he was either playing the violin or tearing over to Moreton to play with pals there. Agnes had already left home and become an assistant in a drapery store.

The big day of our week at our new house was the Sabbath, which began on the Saturday, for that day we got all ready to keep the day as it should be kept. Looking back to those Saturdays in my mind they are associated with the expenditure of prodigious quantities of what Mother called 'elbow grease'. Stainless-steel cutlery and modern polishes make a very little elbow grease go a long way nowadays. Then, knives, forks and spoons were badly stained after a day's use; the knives were cleaned by rubbing on a board roughened by an abrasive called bath brick; it was an arm-aching job to get the polish Mother demanded for use on Sundays. Then there was an array of boots and Father's big square-toed boots made for him by George Ariss of Boddington. Every vestige of dirt had to be removed before they were coated with blacking. This came in bars shaped like a bar of chocolate; a drop of water or a spot of spit was necessary to soften it so that it could be rubbed on the boots. Then a vigorous application of the shining brush very gradually coaxed a shine, but it was a long way round Father's boots and the backs had to shine just as much as the toes; it was a long, arm-aching job that we hated.

In the backyard a few old hens roosted under the steps; they had the run of the yard and outbuildings. The Buff Orpingtons I remember were a dirty lot, and the cows were not at all careful when they were brought into the yard to be milked; so the yard had to be swilled and brushed clean ready for Sunday.

Indoors the girls cleaned the brass door knocker, brass candle-sticks and door handles and the silver teapot and cruet had to be polished so that you could see your face in them. The work was parcelled out so that each one had a regular Saturday morning task; they were tiring and boring jobs and we were incorrigible dodgers, so from time to time attempts were made to slip them.

But Mother scrutinised the work with the eye of an eagle; there was no leaving dirt on the heel of a boot or powder on the spoons, the culprit was sent back to do the job properly.

One day Kate was caught sitting on a low stool at the front door reading a paperback novel she'd hidden under her apron when she should have been cleaning the door knocker. Kate and I especially were voracious readers. We'd read anything, any time: many a time Father has said with an air of disgust, 'Always got your nose in a book'; or, 'You'll get fat on that.' We read in bed by candlelight although it was strictly forbidden; it was very difficult to disobey for in the morning the candle showed just how long it had been alight the previous night and Mother was very, very observant. It could be done only by pinching a candle out of the shop and hiding it in our bedroom, then changing them over in the candlestick.

Sunday began like every day with family prayers as soon as we had finished eating our breakfast. Mother would reach down the Bible from the mantelpiece, the opposite end to the tea tin and place it on the table before Father. It got very fly-blown and grimy outside through the heat and steam of constant cooking operations and, inside, very worn at the Psalms and Matthew, the parts Father constantly read at the table.

He read a psalm or a few verses from one of the gospels, then we all bowed our heads while he prayed for us, the church and all in special need. One phrase he used so often that I still remember it: he prayed, 'That we all may meet around the throne of God in Heaven, an unbroken family.' It is only in later life that I have come to realise the beauty and significance of that prayer Father offered so many times.

At ten o'clock we were at Sunday school for just over an hour under Father's tuition. He believed implicitly that if we learnt to repeat passages of scripture and hymns we should never forget them; so most of the time at school we were expected to learn answers to catechism questions and passages from the Bible. When he called on us to repeat our portions it gave enterprising youngsters an opportunity to indulge their fancy.

I remember one of the Harding boys always affirmed in a loud voice, 'It was better to dwell in a corner of a housetop, than with a brawling woman in a wide house.' My response was to affirm, 'Faithful are the wounds of a friend, but the kisses of an enemy are deceitful.'

And that is about all I remember learning at Sunday school, plus this one incident: the class was reading in rotation verses from Luke 14, the story of the great supper. Harold Kench was reading slowly, 'I have bought a piece of ground and I must needs go and see it. I pray thee have me . . .' and he hesitated at the next word. Frank whispered, 'executed', which Harold at once repeated. The next boy solemnly read, 'I have bought five yoke of oxen and I go to prove them, I pray thee have me executed.'

So by using our wits we were able to extract amusement from the lessons most of us found very boring; for Father did not excel as a teacher and we were anything but helpful.

During the interval between school and dinner Mother sent us to visit old Sally Dancer, the widow who came each week to do our washing. We were strictly charged to enquire how Sally and her son Bill were faring, and we took them some suitable reading matter for the day – the previous week's *Christian Herald* and *Joyful News*. Generally Mother sent a little gift, a pot of jam or a few cakes or tarts. Sunday dinner was a substantial meal, with only very small variations.

When we came to the new house Mother had Plummer, the Byfield tinsmith, make a baking tin to fit the oven of the cooking range. It was a large tin, and the excellence of the Yorkshire pudding it contained always surprised visitors, for Mother always assured them it was made with only one egg. A hefty joint of meat was baked in the same tin, the gravy from this vastly improved the pudding. We had no sweet or cups of tea, but a glass jug of water always formed part of the table equipment. Later in life Mother and Father did have a cup of tea at dinner-time. Mother said: 'I think the time has come when we can indulge ourselves.'

At two o'clock we were back at Sunday school for half an hour before the afternoon service. I can remember nothing of those sessions. It may be that as it followed a hearty meal we were somewhat sleepy, so that our wits did not function as well as during the morning lessons. At 2.30 afternoon service began; it ended anything between 3.30 and four o'clock, according to whether the preacher was short- or long-winded. If he was interesting, we listened, if he wasn't then my wits went wool-gathering or I went to sleep. Old Charlie Prestidge, the cobbler, sat near our pew; he always went to sleep afternoon and evening; sometimes we had to give him a poke to wake him up for the last hymn. We were glad to listen to some of the preachers, for they were born story-tellers. They revelled in the dramatic Old Testament stories and the miracles of Jesus. Percy Edmunds, an aristocratic-looking Banbury man, especially loved the battles the Israelites fought under David's and Gideon's leadership. His graphic descriptions were so real we could hear the clash of arms and the cries of the fallen. No one slept when Percy was preaching or when old Richard Eaves came over from Wardington. Then we knew we were in for a good laugh: in fact as soon as Richard spoke I was bubbling with suppressed laughter; he spoke in such an abject and apologetic tone of voice and his face was so grave that we said he looked like a dying duck in a thunderstorm. He, like Percy, was a born story-teller.

There was much talk about Richard, for no one was quite sure whether all he said sprang from natural simplicity, or whether he was having us on. In telling his story he added the dramatic gestures in such a natural way that he held us young folk spell-bound. The great catch of fish in the Sea of Galilee was illustrated by Richard hanging over the side of the pulpit and slowly heaving in his handkerchief containing the haul of fishes.

Maybe the story of the Good Samaritan was Richard's best effort. We saw the Samaritan look down at the wounded man; we heard him say, 'Oh dear, poor man', then we saw him pour wine and oil on his wounds. 'We think that a funny thing to do', and so the old boy led us to think it was paraffin oil he used, not olive oil. Then Richard showed us how the Samaritan helped the man on to the back of the donkey. As he was very groggy Richard's outstretched arms helped him preserve his balance.

'Mind and not fall off. I'll mind the beastie,' said Richard to reassure him. His theme that day was falling among thieves and he concluded his discourse by quoting instances of men going to London and having their pockets picked. He ended by thanking the Lord that he had never been to London, 'And I doesn't want to go. I should only get run over by one of them motor-bus things.'

We are not sure whether this next quip was Richard's own or whether he got it from one of the Victorian preachers. He was telling of David and Goliath. David put a stone in his sling, walked towards his enemy, then hurled the stone: 'Goliath was so surprised, such a thing had never entered his head before.' Do you wonder we laughed?

All we youngsters thought Richard our best preacher, but Mother always held that his prayers were the best part of the services and that he was not in the same street as his brother, George. Even now, I can shut my eyes and hear old George go stumping up the aisle to the pulpit; he had a peg leg that sounded as if it was tipped with an iron ferrule. I should explain that one leg ended at the knee, and he walked on what looked like a piece of a broomstick. All the older folk reckoned George was a very special preacher; we youngsters thought him one of the dry ones.

About every other Sunday Father was away preaching at one of the villages in the circuit; but if it was our turn to entertain the preacher then Mother did the entertaining so that a newcomer very soon felt at home among us.

Harold Barfield of Banbury, our solicitor, never forgot the first time he came to Eydon as a very young man.

He came in the circuit trap with several others due to preach at nearby villages. As they were talking on the way one of the senior men remarked to Harold, 'So you are going to Eydon, Harold. You'll go to tea at Kench's or Walker's or maybe Tyrrell's.' Then he added an ironical afterthought, 'If you go there, you'll have to keep the conversation going.' Harold laughed over this many a time for Mother was a fluent conversationalist. As Father often said, 'She'd the gift of the gab.' Of the girls he often commented, 'She has the family gift.'

Frequently the sermon at the afternoon service was discussed at the tea table and there were times when the preacher was called to account for something he'd said, for Mother was critical and very outspoken. A text often preached from was Proverbs 22:6: 'Train up a child in the way he should go and when he is old he will not depart from it.' One Sunday afternoon Richard preached on this text. He was a married man but had no family. It always made Mother indignant when such folk laid down the law on how children should be brought up. She held there was a world of difference between knowing and doing. She often quoted Uncle Edward as saying, 'I was a far better father when I was single than when I'd a family to bring up.'

This day at table old Richard heard this and much more. 'It was all very well for folk like him to talk, but really he knew nothing at all about the training of children; if he'd children of his own he'd soon talk very differently.' While Mother was holding forth the old boy sat looking down at his plate and quietly getting on with his meal. When Mother had had her say he looked up, a faint smile on his face, as he remarked, 'I've listened with great interest to what you have to say, Mrs Tyrrell. I think I could preach another sermon on the subject now.'

After the evening service we were free for an hour or two before bedtime. On summer evenings we'd ramble in the fields, often by the brookside, our enjoyment severely restrained by the necessity of keeping our Sunday clothes whole and clean.

During the dark winter evenings the day often ended with hymn-singing round the organ. In this we were joined by Albert Walker and, sometimes, by other musical members of the chapel. This singing did not appeal to me at all; I'd rather have read my book. But there were times when the choir were learning a service of song and, very unwillingly, I was compelled by

Mother to add my bit of alto to the chorus. Whenever I hear the tune 'Diadem' I remember those Sunday evenings, for it was a great favourite whenever there were enough singers to take the different parts. When Percy and Kate left home these musical evenings petered out, for we younger members of the family never rose to the heights or caught the rapture of music as they did.

Indeed we younger members of the family grew up in a different atmosphere from that which our elder brother and sisters had experienced. It was much more genial, for our parents had mellowed over the eighteen years in which they had had small children in the home.

This change of attitude was even more pronounced in the Kench family than in ours. Their two elder boys and Mary were far more restricted after school hours than we were, but Fred, the youngest boy, escaped very early on by making friends with Frank. Mrs Kench once said to Mother, 'Frank can never do anything wrong in Fred's eyes.' The result was that he spent a lot of time at our place with Frank. Father did not approve of us playing in the street, 'I won't have you street urchins,' he used to say. So we did not spend many hours playing with our spinning tops and marbles, but the walk to and from school enabled us to share the games for a limited length of time. During the summer holidays we spent many hours with other youngsters by the brook, bird-nesting, fishing and bathing when the water had warmed up. It was not mixed bathing, as no one possessed a bathing costume in those days. Girls in the party would be shooed away before we stripped, for we were very particular about some things. Of course what two on their own got up to was another matter. We were trespassers, but Thompson the farmer was very good. He laid down the law: 'You keep out of the mowing grass and shut the gates behind you, or I'll lay my stick about you,' he said. We knew very well he would, so we kept the law and there was no trouble. Mother and Father tried to shield us from some of the evils in this world while we were young; they knew full well there were dangers ahead, but by then we should be older and they hoped wiser to meet the temptations of the world around us. 'As long as you put your feet under my table, you'll do what I say,' was a warning Mother often expressed.

When we were wilful or mischievous our parents administered corporal punishment. Mother would tell the wrong-doer before the punishment began, 'It hurts me more than it hurts you.' This, to use one of her own expressions, we took with a pinch of salt. Father always seemed to get sanction to thrash us from the Bible. He would quote, 'Spare the rod and spoil the child,' or, 'Whom the Lord loveth he chasteneth.'

Generally it was his hand that smote the culprit, but his leather slipper did duty on occasions. He had a hot temper and there were occasions when Mother thought he was overdoing the punishment; then she would say, 'That's enough, Joe, that's enough.' John Tomlin held that our parents would have been able to do nothing with us if they'd not administered corporal punishment from time to time.

One day in the backyard Mother smacked one of the elder children and the child ran away crying, 'You didn't hurt me.' This was overheard by Father working just above by an open window. He could move very quickly on occasions and he did this day as he called out, 'If your mother didn't hurt you I'll see what I can do', and the youngster got it 'hot and strong', an expression he often used. I remember Mother smacking Kate when she was quite a big girl, for hanging her head out of a bedroom window to talk to a boy on the street path. We all had it at times from Father or Mother, with the exception of Frank. He was specially favoured, being the youngest in the family. Maybe he never wanted to play in the street, or be naughty or disobedient, but I do know that he very seldom did wrong in the parents' estimation. He was certainly always very sunny-tempered and he'd an amazing knack of getting out of scrapes unhurt.

We were all taught to sing and to perform in public from a very early age – the Band of Hope and school concerts providing regular platforms for us each winter – and we were all given a course of lessons on the family organ. If after about two years' tuition the pupil showed no real interest and had to be forcibly made to do an hour's practice each day then the lessons would cease. Mother would say, 'Well, it's up to you now, you've been given a start.' Mother held that Frank could sing before he could talk and he broke the record by singing a solo on a concert platform before he was three years of age. Later he developed a nice alto voice and some musical folk suggested he was worthy of a place in a cathedral choir. But he never seemed to like music all that much and years later he said to me, 'I'm not musical, I've got good mechanical abilities and the two don't go together.' Percy was the real star. He played the organ and the violin; for three years running he passed examinations in London at the College of Violinists. He joined Fletcher's dance band, and he used to come home in the small hours of the morning after playing at a dance. It was his ambition to play in Dan Godfrey's famous orchestra at Bournemouth. Mother was proud of her children's abilities, but she kept our feet on the ground and poured cold water on Percy's idea. Music, she held, was grand for a hobby but not reliable for a lifetime's work. So each of us was set to learn a trade. Percy and I learnt tailoring and Frank, an apprentice on the railway, became a fitter.

But Percy got very restless at home and was always having rows with Father about the late hours he kept. Both parents had a very lively fear of bad company, drinking and gambling and this led to restrictions which irked Percy and Kate as they passed out of their teens. Percy made many friends of both sexes over at Moreton Pinkney and some we knew were inveterate gamblers. He liked company and there he was one of a lively gang of young folk not bound by the conventions of chapel folk. The uneasiness over his friends galled him and he wanted to get away. When war started in South Africa he wanted to join the army but so much cold water was applied that he could never get up his courage sufficiently to break away.

At last he left home for London to work for a German tailor in Gresham Street and live with Aunt Mary at Leyton. That was a comfort for the old folk. He couldn't go far wrong there, for Aunt Mary was bound to influence him for good. It was the end of playing at dances. Instead he joined the chapel orchestra and found friends there in musical circles.

Whilst the older ones were fretting to be away from home, we younger ones were still at school. When I was eleven, the first day of the twentieth century was heralded by Church and Press with terrific ballyhoo. In their several ways they set out to impress the public that this was the most important day we were ever likely to see. Like Halley's Comet, you were likely to see only one in your lifetime; to see two you would have to live over a hundred years.

I don't remember much about 1900 but I do see that the school log-book records that, 'On July 2nd, 1900 Sydney, Maude and Frank Tyrrell left school at 3.15 this afternoon on account of chapel anniversary tea.'

Although I cannot remember that day, I know we did not like the dressing-up in our Sunday clothes but we did like the tea. I know what we had for tea that day, for the tables, the thick crockery and the eatables were the same for many, many years. Large plates of brown and white bread and butter, currant and seed or spiced plain cake, in abundance. At home we were allowed to eat as much bread and butter with jam as we liked, but only one slice of cake. It was a substantial wedge out of a large round cake, but, no matter how nice it was, it was limited.

So it was a nice change to have a real good tuck-in of cake, and not too much bread and butter. Of course we always had to start the meal with bread and butter, even at tea meetings. That I understand is a sure sign that we are civilised and not like the lesser breeds without the law.

When a scholar was absent, the master often asked the class, 'Does anyone know why so-and-so is not here?' Youngsters are seldom stumped for an answer; if they don't know, they invent a reason. But I emphatically refute the entry: 'Sydney was away helping his father rabbiting.' No doubt I was absent that day, but my father knew better than to take me on that job. My sympathies were on the side of the rabbits; I should have bungled any job he'd set me so badly that the rabbits would have escaped. I don't remember him going rabbiting, but I believe before my time he occasionally had a go with Tomlin and Ted Higham at Lawn Hill. He was a law-abiding man, but had a soft spot in his heart for men who went poaching and, I believe, at times he bought a rabbit cheap and asked no questions.

I can remember being told of the time when the elder three Tyrrells slipped off down to the fields instead of returning to school after the dinner-time break. Hearing the church clock strike and thinking it was four o'clock they trooped back home, but really it was only three o'clock. 'Hello, why are you home so early?' Mother asked them, and a very painful situation developed as they'd no convincing answer ready. Another incident Mother often related was how after long scheming and saving she had taken the two elder children to London for a few days' holiday; buying there very cheap materials to make up for new clothing. On her return the unpacking was done, and the materials laid out on one of the beds. Later on, hearing mysterious sounds coming from the room she rushed upstairs to find Kate sitting on the bed with a broken bottle of hat dye in her hand, the contents sprinkled over the materials and counterpane. 'I sat down and cried,' Mother said. Whether Kate was smacked we were never told; maybe it was too severe a blow to be eased by smacking a naughty child.

Even if my memories of 1900 are blurred I certainly recall 1st January 1901, for that day Agnes was married. I was twelve at the time and remember well that she was married at Marlborough Road, Banbury. Our chapel was not licensed then for weddings and a church wedding with Chapman officiating was un-thinkable.

Agnes had met Jim Gardner when he was Gostick's baker, but now he was working in Northampton. Jim was to come by the evening train the day before and go with us in the morning to Banbury. The train went along the line at the usual time but no Jim arrived. There was consternation at home. Agnes was near tears; what could have happened to keep Jim at Northampton? We all went to the Watchnight Service at chapel but were so anxious that I'm afraid no spiritual uplift came to dispel the doubts and fears present in our minds. Poor Agnes had a bad night and Father and Mother were very uneasy, though I'm pretty sure it did not keep Father awake. Next morning Percy went to meet the first train at Moreton station on his bicycle. In half an hour he was home with the welcome news that Jim had come and was walking here as fast as he could. At once we all set out for Banbury in Herbert's wagonette, with Jim and Percy to follow by train from Woodford. The previous evening Jim had missed the train. He made himself as inconspicuous as possible on his way back to his lodging for everyone round knew he was off to be married that day. Jim had no desire to be raffled by his friends or asked awkward questions by his customers. He and Percy got to Banbury just in time for the ceremony that began a happy partnership which lasted over sixty years.

The year of the wedding was our parents' silver wedding anniversary. We all donned our Sunday best and drove to

Northampton in Herbert's wagonette to have a photograph taken. The elder three children gave them a silver teapot, and I a pair of silver sugar-tongs. We young 'uns look very solemn, but Kate looks to me as if she'd just had a row with Mother; she often got into hot water.

The next year the first grandchild arrived. Olive Kathleen was received with great rejoicing at the Red House, for now there were four generations. Our parents both endorsed the passage in Proverbs: 'Children's children are the glory of old men', and Father often quoted, 'Blessed is the man that hath his quiver full'. He, like the Israelites of old, believed that a family is a sure sign of the approval of the Almighty.

Years before Agnes had left home and become an assistant in a drapery store in St Paul's Churchyard, then gone to a shop in Northampton. When the Red House was built and she heard Mother was having a drapery shop she wrote home proposing she should come home and look after the shop so Mother could get on with the housework. The kind offer met with a speedy rebuff; she was told to stay where she was: Mother was quite capable of managing the shop without her help.

Kate was the next one to be married. She and Jack Harris were united in 1904. This time everything went off happily according to plan, so I've nothing out of the ordinary to record.

But I do remember Percy's wedding in 1909, for it's the one and only occasion I've worn a top hat. At the time Percy was working for Mr Schadler, a German tailor who had first learnt his trade in Berlin and then worked in Paris before he settled in London. Percy had a good chance of taking over the business when he retired (which he did and carried on until he was bombed out in 1942 when he retired). Anyway, in 1909 Percy married Harriet Worsell, the elder daughter of old friends of Grandma Carey at Redhill. Harriet's father had started life as a bricklayer, but he married an ambitious wife and under her guidance and encouragement he had started in the building trade and had prospered. He had three daughters and a son and these three daughters bullied and badgered their poor father to wear a morning coat and top hat when he gave Harriet away. For once their cajoling failed: their father dug his heels in and they had to be satisfied with his lounge suit and bowler hat on the great day. But Percy wore a morning coat and top hat and, as I was best man, I had to don the same garb. The black morning suit and striped trousers were my own, the hat Percy hired or borrowed for me. In his shop I had to practise putting it on my head; for if you get it too near the eyebrows it looks daft, if too far up the forehead it looks as if you have had too much to drink. I only hope I had it on at the right angle at the critical times that day, going to and coming from the church, but I remember I was jolly glad when I could part with it for good. Percy could wear one with dignity and I'm sure Frank would have looked A1 in one, but not yours truly; I'm not cut out that way.

Chapter 9

At work

After Agnes had been married and just before Kate's wedding, I left school. I was fourteen and a half at the time and I brought away about as much knowledge as Father did when he left at nine: the ability to read and write and do simple arithmetic. Those years I spent at school had not been a good period in the school's history; I always think that Agnes, Percy and Kate were much more fortunate. Their master was Andrews, one of the best men ever to serve at Eydon. He left for Byfield soon after I started school. There he spent the rest of his life and there he will be long remembered as an ideal schoolmaster.

During my time we had four masters. They came and very soon decided not to stay, the result being that they had very little interest in the school and their unfortunate pupils. Maybe the parson, Chapman, had something to do with it, for he would appoint them and they would have to fit in with his plans and schemes.

The only prize I ever won was for knowledge of scripture, but as Kate had won five and Percy and Addie two each, that brought me very little glory at home. When I took the book home it only reminded Mother how Kate ought to have had one every year she was at school. But the parson got tired of Kate always being at the top, so they marked her low to give some of the others a chance.

As I had not shown any special aptitude or ability, and no one particularly wanted my services, I left to help Father in the business. When a customer ordered a suit he would be shown patterns of cloths, each bearing a number and price, so arranged that one had to know the code. When the order was booked we would send for the exact length of cloth required. The village carrier brought parcels from Banbury, the merchants there being Stutterd and Pearce. The woollen merchants at Northampton were Quakers named Blunsom and Harris. Their parcels came to Moreton station and we had to fetch them. This was always a job for the boy.

Before my time Percy often went the two miles across the fields for a parcel before he went to school at nine o'clock. He says he used to go at a jog trot and when he reached the stiles he vaulted over. When he got back, Father would say to him, 'My word, boy, you didn't let the grass grow under your feet.'

When it became my job to fetch the parcels, I used the footpath only a few times for I was soon provided with a bicycle, one with solid rubber tyres, called cushion tyres. What an accomplishment it was to be able to ride a bicycle! Only a few venturesome young people were riders and we felt we were joining the élite. To learn, one needed a very active friend to run alongside holding on to the saddle and so keeping the rider upright. The art of balancing was slowly learnt and if the rider could get on, ride and dismount without a fall in about a week it was considered good going.

Everyone wore black clothes at funerals in those days and a death would bring in orders that meant long hours in the workroom to get the clothes made in time for the funeral. I have worked till one o'clock in the morning, then gone to bed for a spell and been back at work before six to get a rush order completed.

The quickest way to get the cloth at these times was for me to cycle to Banbury and bring it back; that took a little over two hours. Most of the cloth came from Northampton and I could go there by train on market days for 1s. 4½d. return; on other days it was 2s. 9d. I liked those trips to Northampton, for there was a change at Blisworth and just this side of Northampton the railway ran close by the Hunsbury Hill iron furnace. It was a thrilling sight to me, with the flames leaping upward from the great towers on a dark night and the glow visible for miles around.

From the time I left school I did all Father's writing, business and private, and the knowledge of our financial position made me very uncomfortable.

We were not exceptional, for at the time many village trades-people were in the same position; they bought and sold to one another for years without any settlement. The merchants and wholesalers in the towns were very long-suffering and patient. They knew whom they could trust and, as long as they received some cash from time to time, the supply of goods was maintained.

The blacksmith at Boddington killed a pig each year and each year the hams were sent to Hoods, the Banbury ironmongers, to reduce his debt. Thus the hams were turned into iron and nails, so the cycle of trade turned.

As we were always pressed for money and bills were never paid, we had very little ready cash in hand. Father made sure that the family ate well, however, by renting a plot of land – one-third of an acre for 5s. It was cheap but it was heavy ground and hard to work. He also turned the outbuildings at the back of the house to good use. Nearest to the house was the wash-house, then the chaff-house and the hovel, and over all ran a hayloft. The hovel just had room for four cows to stand for milking. When Father decided to give up cows he divided the hovel with a wooden partition to make a stable and room for the trap along-side and bought a pony. He bargained with Norman Flowers to break the pony into harness for three guineas. Norman came of a broken-down farming family that for generations had farmed

Tunningham, but now they had neither land nor money. Instead they had great pride that made it difficult for them to settle to regular work. Norman was glad of the job. This was a contract and, after all, breaking in horses was a gentlemanly sort of job.

The pony was christened Kit; she was a Welsh mare, about twelve hands high, brown in colour, with a white spot on her forehead. She was playing with other ponies in a Sulgrave field; she had never been handled by man and was as wild as an eagle. Norman and his helpers had a tough job to get her cornered and a halter on her; when she found she could not escape she kicked and reared in her panic. Norman told us that as a last resort, when she reared he pulled her backwards so that she fell on her back; that quietened her so she was little trouble afterwards.

He brought her home and bedded her down in the stable. The next day he started to give her a mouth. That was the expression he used: he meant a mouth tender enough to be controlled by a bit when she was in harness. First he put a girth round her body and a headstall on her head that held a bit in her mouth; reins ran from the bit to the girth, tight reins that held her head as if in a vice.

The bit was a special one used only for the breaking-in period. It contained several half-loose tags called keys, put there for the express purpose of irritating the poor animal. Poor Kit stood for three or four hours, champing away all the time at those cruel keys. This was continued for several days till her mouth was raw and bleeding, and then she was given a day or two to recover. Then Norman took her out with a plain bit in her mouth and she was soon taught to obey the reins. He had her on a long rein in a field and she was lunged; that is, she was made to trot round him in a circle till she tired. Then she was walked for miles wearing a full set of harness before she was put between the shafts of a trap. The whole process took about a fortnight; by that time Norman considered her safe on the roads. 'As safe as the Bank of England,' he declared.

Father had very little trouble with her, but it was necessary to be on the alert for she was nervous and when she shied she moved like lightning. I soon taught her to like a lump of sugar, for it was a handy lure when I had to catch her in the field. She would nose round my pockets feeling for the sugar; then I would hold a piece between my fingers so that she could not quickly take it, on purpose to feel her silky nose as she strove to get the sugar between her lips. It was my job to fetch her from the field when she was needed for a journey and take her back when the work was done. I hated the breaking-in of Kit for I felt it need not have been such a cruel business, but that was past and Kit and I were settling down nicely when another jar came my way.

At breakfast-time one day Father told me to fetch Kit home, 'for Jack Kilby is coming to dock her'. Kilby was the local veterinary surgeon living at Middleton Cheney. When he arrived Father went into the stable and put a halter on Kit and held her, while Kilby cut her tail with what looked like a pair of garden shears, with short curved blades. He had to use considerable pressure and poor Kit shook and trembled with the pain. Before this began Mother had been given an iron to heat in the kitchen fire. It was a circle of about two inches fixed in a wooden handle. When this was red hot I had to bring it to Kilby and he held it on the cut end of the tail to seal it and stop the bleeding. It was a long, long time before I lost the smell of burning flesh, and I shall never forget Kit's bleeding mouth or the docking of her tail. I hated the matter-of-fact way Father had instituted the proceedings, for docking horses' tails was a fashion that was fading out.

Soon I was able to ride her to and from the field, and to encourage me Father bought a saddle which I used occasionally. I never became a decent rider for I never felt safe on her back, although my long legs were not very far from the ground. I was riding her in the field when a storm came on; a sudden clap of thunder just above us made her jump. One moment I was on her back, the next I hit the ground with the back of my head. My word, it was hard! For a moment I thought I was done for; I literally saw stars and wasn't sure if I was in this world or the next.

What a thrill it was the first time I made Kit gallop in the field! She moved so easily and so gracefully that it was like sitting in a rocking-chair. Later on I put her at the stream in New Zealand and she jumped it beautifully; it was an exhilarating moment and an eye-opener for me. It was all very nice, but Kit never let me think for long that I was master, for something would happen to dispel any illusion of that sort. Riding her home from Hinton I very carelessly failed to see a train that rumbled over the bridge just as we were underneath. She went like a bullet from a gun up the hill to Farndon Gap. By the mercy of providence I did not fall off and she steadied up at the top of the hill, so we arrived home none the worse. The experience gave me a nasty jar; the feeling that for a moment or two I was absolutely helpless, and it made me watch more carefully for trains afterwards.

Usually I could walk up to Kit in the field with a lump of sugar in my left hand and, while she was taking it, get hold of her forelock with the other hand, then slip the halter over her head. Sometimes she'd take the sugar and give me the slip, then I'd try her with a few oats in a bowl. She couldn't grab them like a piece of sugar. Sometimes when she was in the humour both baits would fail to secure her; then the only thing was to drive her into a corner. Often when we were in a hurry and she played that game it was very vexing for it could play havoc with all our arrangements at home. Father and I were cornering Kit on one of these occasions, shooing her with outstretched arms towards the corner where we hoped to secure her. We thought we were getting on well and nearly in the corner when Kit made a dash. I rushed to cut off her escape, but like lightning she dodged and slipped between us. She jumped the brook like a steeplechaser; I burst out laughing, to Father's great indignation. 'What a fool

you are, Syd,' he started off. It has often been my misfortune in
life to laugh in the wrong place and land in hot water.

To make the catching of Kit easier Father bought a headstall
for her to wear in the field. This was a great help for it was
something solid to get hold of, instead of that slippery tuft of
hair between her eyes.

One hot summer we were haymaking in the field. Arthur
Herbert had cut the grass with his machine, and Father, I and
someone else I forget had turned the swarths with wooden hand-
rakes. A couple of hours at that job and my left hand was
blistered and the dry hard ground soon made my feet ache. So
when we had turned it all I suggested we should sit in the shade
and let the sun get on with the job of making hay. Father's face
went red, 'You talk like a fool,' he replied. 'I never heard of such
a thing, sitting down in a hayfield indeed,' he snorted. So we had
to go round again with forks, shaking out where the grass lay
thick, just as they did in the days the grass was cut with scythes.

Henry Peck always helped us get the hay. We did all the
preliminary work, then he came with old Crockwell in the cart
and his boy to help us carry and rick the hay. In return, when his
was ready for carrying, we went and helped him get it in a rick.

Building a rick of loose slippery hay is a skilled job and Henry
fancied himself on top of a rick. 'Keep the middle full,' he kept
on saying to whoever was pitching the hay up to him. They
reckoned he'd had too much to drink the day our rick fell over.
It was seven or eight foot high at the time. He had just come down
the ladder and, as the cart was moved away, the rick slipped over.
Evidently it was leaning against the cart. What a mess it was, and
what a job to make a rick out of that heap of hay. The tale went
round the village, of course, and many had a laugh at Henry's
expense when they heard how the rick he was building fell over.

The part I appreciated most in those haymaking days was
tea-time: sitting in a circle, eating rock cakes faintly flavoured
with ham fat, and drinking hot sweet tea. It was always astonish-

ing when one set a cup of tea down how many little creatures, like grasshoppers, would drown in it, making much skimming with a spoon necessary. At this season of the year Mother always put a hefty piece of ham on the table and the fat that boiled out was used in cooking, so rock cakes came in for a share.

When we shut the field up at the end of April for mowing, Kit would be boarded out in one of Henry's fields, at a charge of about 2s. 6d. a week.

And now it is time we got back to the yard at home, where we kept a few fowls, generally Buff Orpingtons, a fine handsome breed when they are in full feather. They roosted under the back steps till they were three or four years old; by that time their eggs were few and far between, so their days were numbered. An adult could not squeeze through the low door into the roost so it fell to my lot to catch the unfortunate hen sentenced to appear on our dinner-table. When I had secured the bird Father would tie her legs together and hang her on a nail in the hovel beam. Then he'd take his pocket knife out of his pocket and, holding her head with one hand, pierce the neck with his knife. Soon it was all over, the bird ceased fluttering, and my job was to get a bucket of water and swill the blood down the drain. The thatched roof of the hovel and the beam went about 1935, but the drain is still there. It takes rain-water only nowadays into an ancient stone drain.

Each spring a small pig would be housed in the sty and made comfortable with plenty of straw. By the time we dug maincrop potatoes it would have grown and be eating two buckets of potatoes and toppings each day. All the small potatoes and any diseased, with some swedes, were washed and boiled in the copper. Often it was my job to wash and boil the pig's food; then, when it was cooked, put it in a tub and mash it. For the last two months of the pig's life, barley meal was used instead of toppings to finish the fattening process.

If the pig had reached about three hundred pounds in weight by early December, Father would say, 'We'll have the pig in the

house, so there is some pig meat for Christmas.' Mother was glad
to have the extra work done before she got very busy in the shop.
John Howard, the butcher, would be called in, a supply of
wheat straw brought home, the copper filled with water and the
fire lit. John was a very useful man in the village: a good singer
and cricketer, he mended our clocks and watches and killed the
pigs, and he did those things and others, all in the most gentlemanly sort of way.

With a clumsy rough butcher there would be men shouting
and a pig squealing for no end of a time so that all the village
would know what was going on, and the boys would come
from all directions to see the gory spectacle. But John was an
artist at his job. Of course he could not do it without a squeal,
but it was not prolonged and there was no shouting. With his
rope and slip knot all ready he would go into the sty. He'd talk
to the pig and stroke him till they were on good terms, for pigs
love being rubbed. Very gently, John would dangle the noose
by the pig's nose and before you could say Jack Robinson the
rope was in the pig's mouth. The sty door would be opened and
the pig would walk out, John by his side, and they'd quietly walk
up the garden path and John would steer him into the yard
towards the hovel and drain. There he slipped the rope over a
nail on the beam, then pulled till he raised the pig's head. The
rope was given an extra turn round the nail and given to me to
hold. Father was at the other end, holding the pig's tail. John put
a wad of straw on the ground and knelt on it, knife in hand; the
pig gave a gasp and a stream of blood trickled down towards the
drain. Soon it was all over; the pig flopped over and died.

While Father and John got ready for the burning my job was
to gather all the bloodstained straw and take it to the manure
heap in the garden. Then with buckets of water and the yard
broom I had to swill all the blood down the drain; a job I did
with unusual alacrity, for I always heaved a sigh of relief when
the last trace of blood disappeared.

The pig was set up in a crouching position on a bed of straw, then straw was sprinkled lightly till there was quite a heap. When a match was applied there was a lovely blaze for a few minutes; this burnt the hair on the pig's back. The pig had to be moved several times, and more straw burnt before all the hair was cleared. In about an hour the job was done for the day and the pig was hanging by his jaw in the dairy to set for about twenty-four hours. The next day John came and cut up the carcass into hams, sides and numerous smaller joints.

The performance in the yard always attracted a group of boys, for all boys love a fire and many seemed to enjoy seeing the pig killed.

Frank's great friend, Fred Kench, was very friendly with John Howard; he spent hours on Saturdays helping John during the killing season. Frank and Fred were once talking on the subject, discussing the pros and cons, and Frank defined his attitude thus, 'I don't like it, but I stand it.' For once, Frank and I saw eye to eye. I hated it and also Father's apparent indifference to the suffering entailed, whether it was a pig or an old hen. He went down considerably in my opinion.

I remember how I used to be surprised at myself, for very soon after the killing episode I would be enjoying the good things that Mother put on our table. For about three weeks we lived on what Father called 'the fat of the land'. He would smack his lips over the pork pie and say, 'This is the best pig we ever had.' Sure enough, one of us would reply, 'Why, you said that last year.' 'Ah well,' he'd say, 'it's true all the same.'

The pig-killing made Mother a lot of extra work, for she prided herself on making the best of everything. Only those who have seen a pig opened and cut up know how many bits and pieces there are inside. Ours were from 280 lbs. to 320 lbs. in weight. They have to be that weight we reckoned if you want first-rate bacon and ham. Of course the meat in a pig that size is very fat; that can't be helped if you want mature meat, fully flavoured.

The day the pig-killing took place the copper in the wash-house was heated and Mother and Sally set to to clean the chitterlings. Some of these were fried with bacon and eaten for breakfast and some made into sausages. A great slab of pure fat, called the lief, twenty to thirty pounds in weight, was cut into small pieces and melted in the largest saucepan. This was poured into basins and, when cold, became lard that lasted for cooking most of the winter. The lights (lungs) were boiled, chopped up and mixed with meat and liver for faggots.

Mother's special pride were her pork pies, for she raised these by hand, a slow and tedious job. Some of our friends made theirs in cake tins; she thought that a very lazy way, tantamount to an acknowledgement of incompetence in a housewife. Seven or eight were made and taken to the bakehouse to be slowly cooked for some hours. One was always posted to Aunt Mary and some sent to friends here; they sent us a pie when their pig was killed.

Looking after the pig or the pony, fetching and carrying on foot or on my bike – all of this made a good change from sitting indoors learning the trade from Father. But as he got older I had to do more work inside. When I first joined Father to learn tailoring in 1903 he seemed stout and vigorous, although he had often been laid up with bronchitis during the winter season and had developed a large goitre in his neck. The goitre and the bronchitis so impeded his breathing that any effort caused him to puff and blow like a walrus rising out of the water. But he'd been short of breath and had had a hacking cough to clear his throat of phlegm ever since I could remember. You could always hear him coming: the cough always heralded his approach and there were times we were glad to know just where he was. His neck was so large, linen collars had to be specially made for him, size $18\frac{1}{2}$; even then occasionally Mother had to put loops on them to give him an extra inch. His shirts were always made by Mother, for she would have scorned the idea of her Joe wearing a ready-made one.

But by about 1908 his health began to fail and he lost weight rapidly. Dr Hays was called in; he put Father on a strict diet, one that went very hard with him, but Mother kept him to it very strictly. The medicine and diet seemed to do him no good at all, and he appeared to be fading away. Everybody thought the trouble was cancer; we believe the doctor thought so, but he never said so.

Mother was worried, and at last Dr Hays, at his wit's end, suggested that another doctor should be consulted. The great doctor in this area at the time was Dr Buzzard of Northampton, who had a wonderful reputation. Arrangements were made for a consultation and soon Mother went with Father to see him.

In his consulting room Dr Buzzard made Father bend and twist his body in all directions, while he handled him somewhat roughly, poking fingers under poor Father's ribs. When the examination was over Dr Buzzard shook his head and told Mother dieting was no good, but that she should let Father have just what he liked and make him as comfortable as possible for the rest of his life. Mother asked, 'Isn't an operation possible?' and the doctor said, 'No, it is a growth on the bladder.'

And so they came home and faced up to the worst; Father was going to die and nothing could be done about it. Everybody thought his days were numbered, and he looked like it, for he had lost so much flesh his clothes hung on him like sacks. But instead of getting worse he held his own and soon the doctor suggested a complete change would do him good and sea air might be very helpful.

And so, for the first time in their lives, Father and Mother went off for a fortnight's holiday at Bournemouth. Mother had a wonderful capacity for enjoyment; to have leisure and meals prepared was quite a novel experience. The weather was very kind to them, so they let the shadow remain in the background and made the most of Bournemouth; for both firmly believed, 'Sufficient unto the day is the evil thereof.'

What a lot we heard about Bournemouth when they returned home! Mother took it all in, the distances the trams ran, the fishing, Poole Harbour and so forth. We heard all about it, and she told it to the travellers who called for orders and the preachers who came to tea; we heard it so many times that we learnt the geography of that bit of the coast better than any other.

The following year we had two general elections, and Lloyd George was on the warpath creating terrific excitement. I sometimes wonder if that had anything to do with a decided improvement in Father's health. For he slowly improved; he was never first-rate, but he deceived us all by living another twenty-one years. Dr Hays called him a walking miracle and we were reminded that creaking gates hang for many a long day. Father remembered that when he was bending in Dr Buzzard's consulting room he felt something break or give way internally. We firmly believe that something was broken and dispersed and this brought about a very decided improvement in his health.

My firm opinion is that much of Father's ill-health was caused by bolting his food, as if he was in a race and meant to win. I have already recorded my great grandmother, Patience Smith's, maxim: 'quick at eating, quick at work'; Father got into the habit when a boy in the Smith household.

We youngsters noticed that when we had boiled eggs for breakfast, Father ate two before we had eaten our one. At dinner-time he carved the joint and served each one, so that he was the last to start eating, yet his plate was always empty first. Many a time he said, 'Look at my plate, I've finished,' but we never tried to beat him, I'm glad to say.

At the time Father was ill Maude was still at school in Eydon, Frank was at a very up-to-date new council school at Byfield and I was trying to do as much of Father's work as possible. But it was felt that I needed more experience if I was to take over the business so I was sent off to London to learn cutting, a very important part of the tailor's craft. I attended a school in Gerrard Street and lived with Aunt Mary at Leytonstone, travelling each day with Percy up to the City. After a month there I returned home and was then able to take a more responsible part in the business, for Father was able to work only occasionally.

Maude soon became a teacher, graded as 'uncertificated', and when Frank was fourteen he left school and became an apprentice fitter in the locomotive department at Woodford. The first day Frank set out very spick and span in new blue overalls, but when he came home Mother held up her hands in dismay. He looked as if he'd been rolled in oil and grease; he was smothered. It is quite likely he had, for the loco at Woodford had the reputation of being a rough shop in those days. 'I've never handled such washing in my life,' Mother declared, and Sally, her faithful helper, was for once in her life at her wit's end to get Frank's overalls clean. Mother consulted some of the railwaymen's wives and the upshot was that she bought a tub and a dolly, a wooden implement worked by hand and having the same effect as the agitator of a modern washing-machine. So Frank's overalls soon lost the new look, but it wasn't very long before he often came home at the end of the day reasonably clean.

The autumn after Frank started work we decided to have a cycle-camping holiday, for we were both very fond of cycling. With an article in the *Boys' Own Paper* to guide me, I set to work with the sewing-machine. Using a heavy linen I made a tent six foot by five foot and Frank made jointed poles and tent pegs. Our kettle, frying-pan and billy tin were all made of tin for lightness, so that with two blankets, ground sheet and a few spare clothes our total load was thirty-four pounds. This we divided, and packed on our front and back carriers.

We went through Stratford, Gloucester and Monmouth to

Abergavenny, then north through the Black Mountains and home through Hereford and Worcester: about three hundred miles in ten days. We camped at Apperley, near Tewkesbury, by the side of the Severn, with only a narrow belt of osiers between our tent and the river. From a nearby house we were able to hire a boat; we did not tell them we'd never been in a rowing-boat, but did take the precaution of waiting till there was no one in sight before we embarked. It was a good thing for us that the river was wide for our first trip, and that we had it all to ourselves; had there been spectators it would have been a humiliating experience. We tried rowing together, but the boat corkscrewed from side to side; then we tried rowing singly, but that wasn't much better, as we just couldn't keep a straight course. All we learnt that day was that it isn't as easy to row a boat as it looks. We did improve later on and we liked the river there so much we went the next year with Fred, for a bank-holiday weekend.

It was spring, and the first night one sleeps on the ground in a tent sleep is bound to be broken with the newness of the dawn chorus, when every bird near and far away twitters and chirps before the real business of the day begins. There were some birds by the side of the river that we never remember hearing at home – corncrakes. Their raucous calls came from near and far away, for the harsh notes carried in the stillness of the morning with amazing clarity. We had the lovely river nearly to ourselves; very occasionally a tug towing two or three barges would go towards Gloucester. The only small boat we saw was that of two men fishing with a net. Their fish looked so nice we bought several and cooked them for our supper. It was not a success, for there was a nasty earthy taste to those fish that we did not appreciate. We know now that freshwater fish need very careful preparation and cooking if they are to be good eating.

We did all our cooking on a wood fire, gypsy fashion, with the kettle hung above it. By the time the kettle boiled the smoke would be gone and the fire would be a heap of red-hot cinders, just right for a frying-pan and dixie of potatoes. The evening meal was always our main meal. In the morning we boiled the kettle for a drink and at midday we ate a snack by the roadside. Towards evening we bought something in the meat line to fry for supper and I remember calling at a butcher's shop near Gloucester and asking for sausages. They were sold out and the butcher suggested ham, so he cut a thick slice across a home-cured ham and I fried it. Frank and I were tired and hungry, but not too tired to enjoy that delicious fried ham and boiled potatoes as we sat by the fire in the fading light of an August evening.

In the Forest of Dean we camped under the oaks planted when England was at war with Napoleon, with the idea that England would need lots of oak to build ships of war. We were quite close to the Speech House and there we saw small coal mines being worked, some by only three or four men.

For the first time in our lives we encountered real hills, of two or three miles' steady climbing. We rode the easier gradients and walked up the steeper parts pushing our heavy bicycles – at those times we realised how heavy they were. It was hard work but sure enough we had our reward every time, for the uphill road was sure to be followed by a long stretch of freewheeling with brakes hard on. It was on an uphill stretch that we had a tiff, caused by Frank's complaint: 'I don't know what you wanted to come this way for, among these blooming great hills.' Of course I defended myself: 'If you'd taken more interest in the map, you would have known there'd be some big hills on the way.' The squabble ended when we reached the top and a roadside house that sold drinks; a rest and a drink with the prospect of a down-hill ride restored amicable relations.

It was a cheap holiday as we paid nothing for camping sites or firewood, and the boat on the river cost only 1s. or so. Our food cost just about 2s. a day and we lived well at that.

Chapter 10

War

Cycling round the countryside and working in London had made me restless. By 1912, like Percy years before, I had become very dissatisfied with the situation at home. I felt that I needed experience in good-class trade and that could be gained only by going away from home. I felt sure many of our methods and practices were quite out of date. Father had gone in for very cheap work and I felt that in that line of business the factories could beat us any day. There are several different methods of making the pockets in a man's suit, and I found that not one of our methods would have been tolerated in any good-class trade.

My parents tried hard to squash the idea, since they held quite rightly that Father's health was so poor that I was needed at home. I took the line that in the long run it would be for the good of the business if I were more up to date and able to cater for the ladies' trade. I was determined to go, so we took on Ralph Cleaver as apprentice. He was Tommy Cleaver's youngest boy and brother of Jumbo. During the war he joined up and was killed in France.

That was over half a century ago and I feel that it was one of the wisest and best steps I have ever taken. To go among complete strangers where no one knows you or your family is to stand on your own feet, and the experience of finding work and a home to shelter him is valuable experience for any youngster. I hold no brief for boys staying at home to help Father in his business. It is a short-sighted policy that seldom brings lasting good to any of the folk concerned. I answered an advertisement and went to Dunstable to work for Ernest Stebbings, a good ladies' tailor.

The first Sunday I went to the Wesleyan Chapel in the square; there I received a hearty welcome and soon found friends among the young people. It was a church that was very much alive and the fine set of buildings was a hive of activity on Sundays and in the evenings during the week. The much-loved and respected central figure was a saintly old gentleman in the hat trade named Weatherill. It was through his influence and guidance that I became a member of the church. We Wesleyans have no ceremony of confirmation whereby youngsters become members of the church at a certain age. Usually a minister or class leader would ask boys and girls in their teens to become members if they showed some desire for what we called 'good things'. Should the young folk show desire only for the wordly pleasures of life then they would not be pressed to become members.

I spent six months in Dunstable working as an improver, then went on to Epsom as a fully-fledged journeyman tailor. There I did piecework in a shop with a dozen tailors, and there I met for the first time a 'tramping tailor', known as Archibald. He came to work immaculate in a black-tailed coat and striped trousers, and the first thing he did in the workshop was to take them off and don a dilapidated outfit for work. Sitting cross-legged on a bench does not improve the hang of a nice pair of trousers. At that period there were many tailors like Archibald who never settled down for long, but wandered round the country, working a few weeks here and a few weeks there and walking from town to town. Some like Archibald had regular circuits: the hunting shires for the winter trade, racing towns in the spring and seaside resorts for the summer season.

All business was closed on Derby Day, so that we with the rest of Epsom folk could go and see the races. Of course I went too. It was my first race meeting and the year was 1913. I was at Tattenham Corner on the inside rails when the horses came tearing past. My eyes followed them down the course; then when I looked round there was a horse just in front getting on his feet and a jockey and a woman on the ground. Later we learnt that the woman was a suffragette and to draw attention to the Votes for Women campaign, she'd ducked under the rails and run into the racing horses. A few days later she died in Epsom Hospital, but the jockey recovered.

I believe racing folk look on this as the most sensational Derby, for after this accident the first horse home, Craganour, was disqualified for 'barring and boring' and the prize was given to the second horse, Aboyer. It was a thrilling experience to see that bunch of horses go thundering past, with the jockeys perched on their backs looking more like monkeys than men. What a pity it is that horse-racing or any other sport has become so commercialised by big money and the gambling fraternity.

By the end of June work was falling off at Epsom, so I packed up my clothes and asked my landlady to send them on by rail when I could give an address. Then I set off on my cycle for the coast, through Leatherhead and Dorking, calling on some of the tailors on the way in my quest for a job. At Littlehampton I found work with Findley's, a firm busy all the year round, and lodgings with Mrs Brown, a widow, in one of the back streets.

During August her house was filled to overflowing with visitors on holiday, and we nearly slept on the proverbial clothes-line. I believe Mrs Brown slept in the scullery, but as she was last to go to bed and first to rise in the morning it may have been in the passage to the front door. Twice a week there were very cheap day trips from London; these brought crowds of folk to visit our visitors and to add to the congestion. Some whom I am glad to have met were active members of the suffragette movement and workers in the East End of London. Their friend and leader was George Lansbury, that rare combination of politician and saint. One lady in the party was a trade-union organiser who was striving to get the women in the tobacco and cigarette factories into a trade union. One of the men worked with the building staff employed at Westminster Abbey. They found I was interested in their work so we spent hours on the sea front discussing the situation.

They roundly accused us folk within the churches of taking great care that we did not fall into the pit of poverty, rather than taking steps to prevent our weaker brethren falling. They held that the only hope for the future was socialism and that the churches were failing because they did not preach and teach socialism as the practical expression of the Christian gospel. They held that we must take the Sermon on the Mount literally, that the Master's precepts must be taken as commands by his followers, without any ifs or buts.

I was in their company only a few days, but that brief encounter left an influence on my mind that the ensuing years have never erased. At the time of the free trade and fiscal reform controversy I had imbibed some knowledge of political economy. Later I'd been influenced towards socialism by John Ruskin's books and Robert Blatchford's pamphlets. The result of this inoculation of ideas and theories was bound to lead me away from the family allegiance to liberalism.

That autumn I left Littlehampton and came home. I felt much more competent to work up a better-class trade. But no one appeared to be interested in my religious and political ideas. Mother ended the discussion by quoting the old saw, 'There's a lot of difference between staring and going mad.' That was in 1913, the year when the army manœuvres brought the King to Eydon, when clouds dark and menacing were gathering over Europe.

They were by far the largest army manœuvres ever to be held in this country, and about fifty thousand men took part. Aeroplanes and dirigible balloons were used for the first time. One army started from the Thames Valley to attack another army holding part of Buckinghamshire and most of this county. The final battle was fought for Sharman's Hill near Byfield. Officers acted as referees: they decided who was killed, wounded or taken prisoner, but as the dead still walked about and the wounded seemed none the worse and had uncommon good appetites, that part was a very confusing business indeed to us. To this day we don't know which army won, but we still remember the to-do it made here at Eydon, when we were in the forefront of the battle.

Khaki-clad soldiers came first in twos and threes. Then we heard big guns and the crack of rifles. Soon they came in small groups across the fields and before long the lanes and roads were chock-full of men and all the paraphernalia of an army on the march. They did not all stop here, but there must have been several thousand for three or four days. Many of the men were dead beat; they just flopped down on the roadside grass and lay there, tired and hungry. We were told they'd moved so fast the ASC wagons with their rations hadn't been able to keep up. We did what we could for them – many a house had a lively tea-party that day. Wells were emptied to water their horses. Never had bakers' and grocers' shops been so busy. The soldiers bought anything eatable and old stocks were cleared in less than no time. Bakers sold out and set to work at once on another batch of bread, which was eaten long before it got cold. Oh, it was a to-do for days! There was so much going on and so much to see that nobody worked if they could help it. Nowadays we down tools and go for a hunt in the winter, but that's nothing to those days when it seemed as if we'd most of the British army camped in our fields.

One morning Ted Coy and Walt Bromfield set off on their bikes to have a look at some big guns in the Big Ground; they were all right and didn't they make us jump when they were fired! While Ted and Walt were having a look round they saw a group of horsemen coming from Canons Ashby. 'It's the King!' one of the gunners remarked. That was enough – they got on their bikes and tore back to Eydon with the news. 'The King's coming! The King's coming!' But His Majesty King George V was here before the news got properly round, so not many people were in the street when, with his escort and royal standard flying, the King came to Eydon.

There was a group of us down at the Post Office. I remember old Ann Hemmings, the nurse. Well, not exactly a nurse; she looked after births and deaths. And there was Henry Peck, the old coachman who had driven dukes and lords in his day and knew a lot about society. Old Jim Gubbins was there, too. He'd been a London policeman and knew the King very well. The King was in khaki uniform and rode a beautiful black horse and looked just like the pictures we'd seen of him. When he came by us old Henry lifted his bowler hat and held it above his head and we took our caps off and stood looking, very quiet like, when old Ann shouts out, 'God bless King George!' The King smiled and held up his hand to old Ann as she stood on her doorstep. I can see her now, with a little black bonnet on her head, and a big coarse apron tied round where her waist ought to have been.

Well, we followed the King and the generals down to the park, and just as he was going through the gate, if young Norah Ward and Mary Webb didn't come tearing out of the park as if the old man himself was after them, and very nearly ran slap into his horse. As I said before, we'd got friendly with some of the soldiers, but this was specially true of some of the girls – they got friendly with some of the lads in a very short time indeed. That morning Norah and Mary went to the park to see their friends. They found everybody on parade – lines and lines of soldiers standing at attention waiting for the King to come and review them. You'd hardly believe it, those girls had no more sense than to go along the lines of soldiers looking for their friends. When Mary found hers she said, 'You be stuck up this morning, what's the matter with you?' I'm told he stood like a graven image, never so much as smiled, but looked as if he wished Mary was a thousand miles away. Then an officer came towards them, gesticulating wildly and very red in the face. 'The King, the King!' he shouted at Mary. Realising they were not wanted there, those madcaps let out a screech and tore off to see what was going on in the street and nearly ran slap into the King at the gate. Well, we saw him review the troops and when it was over and he was leaving the park, old Jim Gubbins shouts out loud, 'Three cheers for the King!' And we gave him three rousers.

Later in the day the King lunched with the generals in a marquee in old John Henry Ivens's field, Long Leys. When the troops were gone and the excitement died down, old John Henry went about telling everybody it wasn't to be called Long Leys any longer, but King's Meadow. I'm sorry to say nobody took any notice of the old boy; he didn't live many more years and the field is Long Leys to this day.

Oh, I must tell you, the Right Hon. Winston Churchill had intended to be at the review that morning, for he started with the King's party. Unfortunately he had a mishap on the way, for his horse lost a shoe. So when he got to the village he enquired if there was a blacksmith here and was directed to old John Humphries. Then-a-days John was getting old and rheumaticky, and it made him puff and blow to bend himself to shoe a horse, but he wouldn't let anybody down if he could help it. So he put a shoe on Winston's horse for him, and when the job was done Winston paid him, got on the horse and off he went to catch up the King's party. I'm sorry I wasn't there to see the horse shod, but I hope he stood nice and quiet, for if he didn't I know he would get a clout on the ribs with old John's hammer and the old boy would holler, 'Stan' still, will you? Stan' still.' I've seen him do it many a time. He didn't care whose horse it was either – if it had been the King's horse he'd have had to stand still or he'd have had a oner from old John.

Well, all this happened a long time ago, but you know we at Eydon are still glad to remember that old Ann Hemmings shouted out loud, 'God bless King George!' and that when Winston wanted a job done, old John Humphries was here to do it and so help him on his way.

The King and Queen were guests of the Spencers at Althorp for several days. That day, they all motored to Canons Ashby where the King mounted his horse, then rode to Eydon and on to Byfield, while the Queen went on in the car to Woodford Hill. There she was seen later in the day sitting on a cushion in the corner of a field. Looking from that field one has a fine panoramic view of the area where the troops were massing for the final battle for Sharman's Hill. That ended the manoeuvres: the men, guns, horses and transports were put on rail at four stations in the district, one being Woodford Halse. At the time it was considered a splendid feat of organisation on the part of the railway staff. Twenty-four special trains were loaded and despatched to various army depots in twenty-four hours. Never before or since has Woodford Halse station known such a hectic day and night.

The wife of our blacksmith, Mrs John Humphries, had been a lady's maid and had lived in stately mansions in her early years before she married John. He read the *Banbury Guardian* each week and she read *Modern Society* from cover to cover. This kept her fully informed of all that went on in the royal family and in high society. She could reel off the pedigrees of the dukes and duchesses, and the names and titles of their families, and she did it with the reverence due to the angelic host and not to ordinary flesh and blood. Mrs John was one of the few who really claimed to obey the catechism precept, 'To order myself lowly and reverently before my betters'. At this time she was recovering from an illness that sad to say had kept her indoors for weeks, but someone had given her the tip that this was a special day, and something special was going to take place. With great effort she had donned her best black silk dress and hat, added such accessories as a long gold chain and brooches, then set out for the street. Will Ward's daughter, Winnie, told me of the incident. She said, 'I was going down the street when I saw Mrs John coming tottering down the lane, trembling with excitement. I gave her my arm to help her and very slowly we walked down to the corner by the Tudor house. There was quite a crowd there, and soon we noticed a gentleman standing by a big car near Tays Close gate. When the review was over His Majesty came riding out of the park followed by a number of officers. Mrs John knew him of course, but not the other gentlemen, so she asked me very excitedly, "Who's that?" Of course I couldn't tell her. I didn't know any more than she did. Evidently the gentleman the other side of the road saw and heard the old lady, for he came across the road to us and said, "Maybe I can help you, Madam. This is the Duke of Connaught," he said, "and that foreign gentleman is the French military attaché – now comes Prince Arthur." And so he named to us the notabilities as they passed by.'

They had no idea who the gentleman was, but afterwards they were told it was the King's secretary, Colonel Arthur Biggs, afterwards Lord Stamfordham. Little did he know how Mrs John would value and cherish for the rest of her life the help he gave her that day.

After this excitement there was endless talk of war at Eydon. We all feared that it would be a grim struggle. There were few illusions, except that we were quite wrong about its duration. So in July 1914 I decided to have a quick holiday on my bicycle while I had the chance. I decided to explore the Cotswolds, lodging with a smallholder in one of the picturesque cottages at Chipping Camden.

It was showery weather and during a downpour I took shelter in a wagon hovel by the roadside. Soon several farm workers came rushing in out of the rain. 'What's the news this morning?' one asked. 'All reservists are being called up,' I replied. 'It's headlines in all the papers.' 'Ha, ha,' they laughed.

'Old Jarge 'ull ha' to goo;' and they looked at a fresh-faced man sitting on the shafts of a cart. Jarge said nothing; he looked as if he did not relish the prospect ahead. I should have liked to know how he fared, for he looked fine and well, so probably he was one of the 'Old Contemptibles' who bore the brunt of the German onslaught in Flanders.

It would all be over by Christmas, we told ourselves, for we knew that although we had only a small army the French had a big one, as well as a line of fortifications that, we were quite sure, would hold up the advance of any army. Our leaders could see we should have to build up a much bigger army speedily, so General Kitchener was put in charge of recruiting. Great coloured posters appeared on all the hoardings: 'Wanted, 100,000 men for the Army, will you be one?'

Frank and Ted Coy were among the first to join up from Eydon a few weeks after the war started. Frank had just entered on the last year of his apprenticeship on the railway. At Northampton he passed a simple trade test, filing a piece of steel square. This enabled him to get into the Royal Engineers, signals section. His training was done at Thetford and Larkhill camp on Salisbury Plain. The first time he came home on leave he was wearing a sloppy suit of blue serge which, if adorned with a few broad arrows, would have made a very good outfit for a convict.

In those early days men joined the army in such numbers that the supply of khaki cloth ran out, so uniforms were made of any available cloth, and even then some men had to wear their own civilian clothes for weeks after joining up. Some of these details are still fresh in my memory after more than fifty years, but much has faded, so this is a very incomplete record of the part Eydon men took in that titanic struggle. During the first year of hostilities twenty-five men actually left Eydon and enlisted in the army and the number rose to forty in the spring of 1918.

The army in 1914 was only partly mechanised. Horses were still used in large numbers and for transport, and there were many

cavalry regiments. Horses were being requisitioned; an official
went round the farms and hunting stables and picked out suitable
horses. The owners had no option in the matter, although they
were paid for the horses. Pettifers had several horses at the time;
the officer chose a young mare and gave instructions for her to be
delivered to the Remount depot at Weedon.

Bill Edden was working for Pettifers. He was a tall, raw-boned
man of about thirty, very slow in his movements and very splay-
footed. He was sent with the mare to Weedon. There he saw
long lines of tents, hundreds of horses and guns, all the paraphernalia of an army preparing for war. Bill was evidently
much impressed. He handed the mare over and walked back home.
Later he asked for a day off, went to Northampton and enlisted
in the county regiment. It was a great surprise to all of us for no
one had ever dreamt that slow, clumsy old Bill would be a
soldier. We said, 'If they'll take Bill, they'll take anybody.'
Someone asked him, 'Whatever made you do it, Bill?' 'Wall, I
thought I'd like to see a bit of the wurrld,' was his reply. That was
another shock, for no one had ever thought Bill had any aspir-
ations to travel.

In a few weeks he came home, quite smart in khaki uniform,
but still the same splay-footed figure, for they never made a really
smart soldier of Bill. Of course we enquired how he was getting
on, how he liked the army and so forth. He was evidently quite
satisfied, for he ended his remarks by saying, 'I in't done no wurrk
since I left Pettifers.' 'Don't you have to slip into it when you be
digging them there trenches?' we asked. 'Oh, ah,' Bill replied.
'They dooant say ote to you,' and added as an afterthought, 'They
call me ole Bill.' Later he went with his battalion over to France
and little was heard of him, for he was no letter-writer.

In July 1916 we heard that he was wounded, and soon he was
home on convalescent leave, looking fit and well for the wound
in his back was quite healed. 'How did it happen?' we asked. We
learnt that his company were in the trenches not far from the

German lines, and that they had been heavily shelled. Some of the sand bags on the trench parapet had been knocked about and Bill was helping replace them. When lifting one into position Bill showed the small of his back to the enemy, a sniper saw it and fired, giving Bill a flesh wound across his back. 'It were just as if I were 'it with a gret stick, and it bowled me over into the trench,' Bill said, and added after a pause, 'You know it en't none too safe in them trenches.'

When his leave had expired he came to our workroom to say goodbye to Father and me. Mother followed him up the stairs. He shook hands all round and just as he was going, Mother asked a question that should not have been asked. She said, 'You don't mind going back, do you, Bill?' He replied, 'I shouldn't mind going back, but I don't want to be killed.'

Men went out to France lightheartedly the first time, but after months in an out of the trenches, the mud and the slaughter, a man returning knew only too well what lay in front across the Channel. So Bill went back with a heavy heart. Maybe he had a premonition, for he fell in October 1916. No one knows how the end came: he was just 'killed in action'. He and Ralph Cleaver lie in unknown graves. When Ralph fell in August 1916 a letter came to his parents written by D. Pickford, captain of the company, expressing his sympathy and giving this information. They were in a front-line trench which was attacked by the Germans, who secured a section of the trench. Ralph was one of a very small party who volunteered to attempt to drive them out using hand grenades and was killed in the hand-to-hand fighting. This attempt, the captain said, made it possible to achieve victory the following day.

One Sunday afternoon in 1915, Mother and Mrs Kench were walking home from chapel. Mother enquired how Harold was faring, for he had recently enlisted in the Medical Corps. 'He's quite all right,' Mrs Kench said. 'But they've sent him to Salisbury Plain and they say it's so damp there and Harold can't stand damp.' Mrs Kench was so timid, so fearful, little did she know how tough her Harold was. He was at the front for over three years, most of the time in Italy and France, a stretcher-bearer near the enemy lines amid constant shelling. One dark night he fell into a shell hole and injured his elbow and the accident brought him home towards the end of the war. Evidently Harold did a good job of work out in France for he was awarded the Military Medal for bravery in carrying on under heavy shell fire.

During the first eighteen months I went to Northampton twice for medical examination, but both times I was rejected owing to defective sight. Till that time I had not realised how defective my sight was. When I visited an optician and came out of his shop in Northampton Market, wearing glasses for the first time, I had an eye-opener. I looked into shop windows with amazement. I did not know that there were such bright colours or that flowers could be so lovely. When I cycled the roads I knew so well, I saw farmhouses away on the hillsides for the first time in my life. Evidently I'd never had good sight, but there was no occasion to test my eyes till the war and medicals.

After I was rejected in the spring of 1916 I came to the con-clusion they would finish the war without my help and so Nancy and I were married at Boddington on 22nd June 1916. We had just got nicely settled in the old house when the House of Com-mons passed the first Conscription Act, whereby all men between eighteen and forty could be called up for service. The standards for recruits were lowered, so that any man who could walk and wasn't blind could be found a job of some sort in the army. Just a few got exemptions and some got the call-up deferred, but they were very few. Again I was sent a railway warrant to go to Northampton. This time the doctor said, 'You're just the sort of chap we want.' I was passed B1, a category consisting of men fit for garrison duty at home or abroad. On 11th November 1916 I became a gunner in the Royal Garrison Artillery at the old Northampton barracks. Two days later I was one of a party sent to

Rugely camp in Staffordshire. Then followed the dishing out of uniforms and a few drills and route marches; then home on ten days' overseas leave. Back to Rugeley to hard frost and snow, washing in rough shelters exposed to the elements, mercifully for a few days only. Then boarding a train at night, rattling through the hours of darkness to Devonport on a murky morning. We embarked on a captured German boat, the *Huntspill*, and sailed through the Bay of Biscay to land at Gibraltar on 6th December.

It was like going to another world. At home there were short days and long nights, bitter cold weather and darkened lights everywhere. At Gibraltar, lovely sunshine by day and at night a blaze of lights on shore with searchlights lighting up the sea for miles around. There I spent the next two years; at the time it seemed hard lines, but now looking back it takes the form of a very pleasant holiday in another land across the sea. I missed a very severe winter, for the frost and snow that set in here in the middle of November continued with brief breaks till March. Those last two years of the war brought our rations of food to the lowest level since the 'hungry forties' of our grandfathers' days.

Percy was called up in 1917. He was too deaf to do any military duties but they found him a job in the tailors' shop altering uniforms for the smart young men. Making them 'posh', it was called. It was one of those strange strokes of fate that Percy, with his musical abilities, should be going deaf when he was only twenty-five. He went to the best specialists in London for advice and attended hospitals for years; but nothing could be done and he became almost stone deaf. It was thought the trouble began when as a boy he was sliding on the ice one day at Mawbey's brickyard and had a fall that brought on concussion.

Late in 1917 Frank came home on leave and Percy got here at the same time to meet him. They decided to go to Banbury and have their photograph taken in uniform and to meet a second cousin, Tom Mander, home on leave from Mesopotamia. Tom had taken his degree at Oxford and when the war started he was a sub-editor on the *Daily Mail*, a very promising young man. They called for Tom and he was walking up High Street with them when a military policeman met them and, looking very severely at Tom, said, 'Where's your belt, Corporal?' 'Left it hanging on the fence at Baghdad,' Tom replied with a grin. That was Tom's last leave. He went back to his unit and to a grave in the land of the two rivers.

Frank was given one stripe soon after he joined up and in 1917 he was promoted sergeant. Later he was awarded the Military Medal for keeping communications intact under heavy fire. Mother always talked a lot about Frank, and her customers were kept well informed about his progress over the shop counter. Other mothers also had sons on active service and they liked to talk of their boys' welfare. To an onlooker it was highly amusing to hear Mother wear down any opposition on her hearers' part by sheer weight of words, for she was a far better talker than listener.

There were no local men in Frank's company, but twice during the campaign he was able to meet some of the Eydon men in the Northants regiment when they were having a break in the rear of the fighting lines.

In 1910 Viscount Valentia sold the Hall and the estate here to Lady Hesketh, wife of Sir Thomas Hesketh, of Easton Neston. She was a wealthy American, a masterful, domineering woman and it was not surprising that she and Sir Thomas could not live under the same roof for long.

Early on in the war it became fashionable for society ladies to do some useful work to help win the war. I am sure Lady Hesketh never soiled her hands or rolled up her sleeves to do hard work, but she did spend some money in the war effort. The stables at the Hall stood empty, for the horses were turned out to grass; so her ladyship had them converted to make a convalescent home for twenty men. Dr Hays became honorary physician, and an old nurse was installed as matron. Men were sent here from the military hospital at Oxford when they were well on the way to recovery, most of them having been wounded. They were allowed to come into the village at certain times of the day, till one silly man had too much to drink and went back to make a disturbance. There was a to-do at the Hall. Everybody there was terribly alarmed and the culprit was sent back to Oxford the next day in disgrace. From then on the village was put out of bounds and the park became the invalids' prison. I remember one man peering through the iron railings by the lodge saying, 'One cat, one dog in sight in the High Street, what a hole.' In spite of the restrictions George Hawkins (one of the soldiers) managed to meet Harriet Amos and after the war he came back and they were married and settled here. One poor fellow at the home went and died one night, causing such a panic that her ladyship went off the deep end. She had men there to recover and no provision whatever was made for men who did not respond. It was quite unthinkable! I am afraid Lady Hesketh did not derive much comfort from the home, unless from the thought that she was suffering in a good cause.

A storm blew up in the village during 1917 that enlivened the darkest days of the war and gave amusement to many folk and annoyance to a few. These rows do much to enliven village life by arousing controversy that forces us to take sides. It shows very clearly C. J. Thompson's feelings towards the lady of the manor and how he and Father sometimes found themselves standing shoulder to shoulder in agreement. The minute book records that on 30th May 1917 at the parish council meeting C. J. Thompson proposed and J. Tyrrell seconded this resolution to be sent to the County Food Production committee:

At a meeting of this Parish Council held to discuss the question of food production and waste it was unanimously agreed that the attention of the Food Production Committee should be drawn to the fact that while the farmers and allotment holders here are doing their utmost to produce as much food as possible, the greater part of the young rooks at the Eydon Hall Rookery have been allowed to fly away. Horses too which certainly would do well on grass during the summer are living on the best of oats and hay. We think some protest should be made. The rooks have been allowed to increase during the last few years and do a lot of damage to the beans, peas and potatoes in the allotments as well as to the corn and roots in the fields.

Sidney Bricknell, a member of the council, did not vote or take part in the proceedings; in this he was wise, for he was Lady Hesketh's gardener. A month later he resigned, and his resignation was accepted with regret.

The fat was in the fire. Lady Hesketh was wild, her agent Boulton got on the warpath and her London solicitors, Messrs Bird and Bird, got busy with letters to the parish council and the county committee. The parish council sent the clerk Arthur Herbert to Northampton to enlist the help of the county committee in dealing with the onslaught. They could not see their way to intervene in the matter. Letters galore were sent, meetings were held to discuss the situation and on 24th August a very qualified apology was sent to Lady Hesketh. This did not satisfy either her ladyship or Bird and Bird, for they were out for blood. The dispute was settled on 10th September when J. Tyrrell proposed and W. Griffin seconded that an unreserved apology be sent to Lady Hesketh, signed by all the members concerned. So the matter ended with a defeat for the parish council; but they had administered a severe shock to her ladyship, so on balance I consider that the attack was well worth while. I am sure that no one who knew her will disagree when I say that Lady Hesketh was a tyrant, and such people do not go down well in Eydon. It is a surprising fact that while this controversy was raging the Brackley Rural District Council were taking preliminary steps to install a sewerage system in the village. It was done later in the year and it served only a part of the village, but we were fortunate. A drain was laid down our garden straight through Lucks Close to a filter bed built near the ditch. We found it a vast improvement on the old stone drains that had served our houses for generations.

I was still at Gibraltar when Armistice Day came in 1918. At the time I was a range-finder living with another man in a tiny cabin 1,200 foot up the Rock. Our instrument, which half filled our home, was connected to a 9 ft. 2 in. gun lower down the Rock. We had a magnificent panoramic view of about sixty miles of sea and coastline, embracing the Straits and North African coast as well as the southern tip of Spain. Below in the harbour many ships of the Royal Navy lay at anchor, with French and American boats of all types and sizes. That morning we were all waiting for 11 o'clock. On the dot we saw the ball drop on Signal Hill and at the same moment the signal gun was fired and the war was over. Every boat was waiting for the signal and at once they all let out a blast on their sirens: shrill hoots from the small craft and deep-toned blasts from the big ships. The din was terrific, going on for an hour or so at full blast, then gradually fading away, though some had short spells of hooting for the rest of the day. Each ship fetched out every flag on board and hung them, making a glorious riot of colour. All that day boats of the allied navies were coming into harbour after their last patrol, each one gaily decorated with flags and cheerfully hooting to announce her arrival in port.

Discipline went to pieces in the army and navy that day, for everybody, officers and men alike, felt like letting off steam; everybody did let off steam one way or another. Fortunately the supply of beer and spirits was very limited at Gibraltar because of the shortage of shipping facilities but there was enough to enable scores of men to get drunk. There was no change in our duties for some time, as the guns were kept at the ready because it was an armistice and not a declaration of peace. Still, everyone knew there was no earthly chance of Germany restarting hostilities. Soon we began to hear of leave being granted, compassionate leave it was called, but it was given only in exceptional cases.

When I left home in 1916, Father was far from well: stomach trouble and his old enemy chronic bronchitis caused a hacking cough and the constant spitting of phlegm was plaguing him. As a result he was seldom able to do a full day's work. While I was away he was bravely striving to keep the tailoring business going, so that there should be a business here on my return. He had to contend with constantly rising prices, cloth in short supply and with increasing physical weakness. Soon after the armistice Dr Hays gave a certificate on the state of his health and inability to carry on the business. This was sent out to me; I asked to see my CO, Captain Thurman. As I handed him the certificate I explained the situation at home and asked for leave to return home to work in the business. He asked a few questions and granted me twenty-eight days' leave, at the end of which I was to report to Chatham. There were a few days of waiting for a homeward-bound boat, then the saying of goodbyes to a group of friends I'd worked with very happily for two years. This was especially true of the Methodists at Gibraltar, for the Rev. A. B. and Mrs Sackett had been most kind and helpful and their home had been a real godsend to me and many others.

Exactly two years after I'd landed I went on board the *Manitou*, a boat homeward-bound from the Far East. Four days later we feasted our eyes on the white cliffs of the Dorset coast and soon the anchor was dropped. Later we found we were outside Weymouth Harbour. Next morning, as we were lounging on deck and grousing at the delay so near our journey's end, we saw a huge American battleship come slowly steaming through the entrance to the inner harbour. She was followed by four others of the same class. They all set off steaming in line down the

Channel. The next day we read in the newspapers that they were going to meet the boat bringing President Wilson to Europe. He was the first president ever to leave the United States during his term of office. That was the first of many top-level conferences. It was a thrilling sight, those great heavy ships, bristling with huge guns, steaming by so quietly that we heard no sound as they passed our boat. My children will never see such ships, for they are now obsolete; nor are they likely to see a big ship in full sail. During the war several five-masted ships were built in the States, on the theory that they consumed neither coal nor oil. We saw one pass through the Straits in the spring of 1918. She made a glorious picture as she passed in full sail, her spotless white sails standing out against the dark background made by the tree-covered cliffs on the coast of Morocco.

Early the next morning our boat slowly made her way through the Solent and up Southampton Water. By the time she had docked and we'd been through customs the light of the December day was fading. A train was waiting and very soon we were at Waterloo station. Once more we filed through an office to receive a railway warrant home and a ration card for one month. At the end of the month I was to report to the CO at Exeter.

As it was too late to get home I went to Leyton to Aunt Mary's, uncommonly glad to be among the comforts of civilisation again. After two years of drinking tea out of a basin it was a treat to handle a china cup again, and to sit at a table covered with a white cloth was quite refreshing. What a lot there was to talk about. I had my modest story to tell; Aunt Jane gave a vivid description of the Zeppelin raids on London, while Aunt Mary was more interested in Winnie's experiences with the Red Cross out in Egypt.

What a thrill there was in coming home after two years of exile during which I saw no familiar face, nor met anyone who had ever seen Eydon. The train that day from Marylebone seemed very slow; it was a long time before we got to Brackley, then Helmdon went by and soon the signal-box at the junction passed and there on the slope of the hill nestled dear old Eydon and home. It was grand to be home, even though it was December and short days and cold, with Jack Frost just round the corner.

Father had aged considerably since I had been away. His figure was bent, he'd lost flesh and now looked a very old man. Soon I was back in the workroom sitting cross-legged on the board and sewing away for dear life trying to complete the outstanding orders. Cloth was very dear and in short supply, but the government had recently brought in a 'standard' made-to-measure suit. The cloth was a very good serge in grey and blue. It cost us about 13s. a yard and the fixed price for the suit was £4 17s. 6d. They were such good value that we were kept busy, for there was plenty of money about at the time.

The newspapers gave us full details of the government scheme for demobilisation of the millions of men in the forces. It was based on the needs of the various industries at home and the length of service of the individual. It was feared that if men were discharged too rapidly, many would fail to find jobs and unemployment would ensue. The scheme broke down, I believe, through men at home on leave refusing to go overseas again, so there was serious trouble at some of the camps on the south coast. The result was that men at home on leave were getting discharged first, irrespective of their length of service, or whether they were needed in industry.

Knowing what was going on, I carried on at work when my month's leave passed, hoping each day that the postman would bring news of my discharge. Alas, it never came. Instead, one cold frosty morning in the middle of February the Moreton Pinkney policeman came to the house to ask me to go to Brackley with him. He was very good and put it very nicely, so we asked him in and he sat by the fire and drank a cup of tea while I packed my kitbag with a few necessities. Then we walked to Woodford

station and caught the train to Brackley. At the police station
they were quite unprepared for guests, so I sat by the fire in the
constables' room while a fire was lit to warm the cells, for it was
freezing hard. An hour or so later I handed over money, knife and
so on to the sergeant, then was locked up in a cell. The bed was
much more comfortable than many of the army beds I'd slept in,
and I had a very good night. Next morning I was marched into
the court to face a couple of magistrates. After hearing the charge
of being an absentee from the Royal Garrison Artillery I was
remanded, awaiting an escort. That afternoon a corporal and
private of the Devon Regiment turned up, but it was too late to
get to Exeter that day. The next morning we set off to London,
visited a barber's shop and did some shopping, then went on to
Exeter. There I was housed in a cell attached to the guardroom at
the entrance to the barracks. Another culprit and I spent our
time with the men on duty round a huge fire, drinking numerous
mugs of strong, sweet tea. We had to be on the alert for officers
and such-like, and ready to go to our cells and shut the door at a
moment's notice if warned that such were approaching the
guardroom. After two days there I went before the CO charged
with being a defaulter, for which I received seven days confined
to barracks and nine days' pay stopped. Altogether I was at
Exeter for three weeks. Then to Chiseldon, near Swindon, for
discharge early in March and so back home and the daily round
and common task once more.

Father never discussed this escapade with me, but others told
me that it quite upset him, that he felt it was a slur on the family
and that I had let the Tyrrells down. I was vexed at the time; but
I soon looked back on it as an interesting experience, for, after all,
many far better men than I have been prisoners and the war was
over when it occurred.

Yes, the shooting war was over, but such vast changes had
taken place in the four years that we never went back to the 1914
way of life. Now I can see we were silly ever to expect anything

to be the same after such an immense upheaval. There had been talk for years of altering time, so that we had more hours of daylight during the summer, but no one took it seriously, it was an item the newspapers toyed with during the silly season. Now, lo and behold, it was done: the clocks were all altered so that we got up earlier in the summer to the great disgust of many country folk. If we had a wet summer or a hard winter, summertime was blamed. 'It ain't natural,' they said, quite forgetting that during the war years they blamed the gunfire in France for all weather upsets.

We used to walk regularly across grass fields to Culworth, Woodford and Moreton Pinkney. The paths were easy to follow, for they were well trodden, especially the Woodford one across Farmer Lines' fields. The arable fields in the parish were away from the footpaths; they had always been arable, just as the others had been grass in living memory. Now arable fields appeared in the most unexpected places; the paths our forbears made for us were ruthlessly ploughed up to grow corn. The tracks went and the stiles decayed, leaving gaps in the hedges, so that although we still have the right to walk them no one ventures to walk a path that isn't there.

Other casualties here were the flower show and the Foresters' fête held each Whit Monday. Both these events needed the services of the Blakesly Silver Prize Band to be a success, and the band had faded away during the four war years. When the young men went to the war the older men were far too busy to keep up these events, so they just quietly died out. I find that four years is just long enough with us country folk to establish a precedent. We will keep on in the old ways as long as we do it regularly; but if the sequence is broken a new precedent becomes established and then it will need heaven and earth to move us to make a fresh start. Those war years brought on to the scene the agricultural contractor who introduced the tractor, a machine destined to effect a revolution in the countryside. Our farmers were then still very conservative and a few more years had to elapse before they ousted the horse in favour of the tractor.

Chapter 11

The twenties

Whilst I was away at the war and stationed in Gibraltar, Jean, our first child, was born on 9th August 1917. Mrs Pratt had been engaged as nurse and housekeeper. When it was over and Dr Hays had gone back to Woodford Mrs Pratt went next door to report to Mother the birth of a new granddaughter. When Mother heard it was a girl she said to Mrs Pratt, 'Oh, so the honour of the family is reserved for Frank.' Mrs Pratt thought it a bit off and Nancy was not at all pleased with the remark, for Frank was not even engaged.

Mother was proud of her six grandchildren, but as they were the girls' little ones none of them were Tyrrells and now the first Tyrrell grandchild was a girl! So you can imagine what a red-letter day it was for all when Peter was born to us in 1922. He was the first boy of a new generation to bear the family name. Two years later Alan was born. They and Donald Kench were the only grandchildren to live here and they brought a ray of sunshine into my father's and mother's lives when they were old and failing in health.

In 1921, on 21st October, I conducted a service at Wardington Chapel under the fatherly oversight of George Golby, a very able local preacher on Sundays and a capable foreman on Banbury's roads during the week. This was the first step towards becoming a local preacher; study and an examination followed at the end of two years on trial.

To recount how and why I took this step I must go back to 1912 when I had left home to better myself. Whilst I was away at Littlehampton, as I have explained earlier on, I had been greatly influenced by Ruskin and Lansbury towards socialism and away from the family allegiance to liberalism; at the same time my religious convictions had been strengthened. During the war we all had to consign our political ideas to cold storage. Then in the twenties we tried to go back to the pre-war days, but the situation had so altered that we had to learn that the old days and the old ways had gone for ever.

After the war I had lost my faith in liberalism, but it had not been replaced by faith in Labour, the new party then advancing in popular favour by leaps and bounds. When Colonel Kerr became Liberal candidate Frank asked me point blank, 'Where do you stand, Syd?' I had to reply, 'Sorry, I can't support the Colonel.' Father was pleased I was carrying on his work in the Church, but sorry I was not a sound Liberal. He was very gratified that Frank was an ardent Liberal, but sorry he had left the Church. During the last years of his life he often told friends how thankful he was that his three great interests in life – Church, politics and music – were now the interests of his boys and would be carried on after he had gone to rest. Both Frank and I found his interest in our work a tower of strength and an inspiration when the going became hard and discouraging.

When I'd been away from home preaching in a nearby village he would come to my house in his slippers on a Sunday night for a report. He would say, 'What sort of a day have you had, Syd?' He wanted to know about the congregations, where I had been to tea and how all his old friends in the village were faring. Once in conversation with Frank he expressed his regret that Frank had not taken up any work for the Church. Frank replied, 'I think you've done very well. Syd is doing your church work and I'm doing the political work, surely you haven't much to complain of?'

Father could always come to see us very easily, for he lived right next door and when in the 1920s he decided to make his house more comfortable we too decided to make some alterations. It is quite likely my readers will regard them as desecrations, and we may possibly be classed as Philistines in these days of plenty now that money seems to grow on hedges like hips and haws. But the money we gained from them was very helpful at the time, and we were pleased with the alterations, for they made the parlour a much more comfortable room for our use.

When Father bought the property in 1883 he became the owner of the only complete panelled room in the village. He did not value it, and no one else did, for the distinction did not add one penny to the value of the property. Our small parlour was panelled right up to the ceiling. Years before it had been painted and grained; now, faded and dingy, it made the room very dark, so we set no value on it.

Before the war Faulkner, the Banbury antique dealer, had done a deal with Mother. She sold him a pair of Chippendale chairs for £6, so he knew the situation and what we had on the premises in his line of business. I remember it was a nice day in the spring of 1925 when he came and bought, after some haggling with Father, the oak panelling and an oak door for £75. Faulkner explained that although the panelling was oak, the design was quite commonplace. The value lay in a nine- or ten-inch-wide border round the ceiling, which was nicely carved in an elaborate design.

When Kench's men took the panelling down we found on the inside wall a small cupboard complete with door. Naturally our hopes were raised, but, alas, when I opened the door it contained only dust and cobwebs. So when the house was built three small cupboards were made in the walls. I have seen them described as spice cupboards, but Mother called the one upstairs the medicine cupboard. The roughly plastered walls and the hidden cupboard showed that the panelling was not part of the original house, but was added later. Sundry repairs and improvements to the house and making the walls good cost £30. It gave us a more comfortable house to live in, and as Father was £45 in hand we were all very well satisfied with the deal. Now after half a lifetime that deal with Faulkner looks very different. It might have paid us better to keep the panelling in the parlour and set to work to remove the paint, but it would have been a long and tedious job.

I never gave a thought to where the panelling came from until I wrote the preceding paragraph about its sale and then it flickered across my mind where it must have originated. Of course, it came from the old manor house demolished by Annesley in 1788 – old John Browne's manor house. The only other possible source was the demolition of Edgcote House in 1750, but it is not likely that Eydon men worked on that job.

The manor here was a large house, for it had fifteen fireplaces, so it must have had at least twenty or twenty-four rooms in it. There must have been a vast quantity of woodwork and timber, all redundant. The rooms would be low, so no doors or panelling would fit into the plans of the architect for the new mansion. It is quite likely a carpenter lived in my cottage; the old hovel would have made him a very good workshop. He no longer wanted to keep cows or horses in the adjoining building, so he formulated a plan to add part of it to this cottage, and to make a separate cottage of the other part. The door into the building came in the middle of the party wall: he bricked up the aperture and made another entrance by the street wall. Now to make a private parlour he wanted a partition to make a passage from the living-room to the new rooms he was adding to the house.

Probably he worked on the demolition and, when they took down the panelling in John Browne's study and office, he said to the foreman, 'I'll give you five bob for it.' It did the job splendidly, went all round the room and made a thin partition between the parlour and passage into the new rooms. He wanted to make a cupboard upstairs by the side of the great chimney, so he bought a light door for the job for another shilling. It's the folk on the job who get the bargains at such times. If the truth were known, it's likely there are many bits and pieces from that demolition in many houses here today. The oak door we sold was very light and a hefty man could easily have smashed it with his shoulder. It had an ecclesiastical look about it for on the face a narrow beading formed a Gothic arch; it was the sort of door I should expect to see in my lady's boudoir in the seventeenth century. Thank goodness they left in the doorway a strip of three panels, six foot by one foot; it looks me in the face every time I enter the room.

When Father and Mother altered their house next door they set aside two rooms for Frank to live in. Frank did not return from the war until 1919. He had been a tall, good-looking lad still with the bloom of youth on him when he joined up in 1914; when he came home he was a fully mature man of the world. He had borne responsibility and exercised leadership in the fighting line and it had left its mark upon him. Very occasionally he would recount an experience, or recall amusing incidents of officers or men, but not often. In France he had the use of a motor cycle and he liked this new means of transport, so soon after he came home he bought a second-hand Rover fitted with hub gears and a side-car. Later he sold this to Fred and bought an Ariel.

Each man who had served in the armed forces had a sum of

money placed in the Savings Bank for him on discharge, which varied according to rank and length of service. Many a man had more money than he'd ever had before. Many of the younger men invested in a motor cycle, and as Frank was a mechanic by trade his help and advice was often sought. As it is still true that birds of a feather flock together, our yard soon became a combined meeting-place of motor cyclists and repair depot.

The old chaff-house was cleared out and Frank put a window in so that he could use it for a workshop. Soon he was doing quite a business in his spare time, repairing and tuning motor cycles. The Sabbath peace at the Red House was shattered by these gatherings on Sunday mornings in the yard. Mother, busy in the kitchen cooking the Sunday dinner, had the full benefit, while Father the other side of the house got off lightly. After dinner Frank mounted his steed and set off for unknown destinations, returning late at night. While he'd been in the army he'd become very fond of a game of billiards and dancing. The dances he organised for the village hall, at which he was MC, brought him into contact with the dancing fraternity in the nearby villages. He went to their dances and they came to his. We were glad to see a good crowd here, for the funds were growing through his popularity in the district.

The services at the chapel held no attraction for him now, so he cut them out completely. It was evident that those four years in the army had brought a change in him and some of the old landmarks had fallen. Maude and I still attended the two services at chapel each Sunday, as we had always done. It must have been hurtful to Father and Mother, but there were no complaints. Frank had reached manhood so the changed situation was accepted, though with regret.

Father had considerable compensation, for Frank became an enthusiastic supporter of the Liberal candidate. At the Woodford Loco he was working with several young men who were active members of the choir at our chapel. There, under the baton of

Charlie Brooks, musical abilities had been encouraged and developed in the services and in social events on week nights. Frank had an idea: a Liberal concert party to attract audiences and liven up the Liberal meetings. And so the Red-and-White Concert Party was formed, consisting of three ladies and eleven men. Louie Marriott, ALCM, was the pianist, and Billy Preece, who was a born humorist, developed the lighter side of the programmes. He could very soon have the most serious audiences rocking with laughter at his quips and antics. Frank had a good strong bass voice and could sing a solo or make a speech, according to the set-up of the meeting. One of his favourite songs was the cobbler's song from *Chu Chin Chow*.

Mother shared in the good work, for her sewing-machine was soon busily making costumes for the party, of white material decorated with large red pompoms. The party gave concerts all round the district, and in doing so helped the Liberal cause with good music and plenty of clean humour.

On 14th January 1925 Frank married Brenda Smith at Woodford Church. There is no doubt that the romance began when they found they were splendidly matched for dancing. Frank had found his ideal dancing partner at last. Sam Smith, a Woodford driver, was the father of four very attractive girls and Brenda was the eldest. When she married Frank, our youngest, the Tyrrell clan were all fixed up for better or worse. After a while Frank took Brenda to Birmingham to live when he became the Liberal Party agent for the Erdington division there. Later on he moved to Devon, where he worked hard for the Liberal Party for the rest of his life.

Mother saw him married, but she never saw his daughter June, born some years after they'd been wed. The honour of the family was not to be Frank's.

When war broke out in 1939 party politics went into cold storage, so although he was over age Frank joined the Devon Regiment for home defence. He would have been quite happy if they'd left him at Plymouth, but later he was sent to the Isles of Scilly. There, with no politics and no motor to tinker with, he got bored stiff gazing at the restless sea. He had been gassed in the First World War and this left him very chesty, so when he had a bad cold the doctor gave him his ticket and he went back home.

In 1946 an election was held in Greece under the supervision of the United Nations. In an attempt to see fair play by the political parties there, the UN decided to send observers to keep an eye on events and the actual voting. The United States, France and Britain each sent six observers. Someone gave Frank the tip that it was a job he could do, so he sent in an application. He was called to the Foreign Office in London for an interview. There he was asked by one of the officials a question he'd been asked before: 'What school did you go to, Mr Tyrrell?' The questioner wasn't much wiser when Frank replied, 'Eydon National.' He got the job.

The six met in London, went by plane to Paris and there met the Americans and Frenchmen. They all went on to Rome, where they were given a week's briefing on the historical and political set-up in Greece. In Greece he was the guest of a well-to-do merchant for the month during which the elections took place. He found the Greeks' hospitality rather overwhelming, for of course he'd been brought up teetotal. He survived, however, and came home well pleased to see how elections are held in another country. Although he loved the political arena, he came to the conclusion that the Greeks are politically mad.

The next Liberal candidate for North Cornwall was Dingle Foot, a man after his own heart. We had known Dingle's father, Isaac Foot, for years by repute. He was an ardent Methodist and a stalwart Liberal of the old school. It was a great joy to Frank to be a welcome visitor in his home, and to rub shoulders with his four sons, who were true chips off the old block. Frank got on well with Dingle, although they did not always see eye to eye.

They fought elections in 1950–1, but the tide was running out against Liberalism, for Labour was making headway in the West Country. In 1953 Frank became agent in North Dorset for the Hon. Michael Portman. The next year he went into hospital for what we hoped was a minor operation, but the verdict was cancer. They patched him up for the time being so that he was able to carry out his duties in the 1955 election. That was his last political contract: soon after he limped home to Tintagel to die in November, at the age of sixty.

But that is digressing a bit from what happened to all of us after the First World War. Well, Frank, as I've just said, did very well for himself, but Percy turned out to be a bit of a problem. Percy was number two in the family and the eldest son and for several years after his marriage his financial position was the cause of much embarrassment, both to him and to the family.

He rented a room in London at 1 Gresham Street, overlooking the old General Post Office, at a yearly rent of £52. His customers were mostly Stock Exchange and bank clerks and students at the university, some coloured. When old Schadler died Percy entered into a partnership with his son, a commercial traveller. This did not work for long and Percy lost money through its failure. In his room on the third storey the business was done in the following way: a customer was shown patterns of cloth and a suit was ordered; the cloth was obtained from one of the city warehouses and Percy cut the suit and prepared it for a try-on; after this had taken place the coat, waistcoat and trousers were called for by a tailor's runner, often a boy or girl collecting work for father. Most of the London tailors working at home made only one garment – coats or trousers – collecting the orders from many shops in the City. Later the garments were returned; Percy examined them to see that they were up to standard and then paid for the work. He paid 12s. 6d. to the outworker for making

a coat and 5*s*. to 6*s*. for trousers, with more for evening
dress.

In most cases his customers called for the suit, tried it on and
paid. But they did not always pay and often Percy knew only
where a man worked, not where he lived. I remember him
making a suit for a man on the stage. He called for it, put it on
and said it was A1; then he borrowed an attaché case in which he
packed the suit he'd taken off. Percy never saw the case again, or
the money for the suit. He was wild over that do, the loss of the
case adding insult to injury. I fancy that was not the only time
he was done by an actor, for he would have it they were all
rogues. Having bought his experience of the evils and snares of
this wicked world the hard way, Percy slowly started to do a bit
better, but it took quite a long time.

After he'd been married several years, we began to wonder if
they were ever going to have any children. How one particular
conversation began I do not remember, but I well remember
Harriet saying, 'I want a piano, then we may start a family.' She
had the piano as soon as Percy could see his way to buy one, but
they remained childless. It was a shame, for Percy loved little
children.

Although he was almost stone deaf at thirty, in the twenties he
bought a motor cycle and side-car. With Harriet at his side he
drove with full confidence, for he'd learnt to read her lips so well
that she could give him directions on the road. He maintained
that he was a safer driver than we ordinary folk, as all his attention
was concentrated on the road, and that one drives by sight, not
sound. Later they bought a car, but not a common car like a Ford
or an Austin – that wouldn't do for Harriet. So they had an
Armstrong Siddeley. It was Percy's pet till Harriet died in 1946;
then he sold the car, for he dared not drive without her by his
side. We were all relieved when he married an old friend,
Margaret, for his deafness made him a problem to the rest of the
family.

Margaret tried to wrap him up in cotton wool and take great care of him, but he wouldn't have it. She objected to him going up a ladder to paint the bedroom windows. He'd wait till she'd gone shopping, then he'd get on with the job. He was one of the most cheerful and happy men I have ever known, for because of his deafness he lived in a little world of his own. It wasn't quite fair though; he could tell me all his trials and tribulations, but I couldn't tell him mine. There are some things you can't holler, and although he tried various hearing aids, they never seemed in good order when he came to Eydon for his annual holiday.

In 1964 he was eighty-five years old, and that summer he played bowls for his club in Caterham. In the autumn he worked in his garden so that it was in apple-pie order for the winter. When the General Election took place in October he voted and was so interested that he sat up to hear the results till 2.30 in the morning. A month later he fell asleep like a child, never to wake again.

You could call us a long-lived family, for although Frank died when he was sixty Percy lived until he was eighty-five and Father until he was seventy-eight. Towards the last years of his life, Father became rather frail but he was able to enjoy his golden wedding celebrations to the full. We celebrated this in 1926 in the new village hall. All the family were present, twenty-five of us in all, and a few very old friends including Mrs Kench and Mrs Peck. Of course Mrs Walker was there to make the tea. She was indispensable on such occasions. After a substantial meal and a few speeches we sang a couple of Father's favourite hymns and ended with 'Praise God from whom all blessings flow'.

Five weeks after this event Mrs Kench retired for the night and slept the long sleep from which there is no awakening. We all felt the loss of a good friend, but Father felt it especially keenly, for he had been a regular visitor to her house since the death of Thomas. 'All my old friends are passing over the dark river, and I shan't be long,' he said after the funeral. In the class book in which are recorded the members of the chapel, he wrote by her name, Alice Kench, the words, 'Gone Home'. A lovely way of expressing the Christian hope.

In these closing years of his life he spent many hours with the old and infirm folk in the village. To use his phrase, 'now the burden and the heat of the day are over' there was time to spare. The religious and political differences that years ago had isolated him from many people in the village had quite faded away. Some rather surprising friendships blossomed in those years of the late twenties. I remember when he seemed to think very little of Jim Danson, used to call him 'Old-never-sweat'. They seemed to have so little in common, and yet he sat for hours at Jim's fireside, comparing notes and talking of the old days. To hear Jim talk of him after he'd gone, one would have thought they'd been bosom friends all their lives.

Like most old folk he loved to compare the years of his youth with the post-war years; he did it in a spirit of profound thankfulness and very seldom voiced a complaint. One thing he never could forget was the small bundle of clothes he brought to Eydon as a boy; yet now he owned property and was the father of a thriving family. Some of the causes he had espoused when young and energetic were in the doldrums; some had fizzled out after making a brief splash. He felt the Band of Hope had been worthwhile when some of the old boys came to see him during a holiday in the village. It warmed his heart to be assured, 'I've kept the pledge, Mr Tyrrell.' He felt he'd played a small part in the changing habits of men, so that the drunkenness of the 1880s was now like an echo of far-off days: no brawling or fighting in the street now after closing time at The Royal Oak. The allotments he had helped provide in 1887 had not been a success, though good may have been done, for men learnt by experience that it wasn't as easy as they thought to make money cultivating the land.

He could look back to work done in eleven elections, yet in two only had he been on the winning side. But he had the satisfaction now of many open and declared Liberals in the village, in contrast to his early experiences of standing almost alone for the party. Although the party was now at sixes and sevens, they had laid the foundations of the Welfare State. He was devoutly thankful for the old-age pension. 'What a boon and blessing it is,' he often declared.

The outlook at chapel was much brighter than it had been for years. He had seen the congregation slowly diminish through the years till it was only a handful, and the Sunday school had closed in 1908. Boys and girls soon grow up and there were no children in the Methodist homes at that time. There were the usual floating scholars of those days: the children who went to Sunday school a few weeks before the annual treat. After the treat they would go back to the church school. By so doing they partook of two treats a year. At times when we were very young we envied them, for we were so notoriously 'chapel' that one treat a year had to satisfy us.

In the early twenties the situation had altered. A new generation of Kenches and Tyrrells had arrived on the scene and the council houses had brought to the village families of Nonconformist origin. A Sunday school was started by Mary Kench and Nancy, my wife. It went with a swing and soon half the children in the village were on the register. The annual anniversary became quite an event in the village, with concerts held and plays produced. Several youthful artists of great promise were discovered where least expected. The latent talent in children was a discovery we made at that time. It needs love and patience to bring out the best in the little ones, and I'm afraid in these hectic days we tend to exploit it for our own ends. The brighter outlook at chapel and the children at the services was a continual joy to Father in his declining years. He took such a keen interest in the work and was always ready to give a word of appreciation and encouragement to the workers.

The early 1920s were good years for us all. There didn't seem to be a cloud in the sky. They were particularly happy days in our home. Jean was five years older than Peter and mothered him and Alan as much as they would let her. The two boys played together so happily: both full of beans, and what one didn't think of, the other did.

In 1925 I had bought the corner of the next field from Mr. E. R. Wilks. This was to enlarge the garden, for at that time our small garden was divided into four plots, one for each house. In digging the post holes and the mass of brambles and nettles that grew just over the old garden wall, I'd found lots of rough stones. When a large heap had accumulated, I arranged for George Edden to come with a horse and cart to take them away. Mother was busy washing on a nice mild February day when we did the job.

George and I were throwing the stones up into the cart and the two boys were with us helping in their way. They were both dressed in hand-knitted coats and leggings, buff in colour with collars of a contrasting colour.

When we had filled the cart George and I straightened our backs and looked round. 'Where's the boys?' we both said, for they had vanished. I called, no answer; so I walked down the field to see if they had got over the stile into the Long Ground. As I passed the sewerage tank I looked over the fence and there they were floating in the tank. All that was visible were their backs, for they were both face downwards. I shouted for George and hauled them out, both unconscious. Very soon they began to cough and splutter. I carried one boy and George the other and we brought them home, face downwards, as quickly as we could.

Our neighbour, Mrs Walker, came to help Mother and very soon they had the boys in baths of hot water; then they were packed off to bed. Dr Hays was called. He came and dosed them for, as he said, it was no ordinary water they had swallowed, but rank poison.

It made quite a to-do in the village. Folks began to talk and we heard of a couple of lambs that had been drowned in the same tank, but no one had thought a more secure fence necessary. The present fence consisted of posts and rails so that any child or small animal could easily slip through. The liquid in the tank was coated with a solid-looking scum, and whether the boys thought this was ice that would hold them or whether they slipped on the brick wall we were never to find out.

In a few days, the boys were out and about again, apparently little the worse for the escapade. But Alan never fully recovered; for weeks he remained below par. Then an epidemic of whooping-cough came to the village and, in spite of all Mother's efforts to keep the children clear, Alan caught it. The little lad was in no form to stand up against it, and it seemed that neither we nor Dr Hays could do very much to help him. Then early one morning he had a seizure that left him partly paralysed. It was meningitis; at that time, if not fatal, it left the sufferer gravely handicapped physically or mentally. Three weeks later he died in my chair by the kitchen fire.

The death of our youngest was a heavy blow for us all, but especially for Father and Mother, who seemed to take it very hard in their old age. Father's strength began to fail and then Mother became ill. Dr Hays was called in. He soon said 'She has a heart and must go very, very quietly.' Addie, Kate and Maude had a consultation regarding the doctor's verdict, and when they had agreed on a plan they put their proposals before Mother. 'You must have more help in the house,' they said. 'Mrs Castle will come and do your cleaning and Mrs Walker the washing.' They ended by saying, 'You must give up the shop.'

Mother listened patiently to all they had to say, then very deliberately said, 'Well if I've got to give up all the things I've enjoyed doing all these years, to live a bit longer, then I'd rather go home the sooner.' There was no more to be said. Mother unlocked the shop door every morning, attended to the day's customers and locked up at night right to the last. The girls didn't realise that it had become a vital part of Mother's life. It was a regular source of comfort to make a few shillings' profit on the sales, for she had been earning all her life; and above all a few friendly words were exchanged with each customer, so that she kept in touch with the comings and goings in the village.

Father, too, kept in touch with everything that was going on right until the end. He attended his last parish council meeting at the school in 1929. The next four meetings were held at the Red House, for the council came to him when he could no longer get down to the school. He failed very gradually and for a long time we could see his strength ebbing away. As long as he could he'd struggle down the garden leaning heavily on his stick, for he was very interested in my new garden. There is one spot by the old garden wall where I can still see him standing as he said to me, 'When I'm gone, Syd, I expect you'll do so-and-so.' I forget just what it was. He knew very well I'd some drastic alterations in mind for the garden. After all these years, he often comes into my mind in the garden and I feel in some strange way he is not very far away, that he knows what is going on here in the house and garden he loved.

On 3rd September 1930 as he lay dying, Mother sat by the bedside holding one of his hands. Evidently his sight was fading for he said, 'Are you there, Flo?' (That was Mother.) 'Yes, I'm here, my dear,' she replied. There was a long pause, then he said very slowly, 'Ha, just like the Saviour.' So he passed through the Valley of the Shadow of Death, and we believe, like Bunyan's pilgrim, 'The trumpets sounded for him on the other side.'

At the service in chapel our minister, the Rev. W. B. Smith, said of him, 'He believed that even the dusty spheres of politics could be won for the Lord. He was a great Methodist, a great public servant and a great man, and we think of him very proudly, very thankfully and very tenderly this day.'

It was Mother's wish that a memorial tablet should be placed in chapel, so the trustees' sanction was obtained and a bronze tablet ordered. Then Mother took to her bed. Without a doubt she would have recovered if she had put up a fight; but she felt her work was done. For fifty-four years she had tenderly cared for her Joe and now he was laid to rest. During those years they had never been apart for more than a day or two, and the only real holiday had been a fortnight together at Bournemouth. Their business affairs were in perfect order; all had been done that should be done, so she was ready to go to rest.

We managed to get the tablet here in time for her to see it. I carried it upstairs and held it over her bed, and she very slowly read the inscription. She came to the end of the road only five months after we had laid Father to rest, so that they were not parted long.

You will find as you read this record of the family that for some years my parents were in debt. Some folk in these days would not describe a mortgage on a house as a debt; I do, for it means one owns only part of the house. Well, I must tell you that they paid off the last bit of the mortgage on the property in 1920, and very pleased they were to feel it was now their own. When all their debts were paid and the will proved, each of their six children received £100.

A month after my parents had died a little boy was born to us in the Red House. Now I ask you, could we have given him any other name but Joseph? After all, it's a good name in this part of the country and the old book says, 'A good name is rather to be chosen than great riches.'

In writing about the Tyrrell family from one Joseph to another I have covered nearly one hundred years. I wish I could go back further in this record and describe my forbears, but that is impossible because over a century ago the Tyrrells were poor and uneducated and could not even write their own name. But instead I have written about Eydon. I could have written some of it in greater detail but I hope it's enough to enable you to picture it all in your mind. I have tried to give you the material for your imagination to fill in all the details.

I feel a great link with my ancestors for, even though I can read and write, I am not so far removed from them as all that. I too always hanker after the land, and I've always liked to have a plot and a garden. There is one plot of land which I first got to know when I was fifteen years old and which I still had as an allotment when I was sixty. Now it's a good grass field and the only signs of it ever having been anything else are several beds of rhubarb left behind when I went. But I've still got a large garden which keeps me busy.

Every day I must do some work or it will get on top of me; there is no standstill order in operation in a garden. If I dig only a bit as big as a hearth rug, I lie down to sleep at night picturing to myself one scrap of Mother Earth nice and tidy. But in winter when the ground is covered with snow, weeding or digging has to be postponed. Then I saw a bit of wood in the hovel to make a nice blazing fire at night. You can have your gas and electric fires and your smokeless fuels. 'Give me a nice wood fire to sit by, good Lord, as long as you possibly can.' No, I don't want chumps all ready to burn, I want some wood I can chop and saw myself. I have to keep on the right side of a friendly hedge cutter so that I can have some straight out of a hedge. Sometimes he says to me, 'You be a proper old scrounger.' He is quite right; we have had to be scroungers ever since they enclosed the common fields here two centuries ago. While I trace this idiosyncrasy back to my peasant ancestry, it is not fair to blame the Enclosure Act as if that law created the trait. We have always been scroungers, all of us. The lord of the manor and the parson kept their eyes open for anything they could pick up, and we poor folk had to do the same or go hungry. They say that we were all born in sin and they are not far out.